# THE STORY OF RUGBY LEAGUE

# THE STORY OF RUGBY LEAGUE

## Keith Macklin

**STANLEY PAUL**
London Melbourne Sydney Auckland Johannesburg

Stanley Paul & Co. Ltd
An imprint of the Hutchinson Publishing Group

17 – 21 Conway Street, London W1P 6JD

Hutchinson Publishing Group (Australia) Pty Ltd
PO Box 496, 16 – 22 Church Street, Hawthorne, Melbourne, Victoria 3122
PO Box 151, Broadway, New South Wales 2007

Hutchinson Group (NZ) Ltd
32 – 34 View Road, PO Box 40–086, Glenfield, Auckland 10

Hutchinson Group (SA) Pty Ltd
PO Box 337, Bergvlei 2012, South Africa

First published 1984

© Keith Macklin 1984

Phototypeset in Linotron Baskerville by
Input Typesetting Ltd., London

Printed and bound in Great Britain by
Anchor Brendon Ltd, Tiptree, Essex

British Library Cataloguing in Publication Data
Macklin, Keith
    The story of rugby league.
    1. Rugby football——History
    I. Title
    796.33'3'09        GV944.85
        ISBN 0 09 158411 6

To my late father, Arthur Macklin, the
greatest fan of them all

# Contents

# Acknowledgements

The author has received considerable and willing help from many people in the compilation of this book. Special thanks to David Oxley, David Howes and Renee Grant, of Rugby League headquarters; Mrs H. Desser; Peter Edmondson; Raymond Fletcher, Paul Fitzpatrick, David Hodgkinson, John Huxley and members of the Rugby League Writers Association for their own written work and practical help; my mother Jessie Macklin for digging out old cuttings; and countless players, referees, officials and fans who have passed on memories. Thanks also to The Rugby Leaguer, Associated Sports Photography and Sport and General Press Agency for allowing use of copyright photographs.

# Foreword

*by Ray French*

**BBC Rugby League commentator and England international at both codes of rugby**

Every player, administrator and especially spectator will have his own favourite memories of Rugby League. The legendary deeds of Harold Wagstaff and the great Huddersfield 'team of all talents' around the time of the First World War will be forever etched in the memories of a few last remaining stalwarts. The style and grace of Jim Sullivan, Jim Brough and Gus Risman evoke recollections from another generation. For myself, the pleasure of having played in the era of that immortal trio of wingers Brian Bevan, Billy Boston and Tom Van Vollenhoven will be cherished forever. At team level the deeds performed in the Rorke's Drift Test, Prescott's 1958 series and the unforgettable visit of the Australians in 1982 will live long in the annals of our game.

   Such memories are the essence of the game, sadly devoid of real literature until recent years. Tradition and history give standing to a sport, illustrate its modern relevance to the past, and give the game a strength and example to draw upon. What a pleasure then to be able to record the arrival of Keith Macklin's *The Story of Rugby League* which gives the modern supporter a chance to place the game in its rightful context. And what a pleasure to record a history of the sport by a writer and broadcaster so steeped in the origins of the game as Keith Macklin, whose love for the sport is still as strong as when, over twenty-three years ago, he interviewed me, following my first ever game of League, with kindness and consideration. At last our history has been brought up to date: Rugby League's prestige can only be enhanced.

# 1

# The 80s Explosion

It was hard to decide which major sporting organization, the Football League or the Rugby League, was most staggered by the startling news that appeared in the sports' pages early in June 1980. From out of the blue, without anticipatory rumours or inspired leaks, came a *Daily Mail* story that Fulham Football Club was about to apply for membership of the Rugby League.

There had been the odd whisper in northern sporting circles that a new club might enter the 13-a-side code, but no one had imagined that rugby league was about to take root in London SW6. Suddenly, after years of solid retrenchment in Lancashire, Yorkshire and Cumbria, topped up by Eddie Waring's idiosyncratic BBC commentaries, the professional handling code was to sprout in the south of England.

The story was rapidly confirmed. Brian Dalton, a Yorkshireman living in Leeds, and Fulham's financial director, said that a group of 'interested parties' was considering rugby league at Craven Cottage where the football club had just been relegated from division two to division three. Fulham had the ground, the groundstaff and the administrative staff to stage the games, the only question was the financial viability of the proposed Fulham Rugby League Football Club. It was known that a number of well-known rugby-union players in the south would like to turn professional, but were deterred by thoughts of uprooting themselves and their families and having to travel north.

David Oxley, the secretary-general of the Rugby League, gave a measured and guarded reaction: 'The Rugby League is always inter-

ested in attempts to establish the game beyond its northern boundaries,' he commented.

It was a tempting prospect for the Rugby League, a great opportunity to break free from the parochial boundaries that had prevented
the code from achieving national recognition and status. Fulham lost
no time in preparing solid ground for their application to enter the
second division in time for the 1980–81 season. The rumbustious and
outspoken chairman, Ernie Clay, himself a northerner, gave full
support to the venture, and Harold Genders, a northern businessman
and former player, was appointed managing director of the rugby-
league club.

Genders bubbled with optimism, stating that crowds of around
4000 at Craven Cottage would enable Fulham to break even financially. The only additional costs to the club would be the initial capital
outlay on 'good, experienced professionals' and the players' wages as
part-timers.

## *Bowden and Macdonald*

Fulham made two brilliant, astute appointments. Reg Bowden, the
Widnes scrum-half and captain, who had led his side to trophy
after trophy during the 1970s, was appointed player-coach. Malcolm
Macdonald, a charismatic football figure and a former international
centre-forward, was Fulham's marketing executive and he immediately took responsibility for marketing rugby league at Craven
Cottage. Macdonald told *The Times*: 'This is a serious application.
We have the financial backing, and the decision has been made only
after the most careful discussion. We have looked at the problems,
and we believe they can be overcome.' He added that rugby·league
at Fulham would less than double existing travelling expenses.

Rugby League officials were rapidly convinced and became so
enthusiastic about the proposal that they waived a bye-law stating
that applications for membership must be submitted by 31 March
to be considered at the League's summer conference. In a further
newspaper statement Macdonald said, with some degree of hyperbole, 'We have no doubt about our success. In both north and south
we have lit a fire that will take a long, long time to burn out.'

In June 1980, at a special meeting of club representatives at

Harrogate, Fulham were admitted to the second division by a vote twenty-six to nil, with three abstentions. An official announcement from headquarters declared, 'They have opened a whole new chapter in the history of the development of the 13-a-side code.'

Not everyone viewed the Fulham venture with such exuberant enthusiasm. A local residents' association threatened to take out an injunction under the Sunday Observance Act, and furious letters were sent to newspapers. Football pundits conjectured in various branches of the media that the playing of rugby league might damage the turf at Craven Cottage.

Nevertheless, the fire had been lit and on Thursday, 4 September, Fulham held an open day primarily for television, press and radio. On view were an impressive array of players, signed by Harold Genders in consultation with the directors and Reg Bowden. From all-conquering Widnes came Malcolm Aspey, Dave Eckersley, David Hull, Dave Allen and Tony Kinsey, from Bradford Northern the big, turbulent forward, Ian Van Bellen. Other strong-running forwards were Roy Lester from Warrington (the first player to sign for Fulham), Tony Gourley (Salford), Harry Beverley (Workington Town) and Tony Karalius, ex-St Helens and Wigan. Seasoned backs included threequarter Derek Noonan (St Helens), Ian McCorquodale (Workington Town), a prolific goal kicker, and Fulham's first novice, Adrian Cambriani, a Welsh youth international winger from Swansea.

## The big day dawns

Northerner Colin Welland, a director of Fulham and an ebullient propagandist for rugby league, flourished a telegram from his friend Andy Ripley, the Rosslyn Park and England forward. It read: 'Good luck to you and all the boys. Room for everyone.'

Ernie Clay said that the new rugby-league club would help keep alive the football club; he looked forward to an average break-even gate of 3500.

The open day was given massive media coverage, as was Fulham's first league game at home to Wigan on Sunday, 14 September 1980. Fingers were tightly crossed at League headquarters and at Craven Cottage, fine weather was prayed for, and a pre-match programme of curtain raisers, fit to rival the Wembley challenge-cup final, was arranged. The programme included the Dagenham Girl Pipers, a parade of all-time greats from rugby league, and a presentation of the teams to Lord Peart, Opposition leader of the House of Lords. In addition, BBC TV 'Match of the Day' cameras were in attendance to record a momentous occasion on a football ground, and a special instructional commentary was relayed over the public-address system.

The opening game went like a dream, with the scenario rivalling that of a ripping sporting yarn from a schoolboy magazine. Wigan, one of the greatest sides in the history of rugby league, were expected to win promotion to the first division, their natural home. They brought thousands of followers and the attendance was swelled to nearly 10,000.

The Fulham spectators, seeing their first 13-a-side game, roared continuously, cheering every run, tackle and sidestep of their northern-based heroes. There was uproar when McCorquodale kicked a penalty goal to put Fulham ahead, and an endless tumult of cheering whenever the black-and-red jerseys were in possession. The rules of the game were still foreign to the Craven Cottage football fans, but they knew when their side had possession and was going forward. There was more pandemonium when Aspey, the experienced centre from Widnes, sent over the young Cambriani for a try, and yet more when Cambriani followed up his own kick ahead for a touch down.

In the end Fulham won with unexpected ease. Tuffs, formerly of Featherstone Rovers, scored two tries, Allen one, and McCorquodale completed four goals. Eckersley dropped an impudent goal to rub it in, and Fulham won 24–5.

The end of the game brought scenes as euphoric and emotional as the pre-match festivities. Reg Bowden, tears streaming down his cheeks, led his team on a lap of honour as the 9554 spectators stood to applaud. Youngsters, who had hitherto seen rugby league only on television highlights while waiting for the football results, ran onto the field to mob their heroes in black-and-red jerseys.

Back in the dressing room there was champagne, singing and innumerable media interviews. Players towelled themselves down to the accompaniment of lights, microphones and notebooks.

## *Euphoric reaction*

The south reacted to rugby league with fervour bordering on the rhapsodic. Alan Thompson, in the *Daily Express*, wrote: 'The Northern he-man world of Rugby League went to town yesterday, and enthusiastic Londoners voted it a smash-hit.' Peter Batt commented in the *Daily Star*: 'Human elephants like Ian Van Bellen were tramping over the grass once graced by Johnny Haynes and George Best . . . and 9,554 mums, dads and kids were loving every minute of it . . . there wasn't a hooligan in sight.'

It was almost too good to be true, and a week after this wondrous opening day the golden coach suddenly reverted to a pumpkin. Fulham played their second-league game away to Keighley, a struggling second-division side with a poor defensive record and a tally of twenty-two tries against them in three games. It was anticipated that Fulham would have no difficulty following up their first-day triumph with an initial away win.

Keighley had other ideas. They tore into the media idols from the start and, although Fulham led 13–9 at half time, the Lawkholme Lane men dominated the second half. Playing like a leading first-division side rather than a mediocre second-division outfit, Keighley over-ran Fulham to win 24–13.

There was an inquest into what had gone wrong and much hand-wringing at the thought that the Fulham bubble had burst. Fortunately for Messrs Clay, Macdonald, Dalton, Bowden and the Craven Cottage team, the setback was only temporary, and perhaps salutary. The following week, back at Craven Cottage before a good crowd of nearly 6000, Fulham beat the useful Swinton side 25–11, and the show was back on the road.

For the remainder of the season the fairy tale developed on expected lines. The aggressive and inspiring Bowden, talking almost non-stop throughout each game, carried and led his team of northern expatriates and bargain signings to promotion at the first attempt. Fulham finished third, six points behind Wigan and three behind York.

There were the occasional stumbles and in their twenty-eight matches Fulham sustained eight defeats but, by and large, it was a continuous success story, justifying all the hyperbole of the pre-launch claims. The Fulham crowd revelled in the new game and 15,013 people, still a club record, saw the 5–9 defeat against Wakefield in a challenge cup tie. Reg Bowden commented, with dry northern humour: 'Down here they even cheer a knock-on!' Craven Cottage gates averaged 6096 and by the end of the season the spectators had got to grips with knock-ons, forward passes, scrummaging and the offside laws. When Fulham met, and beat, Leeds in a John Player trophy first-round game the crowd was 12,583 at the Cottage, and southern-based journalist David Miller wrote in the *Daily Express*: 'Soccer, the game I have loved for 40 years, is on the run, threatened with exposure of its dull and flabby attitudes by the strident virility of rugby league.'

This splendidly successful opening season ended in style, just as it had begun. Enterprisingly, the Fulham management invited Bradford Northern, the first-division champions, to take part in a pre-Wembley challenge match, with a monetary sidestake, on Friday evening, 1 May. To the exuberant glee of the Fulham supporters the League's newest side won by 20 points to 8 before a crowd of 12,000, an attendance swelled by the influx of thousands of northern fans on their way to the challenge-cup final at Wembley. Dave Allen scored all four tries for Fulham and he and Bowden were carried to the dressing room by adoring home supporters.

## Cardiff and Carlisle

The success of what was still regarded as the Craven Cottage experiment caused several football clubs to examine the prospects for doing likewise. Rugby League headquarters in Leeds received inquiries from Bolton Wanderers, Charlton Athletic, Grimsby Town, Preston North End and Heart of Midlothian. Feelers were also put out by a consortium based in Bristol (centred around the Eastville stadium), and groups of businessmen in Nottingham, Milton Keynes and Luton.

The two positive moves, however, came from opposite ends of the British Isles, from north Cumbria and south Wales. Almost as suddenly as with Fulham, Cardiff City and Carlisle Rugby League Football Clubs came into being.

In two consecutive months, April and May 1981, decisions were made which opened the horizons of rugby league to the Scottish borders and South Wales. In April, at a quickly convened meeting which followed the pattern of events surrounding Fulham's admission, Carlisle were admitted to the second division for the 1982–83 season. A month later, after more feverish behind-the-scenes activity, Cardiff City were admitted. Both teams, like Fulham, were based at football grounds with football clubs as progenitors. The success of Craven Cottage in its first year of rugby league had obviously been closely monitored elsewhere.

The decision to admit Carlisle came at a meeting of club representatives at Headingley on 1 April, and was unanimous. Jim Bendall, chairman of Carlisle United Football Club, said the rugby-league club would be based at Brunton Park, would be called 'Carlisle', and would have a completely separate board of directors, though he would be chairman. Football and rugby league would be run separately at Brunton Park, and solid rugby-league background would be provided by directors Ron Cowan (a former player with Leeds), George Graham, Geoff Holmes and secretary Colin Hutchinson.

On Wednesday, 6 May, the Rugby League council, meeting at Salford, approved the entry of Cardiff City Rugby League Football Club by twenty-seven votes to nil, with one abstention. David Watkins, a Welsh idol of rugby union and former captain of Wales before his fine service with Salford in rugby league, was to be managing director, and another Welsh international at both codes, John Mantle, was to be coach. Ron Grogan was to be chairman and the former Olympic sprinter, Ron Jones, was to be the secretary.

## Nagging doubts

Amid all the excitement surrounding the sudden explosion of rugby league into a nationwide game, there were some nagging, dissentient voices. Those who questioned the wisdom of the double admission of Cardiff City and Carlisle did so on the grounds that there might not be enough experienced talent available to give both clubs a solid launching platform. Fulham, it was felt, had drained away the best available players.

These fears were unfounded. Experienced players in the twilight of their careers were happy enough to be given a new lease of life, and in certain cases clubs were ready to unload gifted players provided the fee was right. The Carlisle coaching team of Allan Agar and Mick Morgan, the latter still in great form as a front-row-forward, foraged in the market shrewdly and well. Cardiff City, anxious to make an impact in rugby-mad South Wales, dropped bombshells among the Welsh Rugby Union establishment figures by signing Steve Fenwick, Tommy David and Paul Ringer, for undisclosed but undoubtedly hefty signing-on fees and offers of lucrative match bonuses.

As with Fulham, Cardiff City and Carlisle measured their costs purely in the signing of players, match fees and travelling expenses. The stadia were there, as were experienced groundstaff.

Amid further media curiosity, gossip and predictions, Carlisle and Cardiff City launched themselves into rugby league with bands, pomp and ceremony. Carlisle entered the lists first, drawing criticism in that it applied for entry to the Lancashire cup in mid-August 1981 rather than waiting for the start of the second-division season. The criticism seemed justified when 2779 spectators, just about break-even point, saw the makeshift Brunton Park team of individuals lose 9–6 after a gallant fight against Wigan.

## *Contrasting fortunes*

In contrast to Carlisle's muted opening Cardiff City went off with a bang. The first match brought Salford to Ninian Park on Sunday 30 August, and the crowd of just under 10,000 provided an exciting, carnival atmosphere to rival the great Craven Cottage opening. The fervent Welsh crowd, augmented by many northerners who had made a holiday trip to South Wales, set up a temendous din in support of the Blue Dragons, and the result was an immensely thrilling, seesaw battle in which Cardiff fought back from 16–4 down to lead 21–16, only for Salford to hit back in the closing stages for victory. Salford built up their 12-point lead at half time with tries from Henney and Fielding and five Rule goals against a try by Barwood (formerly with Wakefield Trinity), and a drop goal from Pritchard, formerly with Huddersfield. In the second half Cardiff surged forward, backed by the crowd, and took a 21–16 lead with tries from Woods, ex-Widnes and Hull, Nicholls, ex-St Helens, and David, with Fenwick kicking four goals. The Blue Dragons could not sustain their efforts, however, and Salford, putting together their collective experience, scored tries through Whitfield and Richards and two more goals from Rule to win 26–21.

On the same day, overshadowed by Cardiff's events, Carlisle won their inaugural second-division match, 10–4, at Bramley. It was a useful performance and good preparation for Carlisle's second launch, the first home league game against their powerful Cumbrian neighbours, Workington Town, the following weekend. This took place on Sunday, 6 September, and the crowd of 5903 saw Carlisle, still struggling to establish their teamwork and understanding, beaten 23–6 by a Town team looking for a good start to their promotion drive. A hopeful sign for Carlisle, in addition to the increased crowd figure, was the fact that Carlisle led 6–2 at half time before Town took charge in the second half.

In the space of one week, fortune turned full circle for Rugby League's two newest clubs. While Carlisle won credit and grounds for optimism in defeat, Cardiff City travelled to Keighley, and suffered the same fate as Fulham twelve months earlier. Keighley tore into the Blue Dragons and swept aside some weak defence to win by 36–8.

From this point onwards, fortune smiled on Carlisle and turned a sour face towards Cardiff City. Fulham, too, began to struggle as the brutal facts of first-division life brought reality and realism to Craven Cottage. Carlisle's progress became as dramatic and irresistible as the Fulham march of the previous season. Attendances at Brunton Park settled down to an eventual season average of 2950, with the highest figure, after the Workington game, of 5644 in a big promotion battle against Oldham in April 1982. Carlisle won nineteen league games in a row in mid-season, and topped the second-division table. In addition their front-row forward, Mick Morgan, who took over as coach from Allan Agar, scored twenty-five tries, a League record for a prop.

Much less spectacular was the progress of Cardiff City after their rousing opening game against Salford. After losing their first two games, the Blue Dragons won four in a row, then began to show a disturbing inconsistency and a tendency to be weak in defence whilst enterprising in attack. Worse, the attendance figures collapsed alarmingly, from an average of more than 3000 in the three home games following the opening to an average of around 1000 for remaining home league games. A ray of light was a gate of 6484 for a cup game against the mighty Widnes, lost understandably by 19 points to 8, but the decline in league attendances troubled David Watkins and the League.

## Rugby Union influence

Watkins and the Cardiff team could cite good reasons for the Blue Dragons' struggle to retain an impact. Rugby Union authorities in South Wales publicly and privately criticized or played down the significance of the 13-a-side's presence in Cardiff. Newspapers, conditioned by a lifetime of reflecting rugby union traditions and mores, often gave minimal coverage to the doings of rugby league at Ninian Park unless the news was unflattering. The presence in the Cardiff team of so many experienced Englishmen, like George Nicholls and Arthur Daley, was held to militate against an all-Welsh profile, and Watkins made it clear that the latter was his ultimate aim once rugby league had settled down in Cardiff.

Fixturing also played its part in reducing the attendance figures. When Cardiff City lost to Halifax 31–21 on 11 October 1981, the attendance was 3147. For various reasons Cardiff's next home fixture was five weeks later, 15 November, and for the game with Huyton, not the greatest attraction in the second division, interest had dwindled to an attendance of 1673; this became the pattern for the remainder of the season. Not all the blame could be laid at the door of external circumstances, however, and Cardiff's unreliable form was a major worry.

Meanwhile, at Craven Cottage, first-division life, and survival, were becoming increasingly hard. The consolation for Harold Genders and the Fulham directors was that gates held up well despite the team's steady drift back to division two. The attendance for the game against Widnes, in which Fulham lost narrowly 15–12, was 6677; when the exciting and phenomenally well-supported Hull side came to Craven Cottage there were 9481 spectators for a challenge-cup second-round tie, won by Hull 11–5 after a close battle.

Fulham showed their enterprise by signing Hussain M'Barki, a Moroccan winger, from the French club, Cahors, for £25,000; he played trials under the name of 'Des Smith'! M'Barki, a quicksilver winger, scored eight tries; Fulham produced some strong and entertaining displays but they only won two games away from home, at Barrow and Whitehaven, and relegation became inevitable early in 1982. It was obvious that Fulham's playing squad was not quite up to first-division standards, but the irrepressible Reg Bowden promised that his team would soon be back, and proved as prophetic as he was confident.

## The harder facts

Fulham took the upswing in the yo-yo existence of the League's three pioneering clubs in 1982–83. They bounced straight back into the first division, though gates dropped from the euphoric heights of the first season. Cardiff City, despite many team permutations designed to produce the dream of an all-Welsh team, again had a mixed season, and attendances remained frustratingly around the 1000 mark. Carlisle, in division one, had such a disastrous season, in almost every respect except loyal support, that the experiment was close to folding up by the end of the season. Only desperate crisis measures, and loyalty beyond the call of duty by some directors, held Carlisle together.

Fulham won the second-division championship, and their game against the brilliant Australian tourists attracted a crowd of 10,432 as Australia won 22–5, M'Barki getting the Fulham try. League gates peaked at 3855 for the visit of Wakefield Trinity in September 1982, and fell to 1050 at the Swinton game in December. The most fraught period for Fulham, a time when relationships with the football club were at a low ebb, was the month of April 1983, when the rugby league were prevented from using the Craven Cottage ground because of soccer problems and requirements. Home games were played at Widnes, producing attendances of only 1050 and 499.

Nevertheless, Fulham were back in the first division and the chirpy Reg Bowden said that his team would 'make a better show than we did last time'. Much less confident at the end of the 1982–83 season were Carlisle, whose decline from the peaks of their opening year was so hectic and catastrophic that they seemed certain to go out of existence. Like Fulham before them, Carlisle found the standards higher and the pace more exacting in division one, and although they started bravely with narrow defeats against Wigan and Castleford, and won a Cumbrian derby against Whitehaven and a tough game against Leigh, they won only three of their remaining thirty-one games. Attendances plummeted, players walked out on the club, and at one stage of the season Carlisle placed eighteen of their players on the transfer list. Only the player-coach, Mick Morgan, and the New Zealand signings, Ian and Dean Bell and Clayton Friend, were not put on offer. Debts mounted, certain directors made clear their disenchantment, and in February the managing director Colin Hutchinson forecast that Carlisle would fold if a consortium could not be found to take over the company and its debts. The Rugby League smacked Hutchinson's, and Carlisle directors', wrists by saying that they were panicking too early, and that two thirds of clubs in the League had financial situations equally as serious as those at Brunton Park. David Oxley, the League's secretary-general, suggested that the Carlisle directors 'should show the same resilience and determination as other club directors in these stringent times'. The response to this reproof was a mass desertion by the directors who resigned en bloc. Subsequently, rugby-league enthusiasts nationwide felt, and in some cases stated openly, that the Brunton Park directors, particularly those without a rugby-league background, were 'rats leaving a sinking ship'. While the going was good they had stayed aboard.

The New Zealanders ultimately returned home, an equally disillusioned Mick Morgan also pulled out and, risking the type of criticism levelled at the directors, was signed by Oldham. Gates dropped to an all-time low of 846 against Warrington, matches were postponed through shortage of players and cash but, miraculously, Carlisle survived, largely through the tireless efforts of two rugby-loving directors, George Graham and Geoff Holmes, and magnificent work by the supporters' club in fund raising.

The struggle for survival was almost equally tough at Ninian Park. The Cardiff and South Wales public obstinately refused to turn up in force to watch the Blue Dragons, and attendances again averaged around the 1000 mark. Yet David Watkins remained outwardly determined and confident and said that, come what may, Cardiff City would keep going for 'at least five years'.

## *Enter Kent Invicta*

The problems of Fulham, Carlisle and Cardiff City might have been expected to daunt further applications for admission but suddenly, from a most unexpected source, came a dramatic and successful application. Paul Faires, a young Kent businessman, and Jim Thompson, chairman of Maidstone United Football Club from the Alliance Premier League, decided to launch rugby league in the garden of England at the London Road ground in Maidstone.

It was a big gamble but Faires, an amateur soccer player with Bromley, Beckenham Town and Croydon, and an amateur rugby-league player with Peckham, bounded with articulate enthusiasm. He pointed out to League officials that Maidstone and its surrounding area was well populated, and that the proposed new club would attempt to get all its players to live in Kent.

The advocacy of Messrs Faires and Thompson was so effective, and a visit by League officials to Maidstone so visually persuasive, that on 6 April 1983 Kent Invicta were admitted to the League by a council vote of twenty-six to three. In his submission to the council, Paul Faires envisaged a possible opening attendance of 8000, with gates settling to around half that figure. His optimism was to prove somewhat misguided on both counts, but council members again took the progressive, expansionary line, and Invicta set out to recruit players. Lynn Hopkins, the record goal-kicking full-back from Workington Town, was the biggest purchase at £20,000, and other experienced signings were Nigel French (ex-Wasps and Barrow), Steve Lane (ex-Hunslet), John Millington (ex-Hull Kingston Rovers), Adrian Alexander and Bob Mordell (former rugby-union players who had played successfully together at Oldham), and Ian Van Bellen and Neil Tuffs who had helped to launch Fulham. From New Zealand came Gary Freeman and Graeme Norton, and from Australia via Peckham came second-row-forward Colin Penola. Two more New Zealanders later joined the club, the speedy winger Mark Elia and Terry O'Shea, a loose-forward. The coach was Bill Goodwin, a southerner who coached Peckham, and the secretary was Bob Fox, from amateur rugby league in Yorkshire.

Kent Invicta opened their league career with a proper blaze of publicity for the game against Cardiff City at London Road, Maidstone, on Sunday 21 August. In addition, the sun shone warmly and brightly, but Paul Faires's estimate of an attendance of 8000 proved staggeringly over-optimistic. The shirt-sleeved crowd totalled 1815; some of the blame was placed at the door of the major counter-attractions of Rochester and Folkestone shows. The gate was disappointing and so was the result, a 31–12 scoreline in favour of Cardiff City, with Invicta scoring one try, through Lane, and four goals from Hopkins against four tries and six Fenwick goals for Cardiff.

The initial high spirits at Maidstone were further deflated when Invicta's second home game, a victory over Doncaster, was watched by only 510 people. The Kent team then went to Batley to win their first away game, 18–8; there were renewed hopes that the supporters would turn out in force for the home game with Workington Town. The attendance was just over 800; Invicta lost narrowly, 11–12.

The crowd figures were, on the surface, shatteringly disappointing, but an examination of Maidstone United's attendances in the Alliance Premier League gave a guide to realism. These averaged between 1000 and 2000, and it had obviously been grossly over-optimistic to talk of 8000 for rugby league.

Invicta's initial problems multiplied when Workington Town, Dewsbury and other clubs in the League complained to headquarters about non-payment of transfer-fee stage-payments for players recruited by the Maidstone club. The League's management committee discussed these matters with Paul Faires and Jim Thompson, and Faires resigned 'to allow for the restructuring on the club's board and finances'. Jim Thompson took over temporary leadership and a search was made for new directors and sponsors.

## Threat to Bramley

Invicta's creditors among the clubs were not disposed to encourage the survival of the new club at their own expense. Hull Kingston Rovers called for the return of their front-row-forward, John Millington, because of the non-payment of the transfer fee and Workington Town, Oldham and Swinton put on similar pressures. Dewsbury threatened to pull out of their fixture at Maidstone on 23 October. Luck was certainly against Invicta because, on 16 October, their train was delayed on the way to a match at Bramley and the match was delayed for forty-five minutes, a fact which, unfortunately, did not help struggling Bramley as they tumbled towards the threat of liquidation.

Invicta received a boost with a gate of more than 2000 for the John Player Special first-round game with St Helens, though they took a 40-point beating. On 21 November 1983 Kent Invicta were unable to raise a team for the second-division game at York, with more than half the side incapacitated by injuries. Nevertheless, it was in November that Jim Thompson went to Leeds to assure the management committee of the League that Invicta had completed their restructure of the board, would survive not merely for the season but for several seasons to come, and might be able to keep going viably on gates of under 1000 with good pruning and housekeeping.

Also in November there came news of yet another suggested venture in new territory. This time the consortium of businessmen came from Mansfield in Nottinghamshire, an area which had been given a glimpse of rugby league by an exhibition match at Nottingham Forest football ground between Hull Kingston Rovers and Cardiff. The consortium's application to the Rugby League chose Mansfield Town football ground, Field Mill, as the base, and looked to nearby south Yorkshire for support. Then, in December, a group based in the Isle of Man put forward a proposal to stage rugby league on the island. The management committee decided not to proceed on this one.

While these missionary moves were in progress, an old-established club, Bramley were struggling desperately to survive. The club was on the verge of liquidation throughout the winter months, with crisis meeting following crisis meeting, fixtures postponed, shareholders' meetings called and adjourned, and dark accusations that Bramley's players were being 'tapped' by other clubs. Hopes of survival alternately rose and fell until, at last, in December, a new consortium took over and fixtures resumed just in time for Christmas.

The 1983–84 season did not end too auspiciously for the four new standard bearers. Fulham made a late effort to avoid relegation, but lost 10–12 to the already doomed Salford at Craven Cottage while Featherstone Rovers pulled clear.

Kent Invicta, after at one stage threatening to make a late bid for promotion, crashed by the amazing score of 80 points to 8 at home to the brilliant second division champions Barrow, conceding 14 tries and 12 goals in an incredible game that shattered, however temporarily, the Maidstone club's morale.

At Ninian Park and Brunton Park, Cardiff City and Carlisle picked up a few victories at the end of the season, but both finished in the mid-to-lower reaches of the second division.

These disappointments did not lessen the enthusiasm of new consortia anxious to enter rugby league, and a meeting of club representatives at Leeds on 18 April considered applications from Mansfield, Sheffield and Runcorn. Mansfield, based at Field Mill football ground, and Sheffield, based at Owlerton greyhound racing and speedway stadium, were admitted subject to stringent financial provisos. Runcorn withdrew their application to allow talks to take place with a view to vandal-ridden Huyton moving from Alt Park to Canal Street, Runcorn. For Huyton it was yet another chapter in an odyssey going back to the thirties through Wigan Highfield, London Highfield, Liverpool Stanley and Liverpool City to Huyton. The club duly moved to Canal Street, and became Runcorn Highfield.

In June one of the pioneers of Fulham, the player-coach Reg Bowden, severed his connection with the London club to replace Kevin Ashcroft as coach of Warrington. His departure, following that of Harold Genders, meant that the two inspirational figures at the birth of Fulham RLFC had left Craven Cottage.

## New Clubs

The new structure of the second division, for the 1984–85 season, placed Sheffield and Mansfield in separate sections, despite their geographical closeness. The 20-team second division was split into eastern and western groups, with Sheffield west of the Pennines among the Lancashire and Cumbria clubs, and Mansfield in the Yorkshire group. Kent Invicta joined the Yorkshire-orientated group one, and Fulham, Cardiff City and Carlisle the western group.

A further twist in the tale of movement and expansion came in June, when it was announced that Southend United had approached Kent Invicta with a view to staging rugby league at the Roots Hall fourth division football ground. This was approved at the League's annual meeting, and Kent Invicta became Southend Invicta, with the injection of new capital and a bigger catchment area.

There were unnerving rumbles from SW6 where the new club explosion began in 1980. League officials revealed that Fulham had been asked for certain assurances following the resignation of Reg Bowden and the transfer-listing of virtually the whole squad of players.

In mid-July there was ominous news from Craven Cottage. The secretary-general of the League, David Oxley, had to delay the compilation of the second division fixtures. The reason was that Fulham were reporting such financial distress that their continuance in 1984/85 was in doubt. The wheel had turned full cycle.

# 2
# How It All Began

The English Rugby Union was formed in 1871, nearly forty years after the Rugby schoolboy, William Webb Ellis, won immortality by picking up a football and running with it. By 1893 there were more than 400 clubs in Rugby Union membership, and in the north of England storm clouds gathered. In the industrial towns of Lancashire and Yorkshire the workers had wages deducted for any time off playing rugby, and in those days factories, pits, shops and offices worked six, and sometimes seven, days a week. Many clubs were faced with incessant, and justifiable, demands from players for 'expenses' to cover time lost from a working shift. Times were hard enough for the miners, the millworkers and the glassblowers, whose wages hardly fed the family, without being stretched to subsidize their sporting pleasures.

To the patrician rulers of Rugby Union, however, the issue was clear cut. The players of the northern clubs were trying to open the door to professionalism, and the very thought was anathema. A clash could not be avoided. At the annual general meeting of the Rugby Football Union in London on 20 September 1893 two Yorkshire representatives, J. A. Millar and M. Newsome, proposed that 'players be allowed compensation for bona-fide loss of time'. It was defeated but 136 delegates out of a total of 418 voted in favour, a strong groundswell. For the next two years many meetings were held and northern club officials, duly encouraged, called a special meeting of club representatives at the George Hotel, Huddersfield, on 29 August 1895. Mr H. H. Waller of Brighouse presided, and clubs represented at this historic meeting were Oldham, Halifax, Leeds, Bradford,

Hull, Huddersfield, Hunslet, Wakefield, Widnes, Broughton Rangers, Batley, St Helens, Leigh, Warrington, Tyldesley, Wigan, Manningham, Rochdale Hornets, Liversedge and Dewsbury.

Only one club, Dewsbury, voted against a proposition that the clubs resign from the Rugby Union to form a Northern Rugby Union in which legitimate 'broken-time' expenses would be paid to players. When Stockport and Runcorn joined the dissentients, twenty-two clubs formed the Northern Union. The first matches were soon played, on Saturday, 7 September 1895, a week before the start of official Rugby Union fixtures. Two senior competitions were formed, one in Lancashire, one in Yorkshire, with 'second team' competitions. The first Northern Union fixtures were: Bradford *v.* Wakefield Trinity, Leigh *v.* Leeds, Tyldesley *v.* Manningham, Batley *v.* Hull, Stockport *v.* Brighouse, Warrington *v.* Hunslet, Liversedge *v.* Halifax, Runcorn *v.* Widnes, St Helens *v.* Rochdale Hornets, and Broughton Rangers *v.* Wigan.

The reaction of the parent Rugby Union was instant and predictable. Clubs in membership were forbidden to play matches with Northern Union clubs, and even more ruthless rules against payments to players were introduced. The rate of 'broken-time' payment was fixed at six shillings (30p) a day, a piffling sum now but a reasonable proportion of Victorian day wages. Wealthier clubs paid more than six shillings for players who were a cut above the average.

## *The gallant youths*

At the end of the first season of Northern Union competition was adjudged to have been keen, playing standards high and crowds good. Runcorn won the Lancashire senior competition and Manningham, a Bradford club, were Yorkshire champions. Sadly, both sides are now defunct and have been so for many years. Many more clubs rushed to join the pioneers for the second season; at the first annual general meeting at the George in August 1896 Mr Waller announced that fifty-nine clubs were in membership, with applications pouring in. Among the new clubs were Swinton, Salford, Morecambe, Bramley, Castleford, Leeds Parish Church, Holbeck and Heckmondwike. In 1896–97 a major development was the launching of the Northern

Union challenge cup for all member clubs, and the first final was at Headingley, Leeds, a superb enclosure then as now, on 1 May 1897.

An excellent crowd of between 13,000 and 14,000 paid £620 to see the game, in which Batley, the Gallant Youths, beat St Helens by two tries and a dropped goal to a try, 10 points to 3, in a game played to standard Rugby Union rules. Lancashire senior-competition champions in the second season were Broughton Rangers, and Brighouse Rangers won the Yorkshire section. It is sadly ironic that the first four clubs to share the competition championships, — Runcorn, Manningham, Broughton Rangers and Brighouse Rangers — are all merely memories.

## *Breakaway laws*

The third season began in September 1897 with a new set of rules marking a distinct break with the parent game. Every goal would count two points, including dropped goals, and the line-out was abandoned. A further host of new clubs entered the Union, many now gone, but including Barrow, lone survivor of that year's crop of entrants. The early part of the season saw the playing of county matches between Lancashire, Yorkshire and Cheshire, in an era when county loyalties were strong and interest high. Lancashire won the first two championships and Yorkshire the third.

Oldham won the Lancashire senior competition in 1897–98, Hunslet taking the Yorkshire title. In the challenge cup the redoubtable fifteen Gallant Youths of Batley again reached Headingley on Saturday, 23 April 1898. Their opponents were Bradford and before a splendid crowd of 27,941, paying £1506, they retained the cup by 7 points to nil. J. B. Goodall scored a try and a dropped goal, Davies adding a further dropped goal.

By now, with the game firmly established in public appeal and gate receipts, the better players were beginning to realize their worth, and were calling for open professionalism and an end to 'broken-time' expenses. The annual meeting of the Northern Union in 1898 accepted the argument and adopted the policy which made professionalism a fundamental part of the northern game.

A four-point charter agreed that professionalism be adopted, players properly registered, players to have 'legitimate' employment in a full time job, and severe penalties imposed for breaches of the charter. The annual meeting also saw an influx of new clubs from Cumberland, with Whitehaven, Maryport, Seaton and Wath Brow joining the ranks.

The 1898–99 season saw many headaches, some with humorous connotations, caused by the rules on professionalism. Shady jobs like billiard-marker, bookies' runner and pub waiter were definitely taboo, and a player named Booth of Radcliffe had his registration suspended when he was found to have no more productive employment than as a public-house barman. A Swinton player who visited a sick relative, thus absenting himself from work, was banned from a Saturday game. The other side of the picture was painted by the *Athletic News* which said some Northern Union players were better paid than soccer professionals, with wages varying between thirty shillings and £4. Inevitably, in their search for good players and success, clubs began to look outside the traditional boundaries, and to rugby union, for captures. Signings were made, always under cloak-and-dagger secrecy in South Wales, the west country and the north-east. Opposition to these moves was particularly bitter in the rugby-union stronghold of South Wales, especially when the brilliant James brothers of Swansea joined Broughton Rangers. Anger seethed and when a man with a strange accent was discovered in Penarth to be a Wigan scout he was ducked in the sea and rolled in the sand. Woodhead, of Elland, and Harry, of Torquay Athletic, were banned from rugby union for life for turning professional.

In the 1898–99 tournaments Broughton Rangers were again Lancashire champions, while Batley took another honour in Yorkshire. Oldham and Hunslet fought out the challenge-cup final at Fallowfield, Manchester, before a crowd of 15,763 paying £1065. Oldham played brilliantly, scoring five tries in a 19–9 victory.

The 1899 annual meeting at Manchester brought a further change in the rules. Kick-offs after tries were to be from the halfway line rather than the 25. The Union's healthy finances led to one or two monetary gestures being made, including payments of £50 to the challenge-cup finalists for the previous two seasons, a gesture which delighted those clubs but miffed Batley who thought the gift could have been given to them for their first two seasons of success. Payments were also made to the four counties, which now included

Cumberland, and to various junior clubs who were struggling for existence.

Runcorn again won the Lancashire senior competition in 1899–1900, and Bradford won the Yorkshire competition. Lancashire won the county championship and Red Rose sides fought out a local derby in the challenge-cup final at Fallowfield, Manchester, on 29 April. The attendance was 17,564, paying £1106, and Swinton won by 16 points to 8. Tom Williams and Pearson scored tries for Salford and Griffiths kicked a goal, but Swinton eventually took control and Messer, Lewis, R. Valentine and Davies touched down, J. Valentine kicking two goals.

## *More changes in the rules*

There were again significant changes in the rules in 1900. In the case of obstruction, the penalty kick was to be taken where the ball dropped, rather than at the point of the offence. Goal-kickers were given clearer opportunities to kick goals, as the charge of defenders was ended. They had to stand on the mark until the kick was taken and this change led to a sudden spurt in successful goal kicks.

A strong move began in 1900–1901 to reduce the number of players in a team from the traditional fifteen to twelve, and this was discussed at a meeting of the professional sub-committee in Manchester during January 1901. The committee passed the buck to the county committees for 'observations', and several clubs took part in friendly 12-a-side games.

A campaign for a 'super league' gathered momentum in 1901. Many clubs felt that county competitions were too parochial and called for a combined top division containing the top clubs. Although the less successful clubs fought against the suggestion the top clubs won their way and in May, 1901, the first combined league was brought into existence, twelve club representatives making the decision at Huddersfield. The twelve, who were given power to add to their number, were Bradford, Batley, Broughton Rangers, Halifax, Huddersfield, Hull, Hunslet, Oldham, Runcorn, Salford, Swinton and Warrington.

A full meeting of the management committee was held on 4 June 1901 and the clubs outside the elite twelve called for a vote. It was a close-run thing, a narrow squeak for the super-league, as the elitists won only by twelve votes to eleven.

While this debate was pursuing its course, the last senior-competition championships were being won. Oldham won in Lancashire, and again Bradford came out on top in Yorkshire. Batley entered their third challenge-cup final in four years and met Warrington at Headingley on Saturday, 27 April 1901, the crowd of more than 30,000 paying £1650. The Batley side again showed their power and consistency and not even the redoubtable Warrington winger, Jack Fish, could pierce the solid defence. Davies and Auty scored tries for Batley, which won by 6 points to nil.

Fifteen clubs were now in membership of the new Northern league, and during the close season of 1901 they evolved further rules and laws. To avoid accusations of a closed shop it was agreed that each season the bottom club would drop out to make way for the winner of a play-off between the Lancashire and Yorkshire senior-competition winners, an early form of promotion and relegation. The knock-on rule was simplified, allowing players to make several attempts to catch the ball, provided it was ultimately held. One new club, South Shields from Durham, was admitted, but Tyldesley and Leeds Parish Church were disbanded.

Attendances were good at the 'super-league' fixtures though, inevitably, crowd figures declined at the devalued senior-competition games and led to many withdrawals in succeeding seasons. The first champions were Broughton Rangers, who produced such irresistible form that they had won the championship by February. Cheshire, with only a handful of teams to select from, won the county championship and Wigan and Leeds were the respective competition winners. Broughton Rangers followed up their championship win by taking the challenge cup and in each case Salford were the runners-up. The cup final, a local derby for the Manchester area, was played at Rochdale on Saturday, 26 April 1902. The crowd was a moderate one, only 15,000, to see Rangers overwhelm their neighbour with brilliant rugby. The score was 25-nil, Wilson scoring a hat-trick of tries, Hogg and Widdeson getting the others. W. James kicked four goals and Oram one.

## Two divisions

The success of the major league system killed for ever any hope of a return to the county competitions. Indeed, in the close season of 1902 a joint meeting of the Northern League and Senior competition club officials at Huddersfield agreed on the first two-division scheme. There would be a first division of eighteen clubs, a second division of twelve clubs, promotion and relegation. Twenty-three clubs applied for places in the second division. The two-division scheme was launched in September 1902; by this time the size of the second division had been increased to eighteen clubs in line with the first. Surprisingly, Leeds, Yorkshire senior-competition winners, did not get enough votes to enter division one. Wigan, the Lancashire winners, were more successful; Leeds had to be satisfied with a second-division place.

The first-division clubs did well at the turnstiles; in the second division the successful clubs broke even, but the unsuccessful teams went into the red.

The first-division championship produced a thrilling battle, with Runcorn, Salford, Broughton Rangers, Halifax and Swinton taking the lead in turn before Halifax clinched it at the death. At the bottom end four newly admitted clubs – Wigan, Widnes, Hull Kingston Rovers and St Helens – finished in the bottom six, with Brighouse Rangers taking the wooden spoon. The winners of the second division were Keighley, with Leeds runner-up. League form was confirmed in the challenge cup when the top two clubs, Halifax and Salford, reached the final. Halifax sought the double while Salford sought to get rid of their unwelcome tag of champion runners-up. The match produced a record crowd of 32,507, paying £1820, at Headingley on Saturday, 25 April 1903. Unfortunately, as a spectacle, it did not live up to its billing.

The record crowd had to wait until the second half for the first points in a dour struggle. Jack Riley forced his way over for a try, which Hadwen goaled, then Hadwen kicked a penalty. Halifax won 7–0, and Salford were again the bridesmaid.

The end of the season brought more sad defections from the Northern Union, and particularly mourned were Manningham, first winners of the Yorkshire senior competition, and Stockport. They were both founder members. For the season of 1903–1904 St Helens and Brighouse Rangers were relegated, and Keighley and Leeds promoted. Pontefract came into a second division of seventeen clubs.

The campaign for 12-a-side rugby received a fillip in 1903–1904 when the county-championship matches were played with teams of twelve, Durham and Northumberland taking part. There were further rule changes in the close season, clubs being forbidden to pack down with more than three in the front row, and the knock-on rule taking a further amendment to allow opposing sides to pick up the ball even if it fell to the ground.

South Shields, the Durham outpost, left the League after a short and unsuccessful stay. Champions in 1903–1904 were Bradford, with Salford in their accustomed second place. Huddersfield and Keighley were relegated and Wakefield Trinity won the second division. St Helens and Holbeck tied for second place. In a play-off St Helens won. This event had dramatic repercussions. Holbeck promptly disbanded as a rugby club and reformed, eventually, as Leeds City Football Club.

The 1904 challenge-cup final saw Halifax beat Warrington 8–3 to win the trophy for the second successive year. A crowd of 17,041 attended the final at Salford on Saturday, 30 April, and receipts were £936. Joe Riley and Morley scored the Halifax tries, Hadwen landing a goal, while the great Jack Fish made a Warrington try for Davies.

Dewsbury won the second-division championship in 1904–1905 in remarkable fashion. Early in the season a smallpox scare swept through the town and opponents refused to fulfil fixtures. Despite an enormous backlog Dewsbury swept through their games to win the title, with Barrow as runners-up. In the first division Oldham were champions, and in the challenge-cup final of 1905 Warrington won consolation for the defeat of the previous year. On Saturday, 29 April, at Headingley, they beat Hull Kingston Rovers by 6 points to nil, Fish getting both tries. The crowd was 19,439 and the receipts £1,261.

## Back to one division

The short-lived two-division scheme was killed by the annual meeting in July 1905. The second-division system was rendering many clubs close to bankruptcy and there had been widespread calls for a return to one division. The close season of 1905 also saw the end of the 'working clause'. No longer need a player prove a weekday *bona fide* job to play on Saturday.

During the season 1905–1906 Northumberland and Durham and Cheshire quit the county championship. To whip up new interest, however, Lancashire and Yorkshire county-challenge cups were instituted. Wigan beat Leigh at Broughton to win the first Lancashire cup, and Hunslet beat Halifax at Bradford.

The fixture tangle in the one-division system caused many problems, since not all clubs could play each other at home and away. The championship was thus awarded to Leigh on a percentage basis after a comparatively undemanding season in which Leigh played only a handful of tough Yorkshire games. Many clubs complained about Leigh's 'easy' fixture list, and in 1906–1907 it was decided a top-four play-off would decide the title.

Salford reached the challenge-cup final yet again on Saturday, 28 April 1906, before a 16,000 crowd paying £920 at Headingley. Bradford were the opponents and Salford were looking to break the long drought in major trophy finals and to get away from the unwelcome label of champion runner-up. It was a dull game with scrum following scrum in monotonous succession. Fifteen minutes from the end the Bradford half-back, Brear, dodged over the Salford line, and when Laidlaw added a penalty goal poor Salford, beaten 5–0, had gone down again.

## 13-a-side

The campaign for a reduction in the number of players in teams gathered fresh momentum at the 1906 annual meeting. St Helens proposed a drop of one player, to fourteen, while Whitehaven Recreation called for twelve. Warrington, backed by Leigh, suggested 13-a-side as a compromise, and this was the figure approved at a Huddersfield meeting, a historic landmark in creating a totally separate personality and character for the northern game.

The first season of 13-a-side won praise and approval for a much more open game; each side was shorn of two tacklers and spoilers. At the end of the season the semi-finals of the first championship play-off attracted good crowds, Halifax confirming their top place by beating the runners-up, Oldham, 18–3 before a 16,000 crowd at Huddersfield.

Oldham also reached the challenge-cup final, meeting Warrington on a rainy day at Broughton on Saturday, 13 April, before an 18,500 attendance. The heavy rain and muddy conditions spoiled the game and at half time it was 3–2 to Oldham, Avery scoring a try against a Fish goal. S. Lees scored a try for Warrington and the brilliant Fish ran from his own half for a spectacular touchdown. Fish kicked two more goals, then Hockenhall added a further try, goaled by Fish in a convincing 17–3 win for Warrington.

The season ended with some momentous news from New Zealand. A syndicate of sportsmen, impressed by Northern Union play and organization during an All Blacks tour of Britain, was planning to sponsor a team to visit Britain and play Northern Union teams in 1907–1908. It was tremendous news and Northern Union officials went into transports of delight as the game took wing internationally.

At club level Liverpool City resigned after one poor season and Bradford re-formed on a new ground as Bradford Northern. But it was in the international sphere that Northern Union made headlines. In Wales, hotbed of rugby, Ebbw Vale and Merthyr Tydfil were admitted for 1907–1908. Not since the pioneering days of 1895 had a season been so eagerly anticipated. In New Zealand the leaders of the international breakaway were A. H. Baskerville of Wellington and George Smith, an All Blacks winger.

# 3
# The First Tour

It was agreed that the New Zealand tourists would receive 70 per cent of gate receipts, with guarantees of £50 for a midweek game and £100 for a Saturday. The tour would be insured against loss.

The proposed tour caused consternation in New Zealand. The All Blacks were stated to have signed assurances that they 'would do nothing contrary to the laws and spirit of rugby union'; indeed, the threat of losing amateur status did not deter the pioneer tourists who set off by sea in midsummer. Among them were four All Blacks – George Smith, D. McGregory, W. Johnston and W. H. Mackrell. Also on board were two players destined to become all-time greats, H. H. 'Dally' Messenger, an Australian 'guest player' from Sydney, and Lance B. Todd, a twenty-two year-old half-back. 'Baskerville's team', the first Australasian tourists, arrived in Britain in October 1907.

The captain was H. R. Wright, of Wellington, and they played their first 13-a-side game at Bramley. They won handsomely, despite having barely found their land legs, and went on to beat Huddersfield, Broughton Rangers before a crowd of 24,000 and Leeds, while drawing at Wakefield. Then the clubs began to get the measure of the tourists and Wigan beat them 12–8. The English winter set in at its muddy, slushy, cold worst and Barrow, Leigh and Oldham also beat the tourists. Runcorn, Bradford and Halifax followed suit and the tour seemed destined to end in anti-climax. The mood of the pioneers was not improved by news from New Zealand that all the players had been suspended *sine die* by the Rugby Union authorities.

Three 'test' matches were played against the New Zealanders, two of them at Cheltenham and Stamford Bridge (Chelsea), as propaganda games. The first Test in Northern Union history was played at Headingley on 25 January 1908, though the gate of 8000 was a disappointment. The teams for this first international were:

*Northern Union*: Taylor (Hull); Hogg (Broughton Rangers), Llewellyn (Oldham), Jenkins, Leytham (Wigan); Jolley (Runcorn), Thomas (Wigan); Ruddick (Broughton Rangers), D. Jones (Merthyr), A. Smith (Oldham), A. Robinson (Halifax), Wilson (Hunslet), Warwick (Salford)

*New Zealand*: Turtill; G. W. Smith, Rowe, Lingley, Todd; Wynyard, Kelly; Wright, Cross, Pearce, Johnston, Gilchrist, Trevarthen

The Northern Union confirmed the poor form shown by the tourists by winning 14–6. Robinson (2), Leytham and Llewellyn scored tries and Jolley kicked a goal. Turtill and Wynyard scored tries for the tourists.

A much better crowd, more than 15,000, turned up at Stamford Bridge for the next Test on 8 February 1908. In the home side Eccles (Halifax), Baxter (Rochdale Hornets), and Thomas (Warrington) replaced Hogg, Thomas (Wigan) and Robinson. New Zealand had Messenger, Tyler and Dunning for Rowe, Kelly and Wright. The result was a shock for the Northern Union and a tremendous and much-needed boost for the tourists who won 18–6. G. Smith, Todd, Johnston and Wynyard touched down, and Messenger landed three goals, against tries from Leytham and Eccles.

For the third and deciding Test at Cheltenham on 15 February Eccles, Llewellyn, Leytham, Baxter, Ruddick, Jones, Thomas and Warwick were replaced by Batten (Hunslet), P. Thomas (Leeds), Tyson, White (Oldham), Clampitt (Broughton Rangers), Birch (Leeds), Spencer (Salford) and Holder (Hull). The New Zealanders made no changes. Conditions were poor and a crowd of no more than 5000 saw the tourists complete the salutary shock to home complacency by winning 8–5 and taking the series. A try by Jolley and a goal from White gave the Union a 5–0 interval lead, but in the second half Messenger and Johnston scored tries and Wrigley kicked a goal. This victory ended a tour in which the tourists had played thirty-five games and won nineteen, including two Tests.

At the end of the tour Oldham signed threequarter George Smith, while Wigan beat several clubs to the signature of the great half-back, Lance B. Todd, later to become a famous player, administrator and commentator on rugby league.

## Australian Moves

In 1908 came the expected Australian breakaway from rugby union. The New South Wales Rugby Union, dissatisfied with official rulings on broken-time and compensation, decided to set up their own set of rules and to send a team to Britain in 1908–1909. Proceeds of the tour would be used to set up a New South Wales Rugby League on the tourists' return. The game in New South Wales was given a boost by three exhibition matches played by the New Zealand tourists on their return home. The matches used Northern Union rules and were well received by the spectators.

The Australian breakaway gathered pace and a meeting took place at Sydney at which the New South Wales president, Harry Hoyle, gave a casting vote for the adoption of Northern Union rules. Interest began to be shown outside New South Wales, in the state of Queensland. In midsummer 1908, a year after the pioneering New Zealand tour, Dally Messenger set sail again, this time with the first Australian tourists.

While these momentous events were happening, the Northern Union's domestic competitions continued successfully. The challenge-cup final of 1908 featured Hull and Hunslet at Huddersfield on Saturday, 25 April. Despite bad weather, a crowd of 18,500 spectators paid £903. The constant blizzard spoiled the game but Hunslet tried hard to handle the ball and create moves. Eagers dropped a goal, Smith scored a try, goaled by Albert Goldthorpe, and then Goldthorpe kicked a second-half goal and Farrar added a try in a 14–0 Hunslet win. Hunslet also reached the championship final, beating Oldham 12–2 at Wakefield on 9 May, in a replay following a 7–7 draw the previous week at Salford. It was the longest season since the Northern Union's inception.

The 1908 annual meeting was understandably a cheerful one and, despite the fact that Ebbw Vale and Merthyr Tydfil had had only moderate seasons, new Welsh clubs in Barry, Aberdare, mid-Rhondda and Treherbert were admitted for 1908–1909.

The Australians, with J. J. Giltinan as secretary-manager and

Dennis Lutge as captain, arrived at Tilbury on Sunday, 27 September 1908. After several mixed-fortune skirmishes against League clubs, they met the Northern Union in the first Test at Park Royal, London, on 12 December. All three internationals had been arranged at 'propaganda venues' but only 9000 turned up at Park Royal. The teams were:

*Northern Union*: Gifford (Barrow); Batten (Hunslet), Jenkins (Wigan), Dickenson (Warrington), Tyson (Oldham); Thomas (Wigan), Brooks (Warrington); A. Smith (Oldham), Longworth (Oldham), Jukes (Hunslet), Robinson (Halifax), Mann, Higson (Bradford)

*Australia*: M. Bolewski; W. Heidke, J. Devereux, S. Deane, H. H. Messenger; A. Butler, A. Holloway; J. Abercrombie, L. O'Malley, A. Burdon, S. Walsh, A. Pearce, J. Courtney. Lutge, who had been out of form, was replaced by Messenger as captain.

Despite the poor attendance the match fulfilled expectations and was an end-to-end thriller. Messenger kicked a goal for Australia, then Thomas and Batten scored tries to give Britain a 6–2 lead. A Devereux try made it 6–5, but Brooks and Batten hit back with tries for Britain and Brooks kicked a goal. Tyson made it 17–5 just after the interval with a fine try, but the Australians rallied. Devereux and O'Malley touched down and Messenger kicked both goals. Robinson replied with a try but Messenger intercepted and created a try for Devereux, his hat trick. Messenger's goal equalized at 20–20. A Messenger goal gave the tourists a two-point lead but, in an exciting finish, Brooks kicked a goal to make it 22–22.

The second Test was played on Saturday, 23 January 1909, in the soccer stronghold of St James Park, Newcastle. This time the match was a much greater propaganda success, with a crowd of 22,000. In the Northern Union side Lomas (Salford), and Silcock (Wigan) were substituted for Dickenson and Jukes.

Australia brought in A. Rosenfeld, F. Frawley, J. Morton, A. Conlon and T. McCabe. The game never reached the heights of the first Test and, although Messenger got a standing ovation for a brilliant individual try for Australia, the Northern Union won comfortably with tries from Thomas, Lomas and Tyson, and three goals from Lomas. The third Test was an anti-climax, played at Villa Park, Birmingham, on Monday, 15 February 1909. The Northern Union

won 6–5 before a crowd of a few thousand, and the game itself
aroused little interest. At the end of their first tour the Australians
had played forty-six games, winning twenty-two and drawing six.
Financially the tour had been a failure, but the Northern Union had
underwritten the tourists' losses. Inevitably, British clubs went for
the signings, Deane and Anlezark going to Oldham, Devereux and
Morton to Hull, and Albert Rosenfeld, a winger with a great future,
to Huddersfield.

## *A Return Invitation*

The Australians proved their optimism for the future of Northern
Union by inviting the Union to send a touring team to Australia.
The invitation was readily accepted, 1910 being the scheduled year.
The game was also growing in New Zealand and, in 1909, a New
Zealand touring side visited Australia.

Hull again reached the final of the challenge cup in 1909, meeting
Wakefield Trinity at Headingley on Saturday, 24 April. A fine crowd
of more than 30,000 attended, producing receipts of £1489. There
were astonishing scenes before the game; large numbers of queueing
spectators became impatient and rushed several gates to break in.
The teams were:

*Hull*: Taylor; Rogers, Connell, Cottrell, Dechan; Anderson,
Wallace, Herridge, Holder, Boylen, Havelock, Britton, Carroll

*Wakefield Trinity:*   Metcalfe; Bennett, Lynch, Sidwell, Simpson;
Slater, Newbould; G. Taylor, Auton, Crosland, Kershaw, Walton,
Beaumont

Referee: J. F. Smirke (Wigan)

Hull, despite fielding an experienced side, were soundly thrashed
17–0 by a young Trinity team, many of whom had worked six successive night shifts in the local pits. 'If we want them fit, we send them
to work,' said a Trinity official. Newbould, Bennett (2), Simpson and
Crosland scored the Wakefield tries and Metcalfe kicked a goal. On
the following Saturday a 12,000 crowd at Salford saw Wigan win the
championship, beating Oldham 7–3 in a mediocre game.

The annual meetings of the parent Northern Union and the
Northern League brought further fresh waves of optimism, although
a slight damper was put on the euphoria by the secession of Barry,

mid-Rhondda and Aberdare. Throughout the close season clubs continued to import players from the 'colonies'. H. S. Turtill, the New Zealand full-back, joined St Helens; Frawley, O'Malley and Stuntz, all Australians, joined Warrington; H. Rowe, an All Blacks winger, signed for Leeds and another New Zealander, Trevarthen, joined Huddersfield. These signings were not too well received in the outposts of empire, where League officials saw their strength being sapped. As a result, transfers could not be effected without the approval of the parent club or without two years' residence in Britain.

J. H. Houghton (St Helens), president of the Union, and J. Clifford, a former president, were named at the start of the 1909–1910 season as managers of the forthcoming historic tour of Australia. The British team was to receive a guaranteed figure to cover expenses, plus a percentage of gate receipts. Clubs were asked to nominate players who would be 'a credit to the Union both on and off the field'; trial matches were played at Headingley and Wigan, and it was agreed that there would be two sailings, one for the bulk of the players, the second for those involved in the major trophies at the end of the season. The following players were eventually chosen for the first-ever Great Britain overseas tour: Ruddick (Broughton Rangers), Shugars (Warrington), Farrar, Smith, Jukes, Batten (Hunslet), Winstanley (Leigh), Davies and Bartholomew (Huddersfield), Riley (Halifax), Jenkins (Ebbw Vale), Lomas, Curzon (Salford), Newbould, Kershaw (Wakefield Trinity), Young, Webster, Ward (Leeds), Boylen (Hull), Helm, Avery (Hull), Ramsdale, Sharrock, Leytham, Jenkins, Thomas (Wigan).

To clear the decks for the tour the challenge-cup final was played on 16 April. Hull (for the second consecutive year,) and Leeds reached the final, played at Fartown, Huddersfield. The match started fifty minutes late because train delays affected both teams, but the 17,000 crowd took the delay patiently. The teams were:

*Hull*: Taylor; Cottrell, Devereux, Morton, Rogers; Wallace, Anderson; Herridge, Osborne, R. Taylor, Connell, Holder, Walton

*Leeds*: Young; Fawcett, Goldthorpe, Gillie, Baron; Ware, Sanders; Biggs, Jarman, Harrison, Topham, Webster, Ward

Referee: H. J. Priestley (Salford)

Hull made another attempt to reward their supporters with a challenge-cup win, but once again they were doomed to failure though

it took a replay to take the cup to Headingley. In the first game the
result was a 7–7 draw after Hull had taken a 7–0 lead with a try by
Cottrell, a drop goal by Wallace and a goal by Rogers. Leeds lost
Sanders in the days before substitutes but came back strongly to tie
the score with a try by Goldthorpe and two goals from Young. The
replay was at the same venue on the following Monday. Both teams
had injury changes, Taylor and Anderson dropping out of the Hull
side and Rowe replacing Sanders in the Leeds line-up. Leeds won
easily 26–12, relaxing after leading 26–0. Webster, Topham, Goldthorpe and Rowe scored tries, and Young got seven goals. For Hull,
Walton and Connell touched down and Rogers landed three goals.

Oldham found better consolation in the championship final. After
three years of disappointment they beat Wigan 13–7 at Broughton.

## *The first tour in Australia*

Thoughts now turned to the momentous tour of Australia. The first
party of seaborne tourists arrived at the end of May 1910, and the
late arrivals on 2 June. The tourists played their first game against
New South Wales on 4 June at Sydney. They lost 28–15, but gate
receipts were good at £1300. Two days later, in an excellent game,
New South Wales won again, 27–20, and a trio of games against the
state team ended the following Saturday. This time the tourists won
23–10 and total gate receipts for the three games were £3600.

The eagerly awaited first Test on Australian soil was at Sydney
on 18 June 1910. A huge crowd of more than 50,000 saw a curtain-
raiser in which the captains, Dally Messenger and James Lomas, had
a goal-kicking competition. Lomas won and followed it up by leading
Northern Union to a 27–20 victory in the Test. Australia went ahead
with a Hickey try and Messenger goal, but Leytham dribbled ahead
to touch down and Lomas goaled. The brilliant Messenger scored a
try and kicked two goals, but tries from Leytham and Thomas made
it 12–11 at half time. There was no holding the tourists in the second
half and Jukes, the powerful Hunslet forward, scored a hat trick of
tries. Batten got a seventh try and Lomas kicked two more goals.
The match was already well won when Australia added two late
tries.

The tourists beat Newcastle and Queensland and, with the receipts totalling more than £6000, the tour was financially safe. The second Test was played at Brisbane on Saturday, 2 July, and the Northern Union won another fine victory after trailing 11–0. Leytham and Thomas touched down and Lomas kicked two goals to pull the score back to 11–10. Then, in the second half, Leytham added three more tries and Kershaw also scored in a final scoreline of 22–17.

As the Test series was now decided it was agreed that the third international should be against a combined Australian and New Zealand side. This took place at Sydney on Saturday, 9 July, before yet another 50,000 crowd, and the result was a draw, the touring team drawing level. V. Farnsworth, Courtney and McKivatt crossed for the combined team and Messenger kicked two goals as Australia led 13–5. Leytham (try) and Lomas (goal) scored for the Northern Union. In the second half the tourists drew level with tries from Avery and Winstanley and a goal from Thomas.

An extra match was arranged for Wednesday, 13 July, against Australasia, and the home side at last found consolation in a 32–15 win. From Australia the tourists went on to New Zealand, where they ran up big scores against the Maoris, Auckland, Rotorua and New Zealand. They beat New Zealand 52–20 at Rotorua and the receipts of £520 brought tour proceeds to £11,000, of which the Union received £6500, a bumper return. There was one final game, a 50–12 hammering of New South Wales on Saturday, 6 August, after which the triumphant tourists set sail from Melbourne in the S. S. *Otranto*.

On the home front two Welsh sides, Treherbert and Merthyr Tydfil, gave up the struggle. Coventry came into the League to give a foothold in the Midlands, but they too found the going hard.

The challenge-cup final of 1911 brought together two Lancashire teams, making a change from the all-Yorkshire finals of three previous seasons. Because of torrential rain and a swamp-like pitch at Salford on Saturday, 29 April, however, the game between Wigan and Broughton Rangers was a big disappointment. Wigan, indeed, asked for a postponement, but the Union decreed that the match should be played; 8000 hardy, soaked souls saw Rangers win 4–0 with two penalty goals from Harris. The sides were:

*Broughton Rangers*: Davidson; Bouch, Wild, Harris, Scott; Barlow, E. Jones; J. Clampitt, B. Clampitt, Ruddick, Gorry, Hirst, Winskill

*Wigan*: Sharrock; Leytham, Jenkins, Todd, Miller; Thomas, Gleave; Seeling, Williams, Cheetham, Ramsdale, Whittaker, Silcock
    Referee: J. F. May (St Helens)
Wigan's hopes of consolation in the championship final a week later were again dashed by Oldham. On a better day, and before a crowd of 20,000, Oldham won 20–7 with Jim Lomas, signed from Salford, having a superb game, scoring two tries, kicking four goals and making a try for White.

## The tour cycle established

Overseas tours were now accepted as part of the Northern Union curriculum, and the Australians arrived in Britain at Tilbury on 16 September, 1911. Managed by C. H. Ford and J. Quinlan, the tourists had twenty-four Australians and four New Zealanders in F. Woodward, A. H. Francis, C. Savoury and G. Gillett. The captain was C. McKivatt and the remainder of the party were:
    C. McMurtrie, P. McCue, W. Noble, A. Broomham, J. Murray, F. Farnsworth, W. Farnsworth, R. Stuart, D. Frawley, C. Russell, H. Gilbert, R. Craig, E. Courtney, R. Williams, C. Sullivan, W. Cann, P. Burge, A. Holloway, T. Berecry, S. Darmody, C. Fraser, W. Neil, H. Hallett. There was no Dally Messenger due to business reasons.
    The tourists began well, beating Midlands and South at Coventry, Broughton Rangers, Wales at Ebbw Vale, and England at Fulham football ground. They beat the Northern League at Everton soccer ground and met their first defeat against Wigan before a 25,000 crowd. The first Test, yet another propaganda vehicle, was at St James Park, Newcastle on Wednesday, 8 November 1911, before a 6000 attendance. Teams were:
*Northern Union*: Sharrock (Wigan); W. Davies (Halifax), Wagstaff (Huddersfield), Jenkins, Miller (Wigan); Thomas (Wigan), Smith (Hunslet); Harrison (Leeds), Burgham (Halifax), J. Clampitt (Broughton Rangers), Gronow (Huddersfield), Winstanley (Wigan), Avery (Oldham)
*Australasia*: Fraser; Broomham, Gilbert, Hallett, Russell; V. Farnsworth, McKivatt; Francis, McCue, Cann, Courtney, Williams, Craig

Davies sidestepped Fraser to put Britain ahead, Thomas goaling, and Thomas added a penalty goal. Suddenly Australasia produced some fine attacking play and Francis, Farnsworth, Hallett and Cann ran in tries, Francis landing two goals. It was 19–7 at half time and the only score of the second half was an unimproved try by Davies for  Britain.

The second Test was at another missionary venue, Edinburgh, on Saturday, 18 December, and the attendance was a moderate 8000. The Northern Union was lucky to escape with an 11–11 draw in a game which the tourists claimed to have won with a penalty goal which, however, was disallowed controversially. Britain made several changes, with Wood (Oldham), Jenkinson (Hunslet), Lomas (Oldham), Batten (Hunslet), Davies (Huddersfield), Clark (Huddersfield), Ramsdale (Wigan) and Woods (Rochdale Hornets) replacing Sharrock, W. Davies, Jenkins, Miller, Thomas, Burgham, Clampitt and Avery. The Northern Union led 11–2 at half time with tries from Wagstaff (2) and Lomas, plus a goal from Wood, against a try by Frawley. In the second half the tourists tied the game at 11–11 with tries from McKivatt and Russell and a goal from Francis. Then came the controversial decision. Francis took a penalty kick at goal and one touch judge, an Australian, put up his flag. The other touch judge, a Northern Union official, put his flag down, and the referee ruled 'no goal' despite fierce Australian protests.

The third Test was played at Villa Park football ground, Birmingham, on New Year's Day 1912. The Union had Jenkins (Wigan) instead of Wagstaff and the tourists replaced Russell by Berecry. The result was a crushing and decisive victory for Australia after the Northern Union had led 8–0. Ramsdale hurt his ankle and left the field, and the tourists took charge. The final score was 33–8. Tries were scored by Farnsworth, with two each from McKivatt, McCue, Berecry, and Frawley, and goals provided by Gilbert and Frawley (2). This victory gave Australia the series.

It was an Australian who took the individual headlines during the season; Huddersfield's flying little winger, Albert Rosenfeld, notched no fewer than eighty tries in 1911–1912, a magnificent record which still stands. Huddersfield also set up a team record with 1183 points, not surprisingly reaching the championship final, beating Wigan 13–5 at Halifax before 15,000 people. The tries came from Rosenfeld, Clark and Davies; Longstaffe and Grey kicked goals. Holland (try) and Thomas (goal) gave Wigan's points.

After the successful tour, more colonial signings were inevitable. Gilbert and Darmody joined Hull, W. Farnsworth came to Oldham and Francis to Wigan, and after hostile verbal exchanges the Union imposed the two-year residential qualification.

Headingley was the venue for the challenge-cup final on Saturday, 27 April 1912, and an attendance of 15,721 paying £853 saw Dewsbury win their first trophy since joining the Union, beating Oldham 8–5. In a tough, hard, tackling game Oldham led 5–2 at half time with a try by Cook and a goal by Ferguson against a penalty goal by Neary. With ten minutes to go Avery, the Oldham forward, was sent off and Dewsbury snatched a try through Rhodes. With two minutes left, from a scrum near the Oldham line, Rhodes squeezed over and Dewsbury won. Teams were:

*Dewsbury*: Jackett; Rhodes, Ware, Ward, Sharples; Neary, Milner; Richardson, Garnett, O'Neill, Hammill, Abbishaw, Evans

*Oldham*: Wood; Cook, Dean, Davies, Williams; Lomas, Anlezark; Ferguson, Smith, Avery, White, Wise, Wiltshire

Referee: B. Ennion (Wigan)

## Huddersfield resplendent

In the 1912–13 season Huddersfield's wonderful teamwork was the talk of everyone throughout the game, and they reached the finals of both challenge cup and championship. Huddersfield met Warrington in the cup final at Headingley on Saturday, 26 April, before a crowd of 22,754 paying £1446. Teams were:

*Huddersfield*: Holland; Rosenfeld, Gleeson, Wagstaff, Moorhouse; Grey, Davies; Higson, Lee, Clark, Gronow, Longstaffe, Chilcott

*Warrington*: Jolley; Brooks, Tranter, Renwick, Bradshaw; Dainteth, Nicholas; G. Thomas, Chesters, Skelhorne, Fearnley, R. Thomas, Cox

Referee: J. F. May (St Helens)

It was expected that the free-flowing Huddersfield attack would take Warrington apart, but the Wirepullers showed determined defence in repelling fast raids and a Bradshaw try and a Jolley touchline goal put Warrington 5–0 ahead. In the second half Hudder-

**THE FIRST CUP WINNERS—BATLEY 1896-97**

Left to Right.
Back Row—Mr. H. Brook (Treasurer), Mr. W. R. Binns (Financial Secretary), Mr. J. Wilson (Trainer), Mr. W. G. Isherwood (Vice-President), Mr. D. Burnley (President), Mr. J. Sheard ("Reporter" Representative), Mr. F. Bennett (Trainer), Mr. J. Goodall (Vice-President), Mr. W. H. Shaw (Correspondence Secretary).
Third Row—G. H. Maine, *T. Wilby, F. Fisher, J. Gath, *F. W. Lowrie, J. Littlewood, J. T. Munns, H. Goodall, *J. Naylor.
Second Row—D. Fitzgerald, A. Garner, J. B. Goodall (Captain), J. Oakland, R. Spurr.
Front Row—*R. Barraclough, *H. Hallas, C. Stubley, W. P. Davies, M. Shackleton, I. Shaw.
* Denotes did not play in Final.

A fading but vintage photograph of the Gallant Youths of Batley, winners of the Northern Union challenge cup in its inaugural season, 1896-97. They beat St Helens 10-3 at Headingley and repeated their success the following year, beating Bradford 7-0 at the same venue

The Cardiff City and former Wales Rugby Union forward Tommy David, gives the Blue Dragons a great send-off with a try in the opening game against Salford at Ninian Park. David clocked up 50 tries by March 1984

Reg Bowden enjoys the familiar taste of champagne after one of Widnes' many trophy successes, the 1980 premiership. He was a founder of Fulham and now coaches Warrington

The Fulham second row forward Martin Herdman flies through the air with the greatest of panache to score a try against Salford

David Watkins, captain of Wales at both Union and League, came north to give long and distinguished service to Salford, and established a seasonal goal-kicking record in 1972-73 with 221 goals for the Red Devils. After a brief spell with Swinton, he launched the Blue Dragons of Ninian Park, Cardiff City, as coach and then managing director

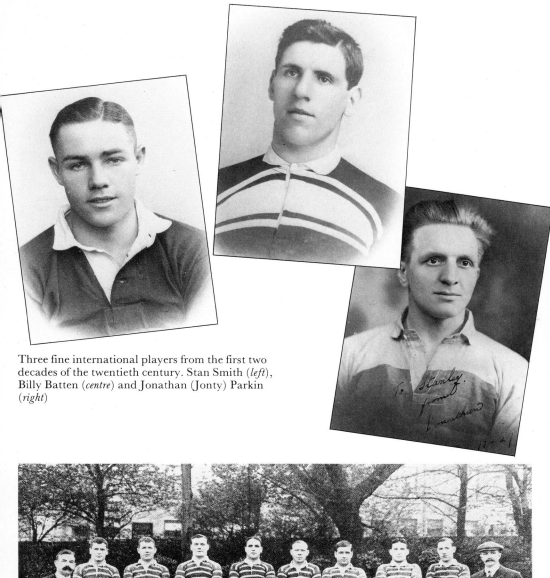

Three fine international players from the first two decades of the twentieth century. Stan Smith (*left*), Billy Batten (*centre*) and Jonathan (Jonty) Parkin (*right*)

One of the greatest teams ever – the Huddersfield 'Team of all the Talents' in 1914–15. Harold Wagstaff is in the centre of the picture, and the Australian record-scoring winger Albert Rosenfeld in the centre of the front row. Rosenfeld scored 80 tries in the 1913-14 season

The 1910 Australasian tourists, the 'Rorke's Drift' heroes. *Back row (left to right):* Clampitt, Clark, Longstaff, Roman, Holland, Smales, Jarman. *Second row:* Hall, Thomas, Guerin, Coldrick, Johnson, Ramsdale, Williams. *Third row:* Robinson, O'Garra, Moorhouse, Mr W.J. Clifford, Wagstaff, Mr J.H. Houghton, Davies, Wood, Jenkins. *Front row:* Francis, Rogers, Mr Murray (trainer), Smith, Prosser

The skilful Australian forward Wally Prigg makes a typical break during the 1936 Test series in Australia, but the formidable figure of Hodgson is waiting

sfield threw everything into attack and Moorhouse ran in for two tries. Warrington tired, and Wagstaff and Moorhouse interpassed for Moorhouse to get his hat-trick. On the following Saturday, before 16,000 at Wakefield, the 'team of all the talents' rounded off the season by once again beating Wigan in the championship final. The score was 27–2, with tries coming at regular intervals from Clark (3), Rosenfeld (2), Davies and Moorhouse, Holland landing three goals.

Huddersfield continued to break records in 1913–14. They pulverized a junior club Swinton Park Rangers, 119–2, in a cup game. Just when it seemed that Huddersfield would again carry all before them, Hull beat Huddersfield 11–3 in the challenge-cup semi-final, and Hull went on to meet Wakefield Trinity, their 1909 conquerors, in the final. With another Australasian tour scheduled in 1914 the final was played on Saturday, 18 April 1914. Teams were:

*Hull*: Rogers; Harrison, Batten, Gilbert, Francis; Devereux, Anderson; Herridge, Holder, Taylor, Hammill, Grice, Darmody

*Wakefield Trinity*: Land; Johnson, Lynch, Poynton, Howarth; J. Parkin, Millican; Dixon, Crosland, Beattie, Kershaw, E. Parkin, A. Burton

Referee: J. F. May (St Helens)

At last Hull gained the challenge-cup victory that had eluded them so many times. Hull had, however, to wait seventy-two minutes to get in front; at that point Kershaw, the Trinity captain, was sent off. Following his dismissal Harrison went over for a try, and two minutes from the end Devereux and Gilbert made a try for Francis. Hull had won 6–0 and at long last Humberside could celebrate.

## Salford at last

The championship final the following week also turned a long-standing bridesmaid into a bride. Salford, the champion runner-up, surprisingly beat the mighty Huddersfield at Headingley. Yet the formality of a Fartown victory seemed certain when Gleeson touched down after a typical move with Wagstaff and Rogers. Salford, however, fought like tigers and tackled like demons. Reese forced his way over and Mesley kicked the goal to give Salford a 5–3 lead. In the second half courageous backs-to-the-wall defending enabled

Salford to hold out. When the whistle finally blew the victorious underdogs were chaired off the field by their supporters.

With the championship final over, the second party of English tourists sailed off to join their colleagues. Managers were again Messrs Houghton and Clifford, with Wagstaff as captain. The full party comprised:

H. Wagstaff, J. H. Rogers, S. Moorhouse, F. Longstaffe, D. Clark and J. Chilcott (Huddersfield), W. Hall, A. E. Wood and D. Holland (Oldham), G. Thomas, B. Jenkins, A. P. Coldrick and R. Ramsdale (Wigan), F. Smith, J. W. Guerin, J. Smales (Hunslet), W. A. Davies, W. Jarman (Leeds), F. Williams, S. Prosser (Halifax), J. E. Robinson, W. Roman (Rochdale Hornets), A. J. Francis (Hull), J. O'Garra, A. Johnson (Widnes), and J. L. Clampitt (Broughton Rangers).

The tour began on Saturday, 14 June 1914, with a 26–10 beating by Metropolis at Sydney. Defeat against New South Wales followed, but the tourists found their land legs and subsequently beat Queensland, Ipswich and Northern Districts. Then came the most remarkable eight-day period in Test history, before or since, culminating in the courageous 'Rorke's Drift' encounter. Three Tests were played at Sydney in this brief period.

Despite injuries Northern Union won the first Test at the Moore Agricultural Ground, Sydney, on 28 June. The crowd was 40,000 and the tourists played superb rugby to win 23–5. Tries came from Moorhouse (2), Clark, Robinson and Hall, with Longstaffe and Robinson each kicking two goals.

The second Test match had been arranged for the King's Birthday two days later. The tourists were further weakened by injuries from the first Test and in a reshuffled side Hall played as threequarter and Rogers played stand-off-half. Britain fought hard and were level 7–7 at the interval. Then Robinson was injured and Australia scored a try and a goal to win 12–7. The series was even and 55,000 had watched the second game, proving that interest was at fever pitch.

Capitalizing on public interest the Australian authorities threw the tourists' plans and preparations into chaos by rearranging the third Test, now vital, from later in the tour to the following Saturday, 4 July. In vain Messrs Houghton and Clifford protested and, when Mr Clifford cabled Northern Union headquarters in Britain, a hastily convened management-committee meeting, in true stiff-upper-lip manner, instructed the tourists to play as requested.

## The Rorke's Drift Test

The message from England concluded with a true Nelson touch. It quoted: 'England expects that every man will do his duty.' Before the match Mr Clifford addressed the players in the dressing room. It was a stirring call to action and Wagstaff later wrote that the players' eyes filled with tears. This was a splendid chapter in the annals of the game. Typical of their spirit was full-back Alf Wood who played with a patched-up broken nose. The teams for this amazing match were:

*Australia*: Hallett; Frawley, Deane, Tidyman, W. Messenger; Fraser, Holloway; Cann, Courtney, Craig, Sullivan, Burge, Pearce

*Northern Union*: Wood; Williams, Hall, Wagstaff, Davies; Smith, Prosser; Holland, Coldrick, Ramsdale, Johnson, Clark, Chilcott

The crowd again topped 40,000 and they witnessed a rearguard action by the British players which was dubbed 'Rorke's Drift' after a Zulu war action in which two British officers and eighty men held out against 4000 Zulu warriors at Rorke's Drift, Zululand, in January 1879. In the first two minutes of the game winger Frank Williams twisted his leg but despite this handicap the tourists led 9–3 at half time, Coldrick scoring a try and Wood three goals. Early in the second half Clark, the Huddersfield forward, broke his collarbone. He tried to resume but had to leave the field. Frank Williams' leg gave out and he left the field. Then Hall suffered concussion going down on a loose ball. Ten tourists faced thirteen Australians, a hopeless task, with thirty minutes to go. Yet the miracle happened. Time and again the Australians attacked and were thrown back. The four-man British scrum heeled the ball from the scrums and, in a makeshift back division, forwards Johnson and Coldrick ran themselves into the ground, tackling and covering. With twenty minutes left, Wagstaff found a gap. He gave the ball to the gallant Johnson who put the ball to his toe, kicked and dribbled half the length of the field and touched down. Wood landed the goal, Hall came staggering back on the field, Britain held out, and at the end of the game the Sydney crowd rose and cheered the Britons off the field. The score was 14–6 and the series had been won against unbelievable odds.

With praises ringing in their ears the tourists left for New Zealand where they won all seven matches, including a 16–3 win over New Zealand at Auckland. After a match at Melbourne against New South Wales the tourists set off for home £2000 up on the 1910 tour. The happy party was to receive a proper heroes' welcome on their return to Britain, but an international event took place which pushed all thought of sporting success into the background. After a series of snowballing squabbles, Europe was plunged into the First World War in August 1914.

## Wartime closures

The outbreak of war caused chaos everywhere and the Northern Union committee had the problem of deciding whether fixtures would begin as scheduled in 1914–15. Most clubs were denuded of players in the rush to volunteer and the Union secretary, Mr J. Platt, said that 'serving King and country is more important than winning medals on the football field'. Amid the disorder the Union decided to open the season as usual, to allow recruiting on grounds and to regard the game as a form of wartime entertainment for the forces and for munitions workers at home. Many well-known players joined the forces. Gwyn Thomas and Bert Jenkins (Wigan), Chick Johnson (Widnes) and G. Ruddick (Broughton Rangers). Sad news came with the deaths of Midgley (Bramley), Twigg (Rochdale Hornets) and Tom Williams (Salford). One town, St Helens, provided more than 13,000 men for various forms of war service.

Despite dwindling crowds and interest the 1914–15 season concluded with challenge-cup and championship finals. The championship final was played first at Wakefield before a 16,000 crowd on Saturday, 24 April 1915, and Huddersfield hammered Leeds 35–2. On Saturday, 1 May, Huddersfield met St Helens at Oldham seeking the four-cups feat, having won the Yorkshire league and county cup in addition to the championship. Only 8000 turned up to see the challenge-cup final which was almost called off when the St Helens players, dissatisfied with their terms, refused to play and were only persuaded to do so by their captain, Tommy Barton. Teams for this last final before the wartime closure were:

*Huddersfield*: Holland; Rosenfeld, Gleeson, Wagstaff, Moorhouse; Rogers, Ganley; Longstaffe, Clark, Gronow, Banks, Lee, Higson

*St Helens*: Roberts; Barton, Flanagan, White, Greenall; Trenwith, Creevey; Daniels, Durkin, Farrimond, Myers, Jackson, Shallcross

Referee: R. Robinson (Bradford)

The St Helens players were, perhaps, too disgruntled to compete and Huddersfield romped home 37–3, scoring nine tries and five goals. The goals were kicked by Ben Gronow who, during this achievement, topped the record of 138 goals in a season previously set by A. Carmichael (Hull KR).

At the annual meeting in June 1915 Union officials decided that there would be no more professional football in wartime. Matches could, however, be arranged on a friendly basis. The Yorkshire clubs showed enterprise in keeping the game alive by organizing 'friendlies' for which the players received two shillings and sixpence 'tea money'. Lancashire clubs followed suit.

Several representative games were played for war charities. Yorkshire met Lancashire and a Yorkshire *v*. New Zealand game was played under Rugby Union rules.

Sad news came from the battlefields as great players like Bill Jarman (Leeds), Fred Longstaffe (Huddersfield), Walter Roman (Rochdale Hornets), George Thom (Salford), J. Harrison (Hull), J. H. Turtill (St Helens) and George Thomas (Warrington), were killed in battle.

With no real gate income many clubs were near bankruptcy as the end of the war neared in 1918. Oldham, Broughton Rangers and Wigan had to sell their grandstands to survive; they were dubbed 'the timber merchants'. One team disappeared from the scene, never to return: Runcorn, Cheshire's last representative and the first winner of the Lancashire senior competition, disbanded.

The Great War ended on 11 November 1918. The Northern Union decided not to rush resumption of play, timed for 1919–20.

## *Back to normal*

The Lancashire and Yorkshire Leagues programmes opened on Saturday, 8 January 1919, and the good attendances both surprised and delighted officials. Australia and New Zealand also opened successfully; their invitation for a postwar tour was accepted for the end of the 1919–20 season. Rochdale Hornets won the Lancashire cup, beating neighbours Oldham 22–0, while Huddersfield carried on where they had left off, beating Dewsbury in the Yorkshire final 14–8 before a bumper 21,500 crowd at Headingley. The respective championships were won by Rochdale and Hull.

The truncated season ended with a happy report to the annual meeting that a full season's resumption, as promised, would take place in 1919–20. Big crowds saw Huddersfield beat Leeds in the Yorkshire cup final and Oldham win revenge over Rochdale in the Lancashire final. The touring party was announced in March 1920. Managers were the Northern League secretary John Wilson and Sidney Foster (Halifax). The players were:

Backs: G. Thomas, H. Wagstaff, J. Rogers (Huddersfield), A. E. Wood, E. Davies (Oldham), E. W. Jones (Rochdale Hornets), D. Hurcombe (Wigan), W. J. Stone (Hull), J. Doyle (Barrow), C. Stacey, E. Lloyd (Halifax), S. Stockwell, J. A. Bacon (Leeds), J. Parkin (Wakefield T.).

Forwards: A. Milnes (Halifax), J. Cartwright (Leigh), J. Bowers (Rochdale Hornets), W. Cunliffe, J. Skelhorne (Warrington), S. Rees (Leeds), A. Johnson, W. Reid (Widnes), B. Gronow, D. Clark (Huddersfield), H. Hilton (Oldham), F. Gallagher (Dewsbury).

There was no holding Huddersfield. They reached the challenge-cup final again, playing Wigan on Saturday, 10 April 1920, in the first final since 1915. Perhaps because of Huddersfield's virtual monopoly of wins, the attendance was a disappointing 14,000 paying £1935. Teams were:

*Huddersfield*: Holland; Pogson, Wagstaff, Gleeson, Todd; Rogers, Habron; Swindon, Naylor, Fenwick, Sherwood, Gronow, Clark

*Wigan*: Jolley; Smith, Hurcombe, F. Prescott, Hall; Hesketh, Jerram; Seeling, Coldrick, Ramsdale, Shaw, T. Prescott, Lowe

Referee: F. Mills (Oldham)

Somewhat anti-climactically, Huddersfield did it again, 21–10.

Wagstaff, Pogson (2), Habron and Todd scored tries, Gronow landing three goals. Hall and Jerram scored tries for Wigan, and Jolley two goals.

Huddersfield were without their tourists for the championship play-offs but reached the final again to play Hull at Headingley on 24 April. The team of all the talents did not sparkle on this occasion and Hull won an unexciting game 3–2, a Batten try against a Holland goal.

The 1920 annual meeting of the Union showed a magnificent balance of £4641, a vast sum in those days, and members paid fulsome tributes to Mr J. Platt who completed his twenty-five years as founder-secretary by announcing his retirement. John Wilson, of Hull Kingston Rovers, who was on tour with the Northern Union party as co-manager, was named as his successor.

The first game of the tour, against Sydney, saw a new record crowd of 65,000 with record receipts of £5500. After a successful series of club and country games, with only one defeat against New South Wales, the tourists met Australia in the first Test at Sydney on 26 June 1920. It was not a good game, both sides playing below form. Gronow kicked two goals to give the Union a 4–0 lead, but Fraser got a try for Australia. In the second half Australia turned on the pressure and their brilliant winger, Harold Horder, cross-kicked for Burge to touch down. Fraser kicked the goal and Australia won 8–4.

The second Test was played at Sydney a week later and Australia regained the Ashes with a convincing and attractive 21–8 victory. Potter, V. Farnsworth, Vest, Horder and Gilbert scored tries and Burge kicked three goals, against tries by Johnson and Gallagher and a goal from Gronow.

The tourists salvaged prestige by winning the third Test at Sydney on 10 July by 23 points to 13. Australia appeared to rest on their laurels and the Northern Union side, at last, played their best rugby. Hilton (2), Stone (2) and Bacon got the tries; Rogers (3), and Stockwell the goals. For Australia Gray, Thompson and Burge touched down, and Burge landed two goals.

Large attendances ensured a thumping profit for the tour, a handsome consolation for defeat. From Australia the tourists went to New Zealand where all three Tests were won, 31–7 at Auckland, 19–3 at Christchurch and 11–10 at Wellington.

## *The post war boom*

The postwar boom was in full spate, during the season of 1920–21, with a record aggregate total of 181,070 at eleven second-round challenge-cup games in March. The final was an inter-county battle between Leigh, making their first appearance, and Halifax, and 25,000 saw the game at Broughton Rangers' ground. Teams were:

*Halifax*: Garforth; Turnbull, Ackroyd, Stacey, Todd; Lloyd, S. Prosser; Gilbson, Milnes, Broadbent, Whiteley, Beames, Schofield

*Leigh*: Clarkson; Hurst, Heaton, Thomas, Braund; Mooney, Parkinson; Cartwright, Winstanley, Darwell, J. T. Prosser, Boardman, Coffey

Referee: F. Renton (Hunslet)

Unfancied Leigh, who had had a poor season, won a surprise but well-deserved victory. Tackling grittily, particularly when Halifax stormed their line in the second half, Leigh won 13–0, with Mooney playing a superb game at half-back and creating all three tries for E. Thomas (2) and Parkinson; Clarkson kicked two goals. The championship final at Headingley on 7 May was a Humberside derby game between Hull and Hull K. R. Hull won a closely fought, typical derby battle 16–14. Cook scored a late try for Rovers to make it 16–14 but, while all Hull fans held their breath, Gibson missed the kick which would have tied the scores.

Featherstone Rovers, later to emerge as a great cup-fighting team from a small mining village, entered the League, and Wigan made one of the greatest signings of all time when they secured a seventeen-year-old full-back, James Sullivan, from Cardiff.

The Australian touring party arrived in Britain on 5 September 1921, with managers S. G. Ball and W. A. Cann, and captain Les Cubitt. The party was:

Backs: C. Fraser, L. C. Cubitt, G. Carstairs, T. Norman, N. Broadfoot, H. Horder, R. Vest, J. H. Craig, E. S. Brown, C. Blinkhorn, H. Peter, C. Caples, A. Laing, D. F. Thompson, A. Johnston.

Forwards: J. Watkins, T. Pearce, B. Gray, F. Burge, R. Townsend, N. Potter, F. Ryan, W. Schultz, B. Latta, E. McGrath, J. C. Ives, C. W. Prentice, W. Richards.

The Australians swept past Salford, Keighley and Hull K. R., rattling up a total of more than 100 points, in the run-up to the first

Test at Headingley on Saturday, 1 October 1921. The crowd was 32,000, paying £3884. Teams were:

*Northern Union*: G. Thomas (Huddersfield); W. J. Stone (Hull), H. Wagstaff (Huddersfield), J. A. Bacon, St. Stockwell (Leeds); J. Rogers (Huddersfield), J. Parkin (Wakefield Trinity); W. Cunliffe (Warrington), J. Cartwright (Leigh), J. Skelhorne (Warrington), E. Morgan (Hull), J. Beames (Halifax), J. Price (Broughton R.)

*Australia*: C. Fraser; H. Horder, R. Vest, J. Craig, C. Blinkhorn; D. Thompson, A. Johnston; C. Prentice, F. Ryan, T. Pearce, F. Burge, B. Gray, J. Watkins

After ten minutes Stone intercepted and raced away to score for Britain. Blinkhorn touched down and a goal by Craig put Australia ahead at half time. In the second half the Northern Union battered the Australian line but Australia tackled magnificently until three minutes from the end when Wagstaff, Rogers, Parkin and Bacon got the ball out to Stockwell who ducked under Horder's tackle to give Britain a dramatic win.

After several club defeats the tourists faced up to Britain for the second Test at Hull on Saturday, 5 November. Before 28,000 spectators the Australians brought in Carstairs, Caples, Schultz and Latta to replace Craig, Johnston, Ryan and Gray. The Northern Union substituted Batten for the injured Wagstaff. Stockwell was hurt early on and Australia grabbed the initiative, but in a bruising game the only first-half scores were a goal each, to Thompson for Australia and Rogers for the Union. Australia, however, cut loose in the second half and tries from Vest, Horder and Blinkhorn (2) and one more Thompson goal tied the series at 16–2.

Britain made six changes for the third Test at Salford on 14 January 1922. Wagstaff, J. Owen (St Helens Recreation), Hurcombe (Wigan), Hilton (Oldham), Taylor (Hull) and Gallagher (Dewsbury) replaced Batten, Stone, Stockwell, Morgan, Beames and Price.

The match, played before 20,000 spectators, was won and lost early on, when Australia lost their full-back 'Chook' Fraser with a broken leg. The tourists fought with courage but Hilton and Gallagher touched down for Britain. The Northern Union had won the series. The tour also paid its way and Australia had won twenty-seven of their thirty-six games.

The champions Hull met Rochdale Hornets in the final of the

challenge cup at Headingley on Saturday, 29 April. There was a
record attendance of 35,500, with receipts of £2964, and the gates
were closed with thousands encroaching on the pitch and having to
be cleared. Teams were:

*Hull*: Holdsworth; Wynne, Kennedy, Batten, Stone; Caswell,
Charles; Beasty, Oliver, Morgan, Wyburn, Taylor, Garratt

*Rochdale Hornets*: Prescott; J. Corsi, McLaughlin, Wild, Fitton;
Kynan, Heaton; Woods, Bennett, Harris, Edwards, Paddon, H. L.
Corsi

Referee: R. Jones (Widnes)

At half time in a well-contested game Hornets led 7–6, Kennedy
and the spectacular Batten getting tries for Hull against Fitton's try
and two Paddon goals. In the second half Fitton got a second try
but Taylor broke through and crashed over to make it 10–9. Stone's
kick curled wide and Hornets won by the odd point. The championship final was held at Broughton the following Saturday, 26,000
paying £1825 to see Wigan beat Oldham 13–2 with goals from
Sullivan (4) and Howley and a Shea try against a goal from Farrar.

# 4

# Goodbye to the Northern Union

The 1922 annual meeting produced two important decisions. The outdated, parochial title, Northern Union, was replaced by Rugby League, and the goal kick from the mark was abolished. This abolition did not affect the marksmanship of the brilliant young Welshman, Jim Sullivan of Wigan, who, while still under twenty, beat Ben Gronow's season total of 147 set up in 1919–20. He kicked 172 goals and also scored ten tries.

The Rugby League challenge-cup final, the first under its new name, was held at Wakefield on Saturday, 28 April 1923, before a crowd of 29,350 (£2390). Hull were in their seventh final, with only one win. Teams were:

*Hull*: Samuel; Stone, Kennedy, Whitty, Holdsworth; Caswell, Gwynne; Oliver, Bowman, Beasty, Morgan, Taylor, Garratt

*Leeds*: Walmsley; Buck, Bowen, Bacon, Lyons; Binks, Brittain; Trusler, Jackson, Dixon, Davis, Thompson, Ashton

Referee: F. Mills (Oldham)

The match was a triumph for the famous 'busy Bs' back division of Leeds, and another disappointment for Hull. Buck, Bowen, Brittain, Walmsley, Davis and Ashton scored tries prompted by Binks, and Thompson kicked five goals. Kennedy scored a try for Hull in a 28–3 Leeds win. Hull K. R. salvaged some Humberside pride in the championship final at Headingley on 5 May. They beat Huddersfield by 15 points to 5 before a crowd of 15,000. It was not a great game; Huddersfield were not the team of old. Rees, Cook and Hoult touched down for Rovers and Osborne kicked two goals against a try by Williams and goal by Gronow.

Wigan Highfield joined the League in 1923–24. This was a club based at Pemberton whose directors were determined to show that there was room for two sides in Wigan. The year 1924 was to be another tour year and after two trial matches the following players were selected:

Backs: J. Sullivan, J. Ring, T. Howley, D. Hurcombe (Wigan), E. Knapman, S. Rix (Oldham), W. Bentham (Broughton R.), J. Bacon (Leeds), C. Carr (Barrow), C. Pollard, J. Parkin (Wakefield T.), F. Evans (Swinton), S. Whitty (Hull), W. Mooney (Leigh).

Forwards: W. Burgess (Barrow), W. Cunliffe (Warrington), H. Bowman (Hull), J. F. Thompson (Leeds), J. Bennett (Rochdale H.), B. Gronow (Huddersfield), A. Brough, R. Sloman (Oldham), J. Darwell (Leigh), F. Gallagher (Batley), J. Price (Wigan), D. Rees (Halifax). 'Jonty' Parkin was skipper, and managers were Messrs H. Dannatt (Hull) and E. Osborne (Warrington).

The challenge-cup final brought together two Lancashire clubs for the first time since 1911. Old rivals, Oldham and Wigan, qualified and huge crowds converged on the Athletic Grounds at Rochdale. Mounted police had to clear the touchlines and the crowd was ultimately totalled at a record 40,786. Teams were:

*Oldham*: Knapman; Rix, Hall, Woodward, J. Corsi; Hesketh, Bates; Collins, Tomkins, Baker, Brough, Hilton

*Wigan*: Sullivan; Ring, Howley, Park, Van Heerden; Jerram, Hurcombe; Webster, Banks, Brown, Van Rooyen, Roffey, Price

Referee: Rev F. Chambers (Huddersfield)

In the Wigan team were two great South African rugby-union players in Van Rooyen and Van Heerden. Roffey and Van Heerden scored fine tries for Wigan, Van Heerden's spectacular effort from his own half including a classic body swerve round a mounted policeman. In the second half Wigan really went to town and tries came from Parker, Ring and Price, Sullivan kicking three goals. For Oldham Knapman and Brough kicked goals.

Wigan also reached the championship final on 3 May but on this occasion the loss of five tourists, including the prodigious Sullivan, proved too much and Batley beat Wigan 13–7. Murray, Leeming and Murray again touched down for Batley and Rees landed two goals. Armstrong (try) and Oakley (two goals) replied for Wigan.

The British tourists arrived in Melbourne on 20 May 1924 and, four days later, beat Victoria 45–3. 'Up-country' victories followed and a crowd of 50,000 at Sydney saw another British victory. Then, suddenly, the tourists' defences cracked and they were hammered by New South Wales, Queensland and Toowoomba.

A win in a further game against New South Wales restored morale and the first Test was played at Sydney on Monday, 23 June 1924, before a 50,000 crowd. There were several Queensland-born players in the Australian side, indicative of the spread of the game. At half time the tourists led 4–3, with two goals by Sullivan against a try by Aynsley. Australia suffered a severe blow with the sending-off of Potter and Britain took charge with tries from Parkin (2), Price and Rix and three more goals from Sullivan.

The second Test was five days later on Saturday, 28 June, and again at Sydney. Despite heavy rain there was a crowd of 34,000 to see a tough, dour, muddy struggle, in which the only first-half score was an Australian try by Aynsley. In the second half Britain slogged away, Australia defended tenaciously, and it was Parkin who did the trick, slipping through for a try minutes from the end. Sullivan's boot supplied the goal and at 5–3 Britain had retained the Ashes.

As so often happens, the third Test brought a consolation victory for the side beaten in the series. It was played at Brisbane in front of a crowd of 28,000. Britain led at half time with a Frank Evans try and Sullivan goal against two goals from Aynsley, but Australia played brilliantly in the second half and Paten, Armbruster and Oxford scored tries with Thompson (2), Aynsley and Oxford kicking goals. In a late burst Parkin and Evans scored tries for Britain. It was a 21–11 win for Australia.

## Kiwi shocks

Receipts had been the highest ever and the tourists went off to New Zealand to receive some rude shocks to their complacency. After some comfortable victories against club sides, Britain were beaten in the first two Tests, 16–8 at Auckland, in a match in which Cunliffe was sent off, and 13–10 at Wellington after Britain had led 11–0. There was small consolation in the third Test at Dunedin, a 31–18 win for the tourists, but the Kiwis had made their point.

Jim Sullivan, the Welsh prodigy, was the leading tour scorer with eighty-four goals, a tour record. His club mate Johnny Ring scored twenty-three tries.

There was a respite from tours during the 1924–25 season, but there was also a significant international development when Other Nationalities met England. This team included men like Van Rooyen and Van Heerden of South Africa and Beattie, Halifax's Scottish forward.

Both Australia and New Zealand applied to tour in 1926 and the Rugby League, remembering New Zealand's series' victory in 1924, surprised Australia by opting for the first full New Zealand tour (the tour in 1907–08 had included Australians).

The star team of 1924–25 were Hull Kingston Rovers who reached both challenge-cup and championship finals. The biggest feat was achieved by Wigan who beat the luckless and hapless Cumbrian amateur team, Flimby and Fothergill, 116–0 in the challenge cup, only three short of Huddersfield's 119 against Swinton Park.

The challenge-cup final was played at Headingley on Saturday, 25 April 1925, with Oldham as Rovers' opponents. The crowd was 28,200 and receipts £2878. Teams were:

*Hull K. R.*: Osborne; Harris, Cook, Hoult, Austin; McIntyre, Raynor; J. Wilkinson, Boagey, J. R. Wilkinson, Westerdale, Bielby, Carmichael

*Oldham*: Knapman; J. Corsi, Rix, Davies, Farrar; Hesketh, Beynon; Collins, Tomkins, Marlor, Sloman, Brough, Hilton

Referee: R. Jones (Widnes)

In a disappointing first half Oldham took a 5–0 lead with a try and goal from Farrar. In the second half Rovers fumbled and faltered and Brough, Corsi and Davies got tries, Farrar kicking a goal. J. H. Wilkinson got a try for Rovers. It was an easy win for Oldham, Rovers still looking for a cup-final success.

Rovers found consolation in the championship final against Swinton at Rochdale the following week, winning 9–5 with a Rhodes try and three Osborne goals against a Bryn Evans try and a Brockbank goal.

New clubs came into the limelight in 1926. Castleford were admitted and Wigan Highfield, who had struggled without much success in the League, accounted for Wakefield Trinity, Huddersfield and Leeds in the challenge cup, all at Pemberton, before losing to

Oldham at Salford in the semi-final by 15 points to 6. The match took Highfield away from their own ground to a neutral ground at Salford. Swinton beat Hull in the other semi-final and the two Lancashire clubs met in the final at Rochdale on Saturday, 1 May 1926. Despite heavy rain the crowd was 27,000 paying £2551. Oldham were making their third successive appearance, while Swinton had reached the final for the first time since 1900. Teams were:

*Oldham*: Knapman; Corsi, Higgs, Rix, Brough; Jones, Hesketh; Lister, Marlor, Read, Sloman, Carter, Baker

*Swinton*: Pearson; F. Evans, Sulway, J. Evans, Brockbank; W. Rees, B. Evans; Strong, Blewer, Morris, Halliwell, Entwistle, Beswick

Referee: A. Brown (Wakefield)

The strong wind made kicking difficult but Morris at last landed one for Swinton and Blewer increased the lead with a try to which Morris added the goal. Morris landed another goal despite the wind and although Oldham, backed by the gale, attacked throughout the second half, their only points came from a try by Corsi. In another all-Lancashire final Wigan won the championship at St Helens, beating Warrington 22–10, Ring getting a hat-trick of tries and Van Heerden crossing twice.

At the 1926 annual meeting another Welsh experiment was tried as Pontypridd were admitted. The New Zealand tourists arrived at Southampton on 2 September, with E. H. Mair and C. H. Ponder as managers and H. Avery as captain.

## Disappointing tour

This first full New Zealand tour was not an outstanding success, with defeat for New Zealand in the Test series and eleven defeats against clubs. The first Test was played at Wigan on 2 October and gate receipts were good at £1650. The Rugby League, remembering the surprise 1924 defeats, chose a strong side and the teams were:

*Great Britain*: J. Sullivan; J. Ring (Wigan), J. Evans (Swinton), C. Carr (Barrow), S. Rix (Oldham); J. Parkin (Wakefield T.), W. Rees (Swinton); W. Burgess (Barrow), J. Bennett (Wigan), W. Cunliffe (Warrington), R. Taylor (Hull), D. Rees (Halifax), F. Gallagher (Batley)

*New Zealand*: E. Gregory; L. Brown, B. Davidson, H. Brisbane, F.

Delgrosso; A. W. Hall, W. Desmond; F. Henry, E. Herring, W. Carroll, L. Mason, H. Avery, N. Mouat

Great Britain went off at a gallop and Carr, Rix, Taylor and Gallagher crossed, with four goals from Sullivan. Avery scored a breakaway try for New Zealand, Mouat landing the goal. In the second half Britain relaxed and Brisbane touched down, Mouat again goaling. Mason and Davidson also scored for New Zealand, but Taylor and Carr replied for Britain in a 28–20 home win.

The second Test at Hull aroused little interest, with receipts a trifling £592, and the match followed a similar pattern to the first. Wallace (Barrow), Fildes (St Helens Recs) and Thomas (Leeds) ran in tries, with two goals from Sullivan against a try by Peterson. At 13–3 Britain took it easy and tries by Avery and Brown and a goal from Gregory rocked them back. Thomas and Fairclough (St Helens) added British tries, however, and Sullivan kicked a goal in a 21–11 victory which clinched the series.

The third Test completed the tourists' disappointment. Britain won 32–17, the tourists' tries only coming when Great Britain sat back. During the game Jim Sullivan kicked four goals and reached his 100 for the season. The unfortunate tourists went home with their tails between their legs, having made a financial loss.

On the home front the championship final was played first, at Warrington, on Saturday, 30 April 1927, before a 24,432 crowd.

St Helens Recreation met Swinton and Swinton, runners-up to the Recs, turned the tables with a 13–8 win, Bryn Evans (2) and Beswick got tries, and Morris kicked two goals. For Recs, Bowen and Innes touched down and Dingsdale landed one goal. This win gave Swinton the chance of the big double, for they met Oldham in the challenge-cup final at Wigan on 7 May before a 35,000 crowd (£3170). Oldham were playing in their fourth successive final and Swinton in their third; the match was a repeat of the 1926 final won by Swinton. Teams were:

*Oldham*: Comm; Johnson, Rix, Higgs, Holliday; Hesketh, Jones; Read, Scaife, Marlor, Sloman, Ashworth, Brough

*Swinton*: Leigh; F. Evans, Halsall, J. Evans, Brockbank; B. Evans, Rees; Strong, Blewer, Cracknell, Morris, Halliwell, Beswick

Referee: R. Robinson (Bradford)

Although Swinton started well with a Brockbank try, Oldham took command. Holliday, a try, and Johnson, two goals, against a penalty by Morris, made it 7–5, and when Swinton resumed without their captain, Hector Halsall, Oldham ran riot with tries from Rix, Brough, Sloman and Holliday (2), in a scoreline of 26–7.

In the close season the annual meeting voted in favour of ending the two-year residence qualification on Australasian stars. Australia and New Zealand protested in vain and top players were soon flooding to Britain. L. Brown, B. Davidson and L. Mason came to Wigan, A. F. O'Rourke and J. Moores to Leeds, A. Carr and S Harris to Huddersfield and Wilson Hall to Hull.

The 1927–28 season brought to an end the Pontypridd experiment. A team of 'exiles' named Glamorgan and Monmouthshire entered the county championship, however.

Managers of the 1928 tour to Australasia were E. Osborne and G. F. Hutchins (Oldham). Jonty Parkin (Wakefield Trinity) was making his third trip and was appointed captain. Other players were:

Backs: J. Sullivan (Wigan), W. Gowers (Rochdale H.), J. Brough, M. Rosser (Leeds), J. Oliver (Batley), A. Ellaby, L. Fairclough, A. Frodsham (St Helens), J. and B. Evans, W. Rees (Swinton), T. Askin (Featherstone Rovers), T. E. Gwynne (Hull), J. Parkin (Wakefield T.).

Forwards: W. Bentham (Wigan Highfield), O. Dolan, B. Halfpenny (St Helens), W. A. Williams (Salford), F. Bowen, A. Fildes (St Helens Recs), W. Burgess (Barrow), H. Bowman (Hull), W. Horton (Wakefield T.), R. Sloman (Oldham), H. Young (Bradford N.), J. F. Thompson (Leeds).


## Swinton ascendancy

Swinton were all-conquering again in 1927–28. They reached the finals of the challenge cup and championship, having won the Lancashire league and cup. They sought to emulate Hunslet and Huddersfield with four cups; the challenge cup was the third hurdle. It was against Warrington at Wigan, before 34,000 paying £3158. Teams were:

*Swinton*: Young; F. Evans, Halsall, J. Evans, Brockbank; Atkinson, Rees; Strong, Blewer, Morris, Hodgson, Cracknell, Beswick

*Warrington*: Frowen; Rhodes, Meredith, Perkins, Davies; Flynn, Kirk; Cunliffe, Peacock, Miller, Williams, Tranter, Seeling

Referee: H. Horsfall (Batley)

Although the game was dour and not much of a spectacle Swinton made the best of windy conditions and Brockbank got a first-half try. Seeling took advantage of a rare Swinton mistake to equalize but Jack Evans dropped a late winning goal for Swinton who then took on Featherstone Rovers in the championship final at Oldham on 5 May, 1928, before a 16,000 attendance. Swinton won comfortably 11–0, with tries from Halsall, Frank Evans and Cracknell and a goal from Young.

The British touring party arrived in Australia at the end of May. Early form in the club and up-country matches was not good and the tourists faced the first Test at Brisbane on Saturday, 23 June, with low confidence. The crowd was 39,200.

Britain were without Parkin and the Evans brothers so Brough and Oliver played centre with Rees at scrum-half and Fairclough at stand-off. Although second favourites, Britain shook the Australians by leading 10–2 at half time with tries from Fairclough and Horton and two goals from Sullivan against a penalty goal by Craig. Armbruster got a fine try for Australia but Britain hit back when superb passing sent Ellaby over. A try and two goals from Aynsley brought the home team back to 13–12 and, amid great excitement, the tourists kept their heads and Sullivan clinched victory with a late penalty goal.

Confidence revived, the tourists went off to pulverize several Queensland sides before the second Test at Sydney on 14 July before a crowd of 45,000. The Australians turned out for this game in the new strip that was to become their hallmark, green and gold. Conditions were dreadful, heavy rain turning the ground into a bog. Britain slogged through it with greater determination and skill, and Parkin and Ellaby scored tries, Sullivan kicking a goal. The 8–0 win clinched the series and retained the Ashes.

Once again the third Test provided consolation, with Australia winning 21–14 before 35,000 at Sydney on 21 July. Horton, the tourist forward, was sent off, and Australia's tries were scored by Wearing (2) and Pearce, with six goals shared by Wearing and Craig. Fairclough got two tries and Sullivan four goals for Britain.

The touring party set off for New Zealand determined to wipe out the memories of 1924, but in the first Test at Auckland they received yet another rude shock, New Zealand coming from 9–3 behind to win 17–13, with tries by Scott (2) and List and goals from Delgrosso (3) and Dufty against tries from Ellaby (2) and Fairclough, and two goals from Sullivan. The second Test at Dunedin was a bit of a roughhouse as tempers ran high; Burgess (the British forward) was sent off and Delgrosso of New Zealand carried off. Britain led 7–5 at half time with a try by Rees and two goals from Sullivan against a Scott try and Delgrosso goal. In the second half the tourists got on top and they squared the series at 13–5 with the flying Ellaby touching down, Bowen also scoring and the defence repelling desperate New Zealand attacks. Crowds of 35,000 and 10,000 had seen the first two Tests and there was a crowd of 20,000, another excellent attendance, for the third at Christchurch on 20 August. Britain won the series in a hard-fought game, 6 points to 5. Fairclough and Askin got a try in each half, Dufty kicked a goal and New Zealand failed to snatch it when Dufty missed the kick at goal from a late try by O'Brien.

The tour had been an outstanding playing and financial success; Sullivan had scored 150 points and Ellaby had scored more than thirty tries.

## *The way to Wembley*

Late in 1928 a movement began which was to have far-reaching, and amazingly successful, repercussions for the game of rugby league. Council members began to search for a permanent home for the great showpiece, the challenge-cup final. Attendances had been rising and the 40,000 crowd at Rochdale had proved almost too much for police and groundstaff. Headingley, stylish and comfortable, was just not big enough. After many meetings with the authorities at the great new Empire Stadium at Wembley, agreement was reached for the first Wembley challenge-cup final to take place in 1929.

The clubs who were destined to take a niche in the history of the game were Dewsbury and Wigan, who met in the first Wembley final on May 1929. The crowd was adequate for the occasion at 41,500 and receipts were £5600, enough to make the experiment seem worthwhile. In the dressing rooms before the game the League chairman, Mr F. Kennedy, urged both teams to be clean and sportsmanlike, since rugby league was on national trial.

Mr R. Robinson was the referee and the teams were:

*Dewsbury*: Davies; Coates, Hirst, Smith, Bailey; Woolmore, Rudd; P. Brown, Rhodes, Robson, Bland, Malkin, Lyman

*Wigan*: Sullivan; Ring, Parker, Kinnear, L. Brown; Abram, Binks; Hodder, Bennett, Beetham, Stephens, Mason, Sherrington

As might have been anticipated, the occasion was just a little too much for the players and it was not a great game. It was certainly clean and sportsmanlike, but not over-exciting. In rare combined moves Abram scored Wembley's first try, Brown the second and Kinnear the third. Sullivan kicked two goals against a drop goal by Davies in a 13–2 Wigan win. At the after-match festivities Mr Kennedy answered the question everyone was asking. He said, 'The council has been satisfied with the experiment which will almost certainly be repeated.'

The championship final between Huddersfield and Leeds attracted 25,604 to Leeds, but was a dull anti-climax, decided by a solitary goal by Brook for Huddersfield.

The Kangaroos arrived at Southampton on the S. S. *Aquitania* on 28 August 1929. Managers were Harry Sunderland, later to become a noted radio commentator on the game, and J. Lorne Dargan. Captain was centre Tom Gorman and the party consisted of:

Backs: F. McMillan, J. Upton, T. Gorman, A. Ridley, W. Spencer, W. Shankland, P. Maher, C. Fifield, F. Laws, H. Finch, A. G. Edwards, J. Holmes, E. Weissell, J. Busch, H. J. Kadwell.

Forwards: G. Treweeke, M. Madsen, A. E. Root, A. J. Justice, G. Bishop, A. H. Henderson, L. V. Armbruster, D. V. O'Dempsey, L. A. Sellers, H. Steinohrt, J. Kingston, W. Brogan, W. Prigg.

The Australians came with a reputation for being a fast, all-round side and they confirmed this with a series of good wins in their early club matches, though losing 14–3 at Wakefield. The first Test was at Craven Park, Hull, on 5 October; Britain was without Parkin, Ellaby and Brough. Teams were:

*Great Britain*: T. Rees (Oldham); A. Frodsham (St Helens), R. Kinnear (Wigan), W. Dingsdale (Warrington), E. Gwynne (Hull); L. Fairclough (St. Helens), W. Rees (Swinton); H. Bowman (Hull),

H. Bentham (Halifax), J. Thompson (Leeds), W Horton (Wakefield T.), A. G. Middleton (Salford), J. Feetham (Hull K. R.)

*Australia*: F. McMillan; W. Spencer, T. Gorman, C. Fifield, W. Shankland; E. Weissell, J. Busch; W. Brogan, G. Bishop, M. Madsen, G. Treweeke, L. V. Armbruster, W. Prigg

The Australians took charge of the first half with some brilliant rugby and sweeping movements put over Treweeke, Shankland and Prigg, with two goals from Weissell. More scintillating combination sent Bishop through, Weissell goaling; with Britain's only reply coming from a Thompson penalty, it was 18–2 at half time. Australia continued to dominate before the 25,000 crowd and, although Middleton got a home try, Shankland, Spencer and Weissell added touch downs for Australia and Weissell kicked a goal. Feetham's try made it a 31–8 rout.

The defeat was a shattering blow to British morale and many changes were made for the second Test at Leeds on 9 November. Only Rees, Dingsdale and the hooker, Bentham, kept their places, and drafted in were Atkinson (Castleford), Sullivan, Ellaby, S. Smith (Wakefield Trinity), Parkin, Burgess, D. Jenkins (Hunslet), Fildes and the Swinton back two of M. Hodgson and F. Butters. Australia brought in Steinohrt and O'Dempsey for Brogan and Armbruster.

The crowd of 32,000 saw a gruelling struggle as Britain got down to the task of holding the Australians. Only once did Australia move the ball clear, and Shankland touched down. Thereafter, Britain ground their way remorselessly to a series-squaring victory, with Parkin and Rees sending the burly Gorman-marker Atkinson over for a try, and Sullivan kicking three goals.

## Busch's 'try'

The vital third Test was played at Swinton on 4 January and a crowd of 33,809 saw a game so controversial that it resulted in demands from Australia for a re-match. Halsall (Swinton), Oster (Leeds) and Thomas (Leeds) came in for Britain and Justice, Brogan, Armbruster joined the Australian pack. With fifteen minutes left there was no score and in that last quarter of an hour the tourists hurled themselves at the British line to try to clinch the Ashes. Loose-forward Butters twice made brilliant try-saving tackles, and then came the incident that is still talked about when Test matches are argued and relived. In the last minute of the game the Kangaroo half-back, Chimpy Busch, jinked past two tackles and went for a narrow gap at the right-hand corner. Busch and the magnificent Butters went for the corner together, Busch to touch down, Butters to nail him before he got there. As Busch hurled himself over the line Butters took his legs from under him and threw him into touch in goal. The touch judge's flag went up, and the referee, Mr Robinson of Bradford, ruled 'no try' despite furious Australian protests that Busch had touched down before entering touch in goal.

## *The fourth Test*

The ebullient touring manager, Harry Sunderland, demanded a fourth Test from the Rugby League council. With the press uniting behind Australian demands, a hastily arranged fourth Test took place at Rochdale on Wednesday, 15 January 1930. In the British team Blinkhorn (Warrington), Brogden (Huddersfield) and B. Evans (Swinton) came into the backs, while Williams (Salford), Crowther (Hunslet) and Young (Huddersfield) were in the pack. Once again the match, before a crowd of 16,743, was a titanic struggle, with defences on top. Bad luck for Australia, however, finally decided the issue. Fifield broke his ankle and, minutes from the end, Brogden sent Smith over for the winning try.

The tourists left for home, still smarting and annoyed, three days later. Immediately, thoughts turned to preparations for the second Wembley final. St Helens and Widnes reached the final, a local derby in which St Helens, star-studded and bristling with 'colonials', were expected to trounce homespun Widnes. The attendance was adequate at 36,544 and the teams were:

*St Helens*: Crooks; Ellaby, Mercer, Lewis, Hardgrave; Fairclough, Groves; Hutt, Clarey, Houghton, Hall, Halfpenny, Harrison

*Widnes*: Fraser; Owen, Topping, Ratcliffe, Dennett; Laughton, Douglas; Silcock, Stevens, Kelsall, Van Rooyen, Hoey, Millington

Referee: F. Peel (Bradford)

Before the match St Helens had played eight games in fifteen days and this may have affected their performance. Great credit must, however, go to the Widnes underdogs who harried and worried the

Saints out of their collective stride. St Helens scored first when Houghton touched down an Ellaby kick, but thereafter the Widnes terriers took a grip on the game. Ratcliffe was awarded an obstruction try and Hoey kicked the goal. Then Dennett scored a try and Ratcliffe landed a penalty. It was 10–3 at half time and, although St Helens fought hard in the second half, Widnes tackled heroically and won a shock victory.

The championship final on 10 May was an all-Yorkshire event between Huddersfield and Leeds at Wakefield. The match was replayed after a dour 2–2 draw, and Huddersfield won 10–0 at the second attempt at Halifax.

At the annual meeting of 1930 it was decreed that the loose-forward no longer had the option of packing down at the side of the scrum, and that defending scrum-halves should have the feed. In the close season more star signings came to Britain. Eric Harris, the Queensland winger to Leeds, Australian centre, Cecil Aynsley, to Rochdale, Bill Shankland, Test winger, and Nelson Hardy, a Sydney centre, to Warrington. Then Leeds really stole the headlines and brought thunder from Australian officialdom by signing the half-back, Chimpy Busch, of Swinton Test-match fame. These signings followed the lifting of the international ban and brought more allegations of British 'poaching'.

The third Wembley final in 1931 brought together two Yorkshire clubs, York and Halifax, and the attendance on Saturday, 2 May , was 40,368, an increase on 1930 but slightly down on 1929. Teams were:

*Halifax*: R. Davies; Higgins, Higgs, Haigh, F. Adams; I. Davies, Harrison; Renton, Rawnsley, Bland, Rees, Norcliffe, Atkinson

*York*: Owen; H. Thomas, Rosser, W. J. Davies, W. Davies; Lloyd, W. Thomas; Pascoe, Myers, W. Davis, H. Davies, Johnson, Layhe

Referee: J. Edden (Swinton)

The Welsh influence on northern rugby league was heavily underlined, with five Davieses, two Thomases, a Lloyd, a Rees and an Owen in the sides. York scored first when Lloyd made a try for Harry Thomas and Pascoe kicked a goal. Then the two Davieses on the York left wing fumbled and Bland scored a gift try, to which Adams landed the goal. Harry Thomas got another try for York, but then York disintegrated. Adams kicked a goal, Dick Davies dropped a goal and Ivor Davies and Higgins (2) scored tries. Thomas kicked two further goals and Halifax won 22–8.

Swinton won the championship for the third time in five years, beating Leeds 14–7 in the final at Wigan on 9 May. The crowd was 31,000.

An attempt at a compromise with Australia over 'poaching' came with a council offer to instruct clubs to pay a fee of between £100 and £200 to the Australian club concerned. Australian reaction was that such a fee was small compensation for the loss of a star player.

The Australasian tour of 1932 caused fixturing problems. To allow the tourists an early departure, the challenge-cup final was brought forward to 9 April 1932. This date was too close to the F. A. cup final and Wembley was not available. The match was played at Central Park, Wigan, when Swinton and Leeds qualified, and a crowd of only 29,000 (instead of the expected 45,000) attended. Teams were:

*Leeds*: Brough; Harris, Moores, O'Rourke, Goulthorpe; E. Williams, Adams; Lowe, Thompson, Smith, Cox, Douglas, Glossop

*Swinton*: Scott; Buckingham, Green, H. Evans, Kenney; B. Evans, Rees; Armitt, Strong, Wright, Hodgson, Beswick, Butters

Referee: F. Peel (Bradford)

The match was a tough struggle, with Leeds attempting to become the first team to score a try against Swinton in the 1931–32 competition. Despite probes by the Australian wing partnership of Moores and Harris, Swinton held out to half time. Thompson, however, compensated for Leeds by kicking four goals against one by Hodgson. A second Hodgson goal made it 8–4 and Swinton stormed forward. Suddenly a Rees pass went astray, Moores pounced on it, gave it to O'Rourke, another Australian, and he passed to Eric Harris, the 'Toowoomba Ghost', who raced away for a thrilling try. Hodgson landed another goal for Swinton but Leeds won 11–8.

Huddersfield again reached the championship final at Wakefield on 7 May, but it was to be St Helens' day. Both sides were without tourists and St Helens won 9–5, with a try by Winnard and three goals from Lewis against a Walker try and Bowkett goal.

The 1932 tourists were managed by Messrs G. F. Hutchins (Oldham) and R. F. Anderton (Warrington) and were captained by

Jim Sullivan (Wigan). They arrived in Australia at the end of May. Players were:

Backs: J. Sullivan (Wigan), A. Ellaby (St Helens), A. J. Risman, B. Hudson (Salford), S. Smith, L. Adams (Leeds), J. Woods (Barrow), A. Atkinson (Castleford), S. Brogden (Huddersfield), W. Dingsdale (Warrington), G. Robinson, E. Pollard (Wakefield T.), I. J. Davies (Halifax), B. Evans (Swinton).

Forwards: N. Silcock (Widnes), J. F. Thompson, J. Lowe (Leeds), W. A. Williams, J. Feetham (Salford), J. Wright, M. Hodgson, F. Butters (Swinton), L. White (Hunslet), N. Fender (York), A. E. Fildes (St Helens Recs), W. Horton (Wakefield T.).

After a series of good wins by the tourists the first Test at Sydney on Monday, 6 June, an Australian public holiday, aroused phenomenal interest and the gates were closed with a world-record attendance of 70,204 in the ground. Teams were:

*Australia*: McMillan; C. Pearce, Norman, Laws, Wilson; Weissell, Gee; Steinohrt, O'Dempsey, Madsen, T. Pearce, Little, Prigg

*Great Britain*: Sullivan; Ellaby, Atkinson, Brogden, Smith; Pollard, Evans; Silcock, White, Thompson, Hodgson, Horton, Feetham

It was a taut, tense match in an electric atmosphere. Ellaby made a typical interception to race away for the first try, but two penalty goals from Weissell, one from halfway, made it 4–3 at half time. Then Ellaby made a try for Atkinson, goaled by Sullivan, and Great Britain hung on despite a sustained flurry of attacks. The tourists were one up and the second Test was played at Brisbane on 18 June before 27,000 spectators.

Australia were quickly in the lead when O'Dempsey sent Gee over and Weissell kicked the goal. Australia stayed on top and tied the series with a 15–6 victory. This brought a decider at Sydney on 16 July; a crowd of 50,000 attended. Britain had Risman, Horton, Fildes and Williams instead of the injured Pollard, Feetham, Fender and Butters, while Australia brought in Neumann on the left wing. Australia made all the early running and led 9–0, O'Connor scoring a try and Weissell landing three goals. Britain hit back and Risman made a try for Smith at the corner.

Early in the second half Weissell kicked another goal but Britain made a successful tactical switch, stand-off-half, Risman, and centre, Brogden, changing places. Evans and Ellaby put Brogden over,

Horton put Smith through, Sullivan goaling. Sullivan and Weissell landed penalties and it was 13–13 with the crowd seething with excitement.

The winning try came to Britain despite the roars backing the Australians. Risman's break sent away Smith and he raced to the corner for his hat-trick. Sullivan banged over the goal from the touchline and, in a dramatic finish, Britain held the Ashes.

Great Britain went on to New Zealand in high spirits and this time made no slips. All three Tests were won, 24–9 at Auckland, 25–14 at Christchurch and 20–18 again at Auckland. A big profit had been made, only two defeats sustained in twenty-six games and the captain Sullivan had totalled 223 points. To rub salt in Australia's wounds, Wigan signed two Test players, J. Wilson and H. Gee.

# 5

# France Enters the Field

A further major international development was the arrival on the
scene of France. Several French rugby-union clubs had been warring
with the French Rugby Union in a similar manner to the English
wrangles which occasioned the 1895 split. In April 1933 a delegation
from French clubs met British Rugby League officials in London
and, in 1933–34, the Australian tourists paid a trip to France.

In Britain, after the 1932 break, the League prepared for a return
to Wembley; the 1933 final could not have been bettered as a crowd-
pulling attraction. Huddersfield and Warrington reached the final
and the Prince of Wales gave it royal patronage. In the event, the
crowd of 42,000 was mildly disappointing but the game was a brilliant
and exciting exhibition. Teams were:

*Huddersfield*: Scourfield; Mills, Brogden, Bowkett, Markham; Richards, Adams; Sherwood, Halliday, Banks, Tiffany, Talbot, Brindle

*Warrington*: Holding; Thompson, Dingsdale, Shankland, Binkhorn;
Oster, Davies; Hardman, Bentham, Miller, Evans, Smith, Seeling

Referee: F. Fairhurst (Wigan)

The game was skilful cut-and-thrust from the start. Bowkett kicked
two penalties for Huddersfield, then Brindle nipped through for a try
and Bowkett goaled. Warrington fought back and Dingsdale ran in
for a try, Holding goaling. Just before half time Davies ran over and
Holding's goal made it 10–9.

The end-to-end play continued. Brindle got another try and
Bowkett two goals to make it 16–10 for Huddersfield. Holding landed
a goal but a Richards's try and another goal to Bowkett seemed to
put Huddersfield out of sight. But Warrington were not finished and

Davies dummied his way over for Holding to kick the goal. Time ran out on Warrington and Huddersfield won a magnificent game 21–17.

The championship final was as disappointing as the cup final had been exhilarating. Swinton and Salford met in a derby game at Wigan before 18,000, but in a scrappy game Salford won 15–5.

## White City gamble

France was not the only territory where expansion was mooted in 1933. From London White City, a greyhound stadium, came an offer from Brigadier A. C. Critchley to stage rugby league; he offered to pay travelling expenses from the north. Wigan Highfield, who had been struggling, agreed to make the move and, as London Highfield, joined the league in 1933–34. Sadly, the gamble was doomed to failure, lasting little more than a season.

The Australian tourists arrived in August 1933, Harry Sunderland making his second trip as manager, W. W. Webb his co-manager, the captain being Frank McMillan. The players were:

F. McMillan, W. Smith, F. Laws, D. Brown, A. Ridley, F. Neaumann, J. Why, S. Gardner, F. Gilbert, V. Hey, C. Pearce, V. Thicknesse, F. Doonar, L. Mead, M. Madsen, S. Pearce, W. Prigg, A. Folwell, M. Glasheen, R. Stehr, D. O'Dempsey, F. O'Connor, F. Curran, J. Doyle, J. Gibbs, H. Denny, J. Little.

The tourists opened up with the longest winning spell of any side in Britain, eleven wins in a row before the first Test at a new venue, Belle Vue Stadium, home of Broughton Rangers, on Saturday, 7 October. A crowd topping 30,000 attended and the sides were:

*Great Britain*: J. Sullivan (Wigan); A. Ellaby (St Helens), A. J. Risman (Salford), S. Brogden (Huddersfield), S. Smith (Leeds); W. J. Davies (Castleford), B. Evans (Swinton); N. Silcock (Widnes), L. White (Hunslet), J. Miller (Warrington), M. Hodgson (Swinton), M. Horton (Wakefield T.), J. Feetham (Salford)

*Australia*: McMillan; Ridley, Brown, C. Pearce, Why; Hey, Thicknesse; Madsen, O'Dempsey, Stehr, O'Connor, S. Pearce, Prigg

After the tourists' great performances in club games their Test display was disappointing. It was a dour game, dominated by the packs, and the only scores were two penalty goals by Sullivan for Britain. After this dreary game the Australians lost six out of ten games before the second Test played at Leeds on 12 November. Australia brought in Smith, Gardner, Folwell, Gibbs and Doyle, while Britain had Hudson (Salford), Dingsdale (Warrington) and Woods (Barrow) replacing Ellaby, Brogden and Smith.

Before a crowd of 29,618 the two teams played a match which was a carbon copy of the dour first Test, strong tackling stifling open play. Sullivan kicked a goal but, in a rare flash of attacking skill, Brown finished off a movement with a try and he himself kicked the goal. A Sullivan goal made it 5–4 and, two minutes from the end, Bryn Evans broke away and Woods crashed over. Britain once again held the Ashes in a stranglehold; interest in the third Test was purely academic. Indeed, only 10,000 saw the third game at Swinton on 16 December, a foggy day. Ironically, this was the best game of the three, both sides throwing the ball about now the series was decided. Britain eventually made a clean sweep, winning 19–16, but it was touch and go until a late penalty goal by Sullivan, his fifth goal of the game. Hodgson, Feetham and Smith scored tries, while Hey and Prigg touched down for Australia and Brown also landed five goals.

## French expansion

Developments continued in France. A Sunday exhibition game was held at the Stade Pershing, Paris (a ground outside the jurisdiction of the French Rugby Union) between Australia and a Great Britain XIII captained by Jim Sullivan. It was held on 31 December 1933, a good crowd saw the game, and it was agreed that a French side, under the leadership of M. Jean Galia, would tour Britain in the spring of 1934. The French team played matches at Wigan, Leeds, Hull, London Highfield and Salford. They won only once, at Hull, but their enthusiasm and open play won them standing ovations everywhere they played.

An 'international' match between France and Great Britain was played at the Buffalo Velodrome, Paris, on 15 April, before 20,000 spectators. Britain won 32–21. After the game British officials met with Jean Galia, Charles Benat and M. Blein to organize a French rugby-league management committee. The next step was a tour of French clubs by Leeds and in August, under assurances of financial and other support from Britain, 'La Ligue Française de Rugby à Treize' was formed at Toulouse.

The first full season began in October, and the founder clubs were Paris Celtic, Bordeaux, Côte Basque, Grenoble, Sport Olympique de Paris, La Rochelle, Pau, Albi, Roanne, S. O. Béziers, Lyons and Villeneuve.

While the game spread its wings in France the home season brought another Wembley final, preceded by a championship final on 28 April 1934. The finalists were Salford and Wigan. Wigan beat the league leaders by 15 points to 3 before a splendid crowd of 31,565 at Warrington. The 1934 Wembley final brought another inter-county duel between Widnes and Hunslet, and the attendance was 41,280. The referee was A. Holbrook (Warrington) and the teams were:

*Hunslet*: Walkington; Dennis, Morrell, Winter, Broughton; Thornton, Todd; Smith, White, Tolson, Crowther, Dawson, Beverley

*Widnes*: Bradley; Owen, Topping, Jacks, Gallimore; Shannon, McCue; Silcock, Jones, Higgins, McDowell, Ratcliffe, Millington

Widnes, facing the strong wind and sun, led 3–2 with a try by McDowell against a goal by Tolson. Then Morrell, the Hunslet centre, broke through and crashed over for a great try. Hunslet, however, lost Morrell injured, had to face the elements, and things looked bleak for them. Nevertheless, Hunslet, with backs-to-the-wall tackling and determined 12-man running, scored tries through Beverley and Smith to win the cup by 11 points to 5.

The June annual meeting introduced two rulings designed to tidy up the game. At the play-the-ball there should be only one acting half-back on each side; in the scrum, the ball must not be hooked until it had reached the foot of the hooker furthest away from the entry of the ball. The other close-season item of note was the winding-up of London Highfield, whose remnant of players came north to re-form as Liverpool Stanley. There was further French activity during the season of 1934–35. Jean Galia brought the Villeneuve club players to play exhibition matches at Warrington, Broughton, Hull, Oldham and Leeds, losing the matches but gaining friends. Salford and Hunslet made short tours of the dissident French clubs.

The first really dramatic boost for the game in France was an international game against Wales at Bordeaux on Tuesday, 1 January 1935. France won 18–11, to the unbounded delight of 15,000 spectators. A short tour by a representative team from the Rugby League followed, and The League presented a trophy to be competed for as the French challenge cup. Another international followed and it was another good result for France. The match was played before a 20,000 crowd at the Buffalo Velodrome and resulted in a 15–15 draw against a strong England side. Rousie kicked three goals for France and Jean Galia got a try, applauded by the English team and officials.

The first representative game against a full French team took place as an international for the Jubilee celebrations of King George V and Queen Mary; a 15,000 attendance at Headingley saw an entertaining game won 25–18 by the Rugby League XIII. It was a good season in France and more teams joined the French League for 1935–36.

The Jubilee celebrations allowed the Rugby League to advertise a 'Jubilee Wembley' in 1935. The publicity campaign did not quite pay off and the crowd for the all-Yorkshire final between Castleford and Huddersfield was just under 40,000, paying £5800. Les Adams, the Castleford scrum-half, was playing in his third final in four years, having won with Leeds and Huddersfield. On the Huddersfield side Adams's opposite number was D. M. Davies who had played against Adams with Warrington in 1933. Teams were:

*Castleford*: Lewis; Cunniffe, Atkinson, Croston, Askin; W. J. Davies, Adams; McManus, Haley, Taylor, F. Smith, Crossley, Sadler

*Huddersfield*: Scourfield; Mountain, Towill, Fiddes, Markham; Richards, D. M. Davies; Roberts, Watson, Sherwood, Tiffany, Fuller, Talbot

Referee: A. E. Harding (Broughton)

The match was not a great one and Huddersfield's performance was well below their brilliant 1933 display. Castleford won 11–8 with tries from Askin, Adams and Cunniffe and a goal from Atkinson, against tries from Towill and Fiddes and a Sherwood goal; victory went to the better side.

The championship final at Wigan on 11 May saw Swinton beat Warrington by 14 points to 3 before a 27,000 crowd. It was a comfortable win, with Swinton rarely extended.

## London experiments

The annual meeting at Manchester in June brought two more surprise entries into the League. Sporting businessmen in London launched two sides with the cumbersome names of Acton and Willesden, and Streatham and Mitcham. In 1935–36 Swinton and a Rugby League XIII made tours of France, and France entered the international championship, losing both their games, to Wales at Llanelly and England at the Buffalo Velodrome. Receipts for the Paris game were £2510, a good figure and a happy augury.

The two new London clubs had fairly successful openings. Crowds were not large but the two teams, stiffened with experienced players, won several impressive victories. Streatham and Mitcham showed enterprise by signing five New Zealanders, including a Maori full-back, George Nepia.

Managers of the 1936 tour to Australasia were Messrs R. F. Anderton (Warrington) and W. Popplewell (Bramley). Making his fourth trip, a record, was Jim Sullivan who was again captain. Players were:

Backs: J. Sullivan, J. Morley (Wigan), J. Brough, S. Smith, F. Harris, S. Brogden (Leeds), B. Hudson, A. Edwards, A. J. Risman, E. Jenkins, W. Watkins (Salford), A. Atkinson (Castleford), W. Belshaw (Liverpool Stanley), T. McCue (Widnes).

Forwards: N. Silcock (Widnes), H. Woods (Liverpool Stanley), H. Field (York), T. Armitt, M. Hodgson (Swinton), J. Miller, J. Arkwright (Warrington), H. Jones (Keighley), L. A. Troup (Barrow), G. H. Exley (Wakefield T.), H. Beverley (Hunslet), H. Ellerington (Hull). To this party fell the responsibility of maintaining Britain's sixteen-year immunity from defeat by Australia in a Test series.

The first party of tourists left on 17 April and the challenge-cup final at Wembley was played on the following day between Leeds and Warrington. The attendance was the best yet, 51,250, and the receipts of £7200 were a British gate record. Teams were:

*Leeds*: Brough; E. Harris, F. Harris, Parker, Brogden; Ralph, Williams; Hall, Satterthwaite, Dyer, Jubb, Casewell, Isaac

*Warrington*: Shankland; Garrett, Hawker, Dingsdale, G. Jenkins; Newcombe, Goodall; Hardman, Cotton, Miller, Flannery, Arkwright, Chadwick

Referee: A. S. Dobson (Featherstone)

The large crowd did not see a particularly good final, the tension of the occasion causing fumbles and misplaced passes. Leeds, however, showed the greater inventiveness in attack and after Harris had cross-kicked for Isaac to score, the 'other Harris', Englishman Fred, raced through for a brilliant individual try. In the second half Eric Harris and Parker scored further tries, Williams completed three goals and Leeds won 18–2, equalling Huddersfield's record of four victories.

The championship final at Huddersfield was fought out between Hull and Widnes and the trophy went to Humberside. It was 2–2 at half time, but the Chemics collapsed startlingly in the second half and Hull won 21–2, with Joe Oliver, the Hull captain, scoring two tries and five goals.

After sixteen years of British domination Australia were determined to win a series. The early games of the 1936 tour were tough and bitterly fought, giving ample warning to the tourists as they reached Sydney Cricket Ground on 29 June for the first Test before a crowd topping 40,000. Australia won possession from the early scrums and pounded the British line but Britain scored first in a breakaway when Beverley ended good handling by crashing over. Brown kicked two penalties to give Australia a 4–3 half-time lead, and in the second half the green-and-gold jerseys took over. Ridley ended a seven-man move with a try and Brown, Pearce and Brown again ran in fine tries. Brown completed three goals and Beaton three in a 24–8 win for Australia, Beverley getting a second try for the tourists and Hodgson a goal.

Australia meant business and Britain buckled down to the second Test at Brisbane on the following Saturday. A crowd of 30,000 saw a game in which Brough, Arkwright, Risman, Watkins and Armitt were brought in by Britain replacing Morley, Atkinson, McCue, Field and Miller.

It was Britain's turn to start determinedly and, after Edwards had touched down, Risman kicked a goal. The tourists' enterprising play backfired when, during a passing movement, Crippin, the Australian winger, seized on a dropped ball and scored a spectacular try goaled by Beaton. In the second half Britain went into the lead when Edwards scored again and Risman goaled from touch. Brown kicked a penalty goal for Australia but a penalty from Hodgson made it

12–7 and Britain, tackling fiercely, tied the series. So the Ashes were at stake when the third Test was played at Sydney on 18 July 1936, a crowd of 53,000 paying £4299.

The first half was marred by some rough exchanges and a personal feud between Stehr and Arkwright resulted in the two forwards being sent off. At half time Britain led 5–2, Hudson scoring a try and Hodgson a goal against a Brown penalty goal. In the second half Australia fought hard to get on terms and break the hoodoo against Britain, but Britain came away from defence when Brogden took Jenkins's pass to score. Hodgson kicked two goals and, although a great run by Prigg gave Hey a try for Australia, Brown kicking the goal, it was too late, and a 12–7 scoreline, the second in successive Tests, clinched yet another series for Britain.

The tourists, having won thirteen out of sixteen games, set off for New Zealand where they won one 'warm-up' game against South Auckland with only nine men left on the field at the end. Ellerington and Exley were hurt, Hodgson was sent off and Beverley walked off with an injury near the end.

The first Test against the Kiwis, at Auckland on 8 August, saw Great Britain field both hookers, Armitt and Field, with Troup coming in at loose-forward. The referee penalized Britain incessantly but Hemi and Watene wasted goal-kicking chances. As a result Edwards and Jenkins scored tries for Britain, and Hodgson scored two goals to give Britain a narrow 10–8 victory, Watene (3) and Trevarthen landing goals for the Kiwis.

The second and final Test at Auckland a week later brought a more convincing 23–11 win for the tourists; in the British back division were five Salford players, Risman, Watkins, Jenkins, Hudson and Edwards. The 1936 tour ended successfully, with a profit of more than £8000.

The 1936–37 season began with the end of one experiment and the launching of another. The Acton and Willesden club disbanded after one season; into their place came a north-eastern club, Newcastle. Unfortunately, Newcastle staggered from defeat to defeat, losing their first thirteen games. Then came an outstanding result, Newcastle beating the reigning champions 13–0! It was a momentary revival – the writing was on the wall for Newcastle.

Meanwhile, Streatham and Mitcham began to fly financial distress signals and midway through the season the general manager, Ivor Halstead, announced his club's retirement from the League.

## Continued French growth

While home ventures foundered, the game continued to grow in France. Côte Basque made a short tour in Britain under their English coach, Tom Parker, a former Wigan player, and a big fillip for the game in France was the admission of the French League to the Fédération Nationale des Sports. A triangular international tournament was again held and, although both England and Wales again beat France, the games were well supported and the French side showed continued improvement.

The 1937 challenge-cup final brought together Widnes, playing their third final in eight years, and Keighley, playing in their first. The championship final, between Salford and Warrington, was played first at Wigan on Saturday, 1 May 1937. The first try came after seventy minutes, the score tied 8–8 from four penalty goals each. Cotton slipped over for an unimproved Warrington try but Salford snatched victory when Hudson went over in the corner and Risman kicked a great goal.

The challenge-cup final the following Saturday attracted 48,000 to Wembley. Keighley were led by D. M. Davies, beaten finalist with Huddersfield and Warrington. Teams were:

*Keighley*: Herbert; Sherburn, Towill, Parker, Lloyd; Bevan, Davies; Traill, Halliday, H. Jones, Talbot, Dixon, Gill

*Widnes*: Bradley; Whyte, Topping, Barner, Evans; Shannon, McCue; Silcock, J. Jones, Higgins, McDowell, Roberts, Millington

Referee: P. Cowell (Warrington)

Widnes were ahead in ten minutes when a McCue break sent in Shannon, Topping landing the goal. Then McCue jinked through for a great try; Keighley's only first-half reply was a goal by Sherburn. In the second half Barber intercepted between Bevan and Towill to score, Topping adding the goal. Lloyd got a late try for beaten Keighley.

The Australian tourists arrived at Southampton on 15 September. One big name missing was the powerfully built stand-off-half, Vic Hey, who had joined Leeds. Harry Sunderland was making his third managerial trip, with R. E. Savage as co-manager. Only Gilbert, Stehr, Curran, Gibbs and Prigg were experienced tourists in a young side. Players were:

Backs: L. Ward, H. Robinson, C. Hazelton, L. Dawson, J. Beaton, B. Williams, R. McKinnon, E. Norman, P. Williams, L. Thompson, G. Whittle, D. McLean, J. Reardon, F. Gilbert.

Forwards: F. Nolan, P. Fairall, R. Stehr, F. Curran, J. Gibbs, H. Narvo, E. Lewis, W. Prigg, A. Norval, R. McLenna, H. Pierce, F. Griffiths, L. Heidke, E. Collins.

The Australians won six and lost two of their pre-Test games. The first Test took place at Leeds on Saturday, 16 October, before a 32,000 crowd. The teams were:

*Great Britain*: W. Belshaw (Liverpool S.); C. Cunniffe, A. J. Croston (Castleford), A. J. Risman (Salford), J. Morley (Wigan); E. Jenkins (Salford), T. McCue (Widnes); N. Silcock (Widnes), T. Armitt (Swinton), H. Woods (Leeds), J. Arkwright (Warrington), M. Hodgson (Swinton), H. Beverley (Hunslet)

*Australia*: Ward; Reardon, Beaton, McKinnon, B. Williams; Norman, P. Williams; Curran, Pierce, Stehr, Gibbs, Lewis, Prigg

Great Britain's long-running defence of the Ashes made a bad start, with dreary, plodding play, and it was only poor finishing that prevented the tourists from taking a big half-time lead. It was 4–2 at the interval, two goals from Beaton against one from Hodgson. Australia paid the price of these errors in the second half, when the only score was a try to Britain by Jenkins. Britain had scrambled an unconvincing 5–4 win.

Changes were inevitably made for the second Test at Swinton on 20 November. Hudson, Watkins, Brogden and Edwards replaced Cunniffe, Croston, McCue and Morley in the backs, while Higgins (Widnes) and Jubb (Leeds) took over from Woods and Hodgson in the pack.

Australia had injuries to Stehr and McKinnon. Dawson came into the backs, and Narvo and Heidke replaced Curran and Stehr. The changes worked better for Britain than for Australia, and Britain made no mistake before an attendance of 31,724. Edwards got a try in the first half and Edwards and Hudson crossed in the second, with Risman's two goals giving Salford players all the British points. Dawson got a try for Australia.

Once again Britain had taken the series and fewer than 10,000 saw the third Test at Huddersfield on 18 December 1937. The match, played in poor weather, was belated consolation for the tourists who won 13–3. Norval, Reardon and Narvo scored tries against a home team resting on its laurels, and Beaton kicked two goals. Hudson got a try for Britain. The victory came too late to save the Ashes or, indeed, the tour finances, for takings were nearly £10,000 down on the 1933 figure, due to a shorter tour and eleven defeats in twenty-four games.

## Elland Road championship

The 1937–38 domestic competitions brought an unusual venue choice for the championship final. Two Leeds clubs, Hunslet and Leeds, reached the play-off; after representations from the clubs the venue was switched from Wakefield to the spacious Elland Road football ground, home of Leeds United. When the game was played on 30 April 1938 the attendance was more than 54,000, a record for a rugby-league game in England. The match was a hard-fought local derby, Hunslet winning the title by 8 points to 2. Winter and O'Sullivan scored tries and Walkington a goal for Hunslet, while Tattersfield landed a goal for Leeds.

The following Saturday was Wembley day, Barrow and Salford competing before an excellent crowd of 53,000. The match was to produce a sensational finish and major talking point. Teams were:

*Barrow*: French; Cumberbatch, Higgins, McDonnell, Thornburrow; Lloyd, Little; Rawlings, McKeating, Skelly, Troup, Ayres, Marklew

*Salford*: Osbaldestin; Hudson, Brown, Gear, Edwards; Risman, Watkins; Williams, Day, Davies, Thomas, Dalton, Feetham

Referee: F. Peel (Bradford)

Defences were on top throughout the game, Salford having conceded only one try in their challenge-cup run. Barrow were equally tenacious. French kicked a penalty for Barrow but Risman replied with a dropped goal and a penalty. The second half was equally dour and Salford seemed likely to hold out until Little dropped a fine goal to bring the scores level at 4–4. The crowds were streaming towards the exits anticipating a replay at Wigan when

Troup, under pressure, rolled out a bad pass near his own line. Gear, the Salford centre, pounced on the ball and forced his way over the line with half the Barrow team clinging on like limpets. Mr Peel awarded a try, despite fierce protests that Gear had not grounded, and Salford won 7–4.

The 1938–39 season began without Newcastle whose brief and unhappy career terminated at the 1938 annual meeting. This was to be the last season before the outbreak of the Second World War and, ironically, it heralded the 'arrival' of France as an international force. France beat England 12–9 at Swinton and then beat Wales 16–10 at Bordeaux to win the championship, an achievement hailed in France and applauded in Britain.

The consistent Salford side again won through to Wembley, where they met Halifax, and the championship final, where Castleford were their opponents. The last pre-war Wembley brought a new record crowd for Britain of 55,543. The match was played on Saturday, 6 May, with George Phillips of Widnes as referee. Teams were:

*Halifax*: Lockwood; Bevan, Smith, Treen, Bassett; Todd, Goodall; Baynham, Field, Irvin, Cox, Chadwick, Beverley

*Salford*: Osbaldestin; Hudson, Miller, Risman, Edwards; Kenny, Watkins; Davies, Day, Bradbury, Thomas, Dalton, Feetham

If Halifax were impressed by Salford's reputation they showed few signs of it, and took charge of the game. Osbaldestin was hurt and left the field for the last thirty minutes, but even before then Salford were second best.

Good Halifax moves sent Smith and Treen over for first-half tries, Lockwood adding the goals. Risman pulled back three points with a try, but after Osbaldestin's retirement from the field Todd and Bevan touched down and Lockwood kicked both goals. Halifax won 20–3 and Mr Phillips's final whistle rang down the curtain at Wembley for seven years. It seems ironical that this last pre-war season ended with the game on a tide of mounting popularity. The championship final between Castleford and Salford was played at Maine Road, Manchester, and set up another crowd record with more than 70,000 present. Castleford held on grimly to a 6–5 lead, with tries by Brindle and Robinson against a try by Kenny and goal by Risman, until late in the game when swift Salford handling gave Edwards the winning try.

## Untimely deaths

The summer of 1939 brought the passing of a good club and the death of one of the game's 'immortals'. St Helens Recreation, the works team from Pilkington Bros., disbanded because of heavy financial losses and, in July 1939, Harold Wagstaff, the great Huddersfield and Great Britain centre, and one of the finest players the game has known, died.

The 1939 annual meeting made two important rule changes. The hooker was allowed to strike with either foot, and scrums would form ten yards from the touchline. These changes were made as war clouds gathered and a sense of foreboding and inevitability moved across Europe.

# 6

# The War and the Post-War Boom

The Second World War shattered and disrupted sport just as the First World War had done. Football and rugby-league programmes were cancelled and replaced first with friendlies and eventually with patched-up wartime competitions. Hardest hit were the New Zealand tourists, under managers R. Doble and J. A. Redwood, who arrived in Britain on 29 August and then had to return on the outbreak of war after playing two games at Dewsbury and St Helens.

The Rugby Union made a welcome gesture to Rugby League. The ban on Union players appearing alongside League players was lifted for the duration of the war, and services' teams soon testified to the value of the decision. The League permitted players to 'guest' with teams near their service bases; Dewsbury were to benefit greatly from this ruling during the war years.

There were no challenge-cup or championship games in 1939–40, but the county cups were held. Swinton beat Widnes in a home-and-away two-leg Lancashire final, while Featherstone Rovers beat Wakefield Trinity 12–9 at Odsal. In an 'emergency' play-off the Yorkshire champions Bradford Northern beat their Lancashire counterparts, Swinton, in home-and-away ties.

The first wartime annual meeting of the League was at Leeds on 12 June 1940. The meeting was short and a slight loss was reported. When clubs lined up for the second wartime season there were nine in the truncated Lancashire league and fourteen in Yorkshire. Clubs which had withdrawn included Barrow, Widnes, Rochdale Hornets and Hull K. R.

The season of 1940–41 was not a very long one and Salford and

Warrington withdrew midway through it. No Lancashire cup was competed for, but Oldham and Wigan were accepted in the Yorkshire cup which was won by Bradford Northern who beat Dewsbury 15–5. The depleted Lancashire competition was won by Wigan, and the Yorkshire title by Bradford Northern who swept the board when they beat Wigan home-and-away in the play-off.

The challenge cup was revived as a further wartime 'emergency' competition in 1941. The popularity of the game even in wartime was emphasized by a crowd of 29,000 at Odsal on 19 May to see Leeds beat Halifax 19–2.

The council decided that the two county competitions would be fused into one in 1941–42. Rugby League suffered an international blow in November 1941 when the French puppet Government, under Marshal Pétain, banned rugby league in France and transferred all the League's property and funds to the Fédération Nationale des Sports. During the remainder of the war years the game was kept alive by village teams playing furtively in areas of lax German rule.

## United in service

One of the features of the war years was the quality of services' rugby, the best union and league men playing alongside each other. In an RAF *v.* Army game at Rosslyn Park in January 1942, the RAF included Edwards (Salford), W. T. H. Davies (Bradford N.) and E. Watkins (Wigan) while the Army fielded S. Brogden (Hull), A. J. Risman (Salford), T. Foster, E. Hodgson (Bradford N.), K. Jubb (Leeds) and G. Williams (Wigan). There were matches between England and Wales involving league players, and between Lancashire services and Yorkshire services.

A particularly interesting wartime game was a Northern Command *v.* Rugby League match under league rules at Thrum Hall in March 1942. The Command team consisted entirely of league players and before a 7000 crowd they beat the Rugby League XIII by 22 points to 18. Ernest Ward (Bradford N.) kicked five goals and Francis, Pepperell, Case and Walsh scored tries. Chapman (2) and Lawrenson (2) scored tries for the League team and Lockwood kicked three goals.

Severe weather during 1941–42 caused the extension of the third wartime season to 6 June when the challenge cup final was played. Dewsbury won the emergency championship by beating Bradford Northern at Headingley.

A crowd of 15,250 saw the wartime challenge-cup final at Odsal. It was a repeat of the previous year and once again Leeds beat Halifax, this time 15–10. A wartime oddity was that Edwards and Risman played for Leeds after 'guesting' for Dewsbury. In 1942–43 Castleford, Bramley, Hunslet and Broughton Rangers decided not to continue, reducing the League competition to fourteen teams. On 23 January 1943, at Headingley, and before 8000 spectators, there was a League *v.* Union match. The Northern Command union and League teams met under union rules, and after a great game the League won 18–11 after being eight points down. The League team scored six unimproved tries through Mills (2), Jubb (2), Tattersfield and Chapman.

Dewsbury won the two-leg Yorkshire cup in 1942–43 and were again finalists for the wartime challenge cup, a two-leg game between Dewsbury and Leeds. In the first leg at Dewsbury on 24 April 1943 it won 16–9 before 12,000 spectators and, two days later, in a dour and unrelenting battle at Headingley, three penalty goals gave Leeds a 6–0 victory, the overall honours going to Dewsbury by one point. Dewsbury, with the pick of the services' stars, cleaned up the honours by beating Halifax home and-away in the championship final.

## *Dewsbury fined*

Dewsbury's elation turned to consternation at the meeting of the League's war-emergency committee at Leeds on 7 July. Bradford Northern complained that Dewsbury had played an ineligible player, Smith of Castleford, in its semi-final championship game with Northern. The committee declared the championship null and void and fined Dewsbury £100.

Barrow and Hunslet clubs returned to the fold for the season of 1943–44. Bradford Northern beat Keighley in the Yorkshire-cup final. In the challenge-cup final it lost 3–0 at Wigan, but won 8–0 against Wigan at Odsal. Wigan again challenged the wartime Yorkshire monopoly in the championship final. They beat Dewsbury 13–9 at Central Park and then delighted their fans by winning 12–5 at Crown

Flatt to become the first Lancashire club to win a wartime title. Jim Sullivan, who had first played for Wigan twenty-three years before kicked three goals in the second leg against a team for which he, too, had guested.

A new team was admitted in 1945, as Europe looked forward to the end of the war and the resumption of normal sporting activities. Workington Town came in from Cumbria, with good potential support on the west Cumbrian coast and under the chairmanship of Mr F. Meageen.

During the season of 1944–45, the last in wartime, Halifax beat Hunslet in the Yorkshire cup. Huddersfield beat Bradford Northern in the two-leg challenge cup, with Bawden the Huddersfield scoring hero, and Bradford Northern beat Halifax in the two-leg championship. On Monday, 30 May 1945, club representatives met at Leeds to recommend that full activity resume in 1945–46.

## The crowds return

The first league games were played on 25 August 1945. Two clubs, Wigan and Hunslet, appointed famous former players, Jim Sullivan and Jack Walkington, as coaches. In the early weeks there was every sign of returning crowd enthusiasm, with 16,000 at Wigan, 12,000 at Odsal and big crowds at Barrow and Headingley. The county-cup matches were played to bigger crowds than pre-war. In Australia 50,000 watched New South Wales and Queensland play at Sydney. In France the indefatigable Jean Galia arranged for a tour by Castleford as the French League rapidly revived after the occupation.

Australia quickly asked for a British tour in 1946. The problem was transport, with so many ships requisitioned for the war effort, but the Rugby League agreed. Eventually the team travelled by the aircraft carrier *Indomitable*.

England played Wales, a form of Test trial, on 24 November 1945. The game was played at Swansea before a splendid attendance of 30,000, and Wales won 11–3 with tries from G. Price (2) and Phillips, plus a goal by Risman, against a Nicholson try.

John Wilson retired as secretary of the Rugby League after twenty-five years' service, and William Fallowfield took over to become the League's third secretary in half a century.

England beat France in Paris and at Swinton before good crowds and Wigan set the pattern for overseas signings by bringing over from New Zealand two players destined to make big impacts on the game in England, winger Brian Nordgren and half-back Cecil Mountford.

After two more Test trials at Wigan and Leeds the tour party was announced, under the management of Messrs W. M. Gabbatt (Barrow) and W. Popplewell (Bramley). They were:

Backs: M. Ryan, Ted Ward (Wigan), J. Jones, W. Horne, J. Lewthwaite, B. Knowelden (Barrow), E. Batten, J. Kitching, E. Ward (Bradford Northern), A. J. Risman, capt. (Salford), A. Bassett (Halifax), A. Johnson (Warrington), T. McCue (Widnes), D. Jenkins (Leeds), W. H. T. Davies (Bradford Northern).

Forwards: K. Gee, J. Egan (Wigan), G. Curran (Salford), F. Whitcombe, T. Foster (Bradford Northern), F. Hughes (Workington Town), D. Phillips (Oldham), R. Nicholson (Huddersfield), L. White (York), I. Owens (Leeds), H. Murphy (Wakefield T.).

The 'Indomitables' sailed in April, along with returning Australian servicemen, on the aircraft carrier. The early departure created problems for the clubs engaged in challenge-cup and championship finals. Worst hit was Wigan which reached both trophy finals with four players on tour. Yet, such was Wigan's reserve strength that they put out strong sides for the Wembley final against Wakefield Trinity and the championship final against Huddersfield at Maine Road, Manchester.

## Wembley and the 'Lance Todd'

The challenge-cup final returned to Wembley on 4 May 1946, an excellent crowd, totalling 54,730, paid world-record receipts of £11,995. Teams were:

*Wakefield Trinity*: Teall; Rylance, Stott, Croston, Baddeley; Jones, Goodfellow; Wilkinson, Marson, Higgins, Exley, Howes, Bratley

*Wigan*: Cunliffe; Nordgren, Ratcliffe, Ashcroft, Jolley; Lowry, Bradshaw, Banks, J. Blan, Barton, Watkins, Atkinson, W. Blan

Referee: A. Hill (Leeds)

The match provided eighty minutes of sustained excitement and fluctuating play, and ended breathtakingly. Wigan secured a one-point lead at half time, Nordgren and J. Blan running in tries against a try and a goal from Stott, the centre secured from Oldham for £90. As play swung from end to end, both sides scored two unimproved tries, Jolley and Nordgren for Wigan, Croston and Rylance for Trinity.

With only ninety seconds left Mr Hill awarded Wakefield a penalty, a long way out and at an angle. Wigan led 12–11 and every spectator held his breath as Stott walked slowly back, took careful aim, and sent the ball straight through the middle of the Wigan posts. Trinity won 13–12 and Billy Stott, the giveaway transfer, became the first recipient of the Lance Todd trophy, named after the great New Zealand player and administrator who was killed in a car crash in 1941.

Wigan sought consolation in the championship final which attracted a massive crowd of 67,136 to Maine Road on 18 May. Wigan won 13–4, the star being full-back Jackie Cunliffe who was dazed in a tackle, went to half-back and scored a great try. Ashcroft got two tries and Nordgren two goals, while Bawden kicked two goals for Huddersfield.

In Australia the tourists prepared for the first post-war Test with warm-up games 'out in the sticks' and against the state sides. The first Test was at Sydney on Monday, 17 June 1946, and Britain were without both full-backs, Ryan and Jones, through injury. Teams were:

*Australia*: Parkinson; Newham, Cooper, Jorgenson, Bailey; Devery, Grice; Westaway, Watt, Farrell, Clues, Kay, Mulligan

*Great Britain*: Risman; Batten, Ernest Ward, Kitching, Johnson; Horne, McCue; Gee, Egan, Whitcombe, Phillips, White, Owens

The game pulled in 64,000 spectators and ended in an 8–8 draw. Britain should have won but Risman missed eight out of nine kicks at goal. Britain led 6–2 at half time, Horne nipping over and the mighty Whitcombe ploughing over for tries against a Jorgenson goal for Australia. Britain played the second half with twelve men, Kitching having been sent off after an alleged 'bite' by Jorgenson had brought retaliation. Bailey scored a try for Australia, Risman kicked his only goal, but Cooper brought the house down, running powerfully from his own half for the equalizing try. Jorgenson missed the kick and later missed another simple chance.

Badly hit by injuries, Britain had Ernest Ward at full-back for the second Test before 45,000 at Brisbane on Saturday, 6 July. The big crowd, with thousands locked out, saw Britain rise magnificently to the occasion.

Bassett, the big Halifax policeman on the wing, ran in a great hat-trick and Johnson scored a spectacular individual try, Ward landing one goal. Cooper got a try for Australia and Jorgenson a goal, but Britain won 14–5 and were one up with one to play.

The 'Indomitables' clinched the series in the final Test at Sydney on 20 July before a crowd of 35,000. The score was a convincing 20 points to 7 after Australia had led 7–2 at half time with a Kennedy try and two Jorgenson goals, against a Risman goal. In the second half there was a transformation as Britain played great football to score tries through Bassett twice, Curran and Owens, Risman landing three goals. After this unbeaten series in Australia the tourists went to New Zealand for an ego-deflating shock in the only Test match at Auckland. The ground was like a swamp, hampering Britain's back play, and the referee penalized Britain so often that all New Zealand's points in a 13–8 win came as the result of penalty kicks. Clarke kicked four goals and added a goal after a penalty had hit the woodwork and rebounded to Graham who touched down. Ernest Ward and Batten scored tries for Britain and Ward kicked a goal.

The tour over, the party left Wellington on 14 August on the S. S. *Rangitiki*. The tour saw the end of Gus Risman's long connection with Salford for, after his return, he signed as player-manager with the new club, Workington Town. The 1946–47 season opened with more overseas signings from Australia. Arthur Clues, a forward, and Bert Cook, a full-back, joined Leeds, and Huddersfield signed up backs Johnny Hunter and Pat Devery.

## The long season

The Australians arrived to find British weather about to do its worst. The winter was so snowbound that postponements were legion; the season was extended to 21 June, when the championship final took place. Challenge-cup ties were played as, and when, grounds became available but, nevertheless, the final was played at Wembley on time, on 3 May 1947. Interest in the event was the highest ever and

Wembley at last produced an attendance worthy of the stadium, more than 77,000 paying £17,605 to see a Bradford Northern *v.* Leeds battle.

Paul Cowell (Warrington) was the referee and the teams were:

*Bradford Northern*; Carmichael; Batten, E. Ward, Kitching, Walters; Davies, D. Ward; Whitcombe, Darlison, Smith, Tyler, Foster, Evans

*Leeds*: Cook; Cornelius, Price, T. Williams, Whitehead; R. Williams, Jenkins; Prosser, Murphy, Brereton, Watson, Clues, Owens

The final was a disappointing affair, Leeds, in particular, being below their best. Willie Davies won the Lance Todd trophy for his untiring efforts at half-back for Northern. Walters and Foster scored the Northern tries and Ernest Ward landed a goal. Leeds's points came from two goals from Cook.

The delayed championship final at Maine Road on 21 June brought together Wigan and Dewsbury, and again the match was something of a disappointment. A Ledgard goal gave Dewsbury an interval lead but, in the second half, Wigan livened up and Nordgren, Lawrenson and Bradshaw went in for tries, Ward kicking a goal. A dropped goal by Holt for Dewsbury made it 13–4 to Wigan.

The 1947 close season brought more industry in the transfer market. A stream of overseas players included Harry Bath, a forward who joined Barrow and later Warrington, Duncan Jackson, half-back and Bruce Ryan, winger, who both went to Hull, Don Graham, back, to Hunslet, Dinny Boocker, back, to Wakefield Trinity, and Len Kenny and Ted Verrenkamp, threequarters, to Leeds. The flood of overseas signings led to renewed protests from Australia and New Zealand and the council placed a five-year ban on overseas signings.

## A longer Kiwi tour

The 1947–48 season brought the visit to Britain of New Zealand, whose 1939 tour had been cut to two matches by the outbreak of war. Managers were Messrs J. Redwood and C. Hunter, with forward P. Smith as captain. Former Great Britain full-back and centre, Jim Brough, was appointed adviser to the New Zealanders. Players were:

P. Smith, D. Barchard, J. Haig, J. Hancox, R. Nuttall, W. S. Clarke, R. Clark, T. Hardwick, M. Robertson, J. Forrest, D.

Anderson, A. McInnarney, R. Cunningham, L. Jordan, L. Pye, G. Davidson, G. Johnson, A. Gilman, J. Newton, K. Mountford, C. McBride, A. Graham, R. Aynsley, J. Johnson, A. W. McKenzie.

It was a hectic tour for the Kiwis who played their first Test only a fortnight after arrival. The match took place at Headingley and a big crowd of 28,445 saw Great Britain win narrowly, and luckily, 11–10 after being outplayed for most of the game. With ten minutes left the tourists led deservedly 10–8 with tries by McGregory and Forrest and two goals from Clarke, against British tries by Aston (St Helens) and Gwyther (Belle Vue Rangers) and a goal from Ernest Ward (Bradford N.). With the minutes ticking away Stott, the St Helens centre, appeared to knock-on before kicking ahead, but play was waved on and Johnson, the Warrington winger, touched down to give Britain a lucky win.

The Kiwis deservedly squared the series by winning the second Test 10–7 at Swinton on Saturday, 8 November. Although out-hooked in the scrums, New Zealand tackled and ran well. They scored tries through Forrest and Newton and two goals from Clarke, against a try by Jenkins (Leeds) and two goals from Ledgard.

Interest was high for the third and final Test at Odsal on 20 December, and 45,000 paid £5800 to see it. Alas, the game was an anti-climax for Great Britain played brilliant football and outclassed the Kiwis, winning 25–9 with five tries and five goals against a try and three goals. Consolation for the tourists was a profit of £6000.

## The International Board

The Rugby League International Board was set up at a meeting in Bordeaux in 1948. It consisted of representatives of Australia, Great Britain, New Zealand and France.

The 1948 challenge-cup final brought a clash between the two post-war giants, Bradford Northern and Wigan. It was a 'natural' for Wembley and a tremendous crowd of 92,500 swarmed to the stadium in early May. Teams were:

*Bradford Northern*: Leake; Batten, Case, E. Ward, Edwards; Davies, D. Ward; Whitcombe, Darlison, Smith, Foster, Tyler, Traill

*Wigan*: Ryan; Ratcliffe, Ted Ward, Ashcroft, Hilton; Mountford, Bradshaw; Gee, Egan, Barton, White, W. Blan, Hudson

Cec Mountford won fame and popularity as a fast and skilful stand-off half with Wigan. He later became a coach and manager with Warrington and, when he returned to New Zealand, enhanced his status by becoming the manager of the national squad. Here he is (*second from right, front row*) with the Kiwis 1970 World Cup squad

Alan Hardisty gave great service to Castleford, Leeds and Great Britain as a stand-off half, and had a spell playing in Australia. He leaves Salford defenders behind him as he touches down for a typical try for Castleford

Graeme Langlands broke goal-scoring records with the Kangaroos. Another successful kick is on target during the 1973 tour on which Langlands was captain

Billy Benyon coached his former club, St Helens, after a successful coaching spell with Warrington. In his playing days with Saints he scored many fine tries, including this one in a cup game against Doncaster

Keith Elwell, the diminutive Widnes hooker whose burrowing style won him the nickname 'The Mole', set up a world record of consecutive club appearances with Widnes, his 239 beating the previous record set up by Gilbert Austin of Hull Kingston Rovers, the winger who totalled 190 games in a row

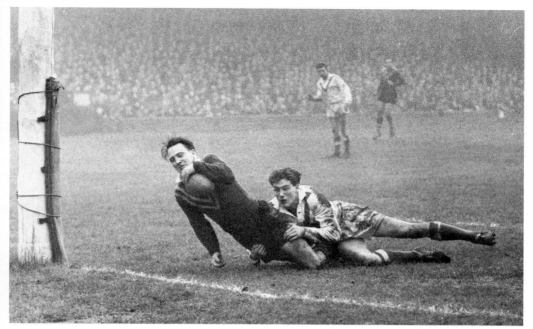

The 1959 Headingley Test between Great Britain and Australia produced a dramatic finish with a last-gasp English victory. Australia led 10-6 late into the game, with Brian Carlson's finishing power producing this Kangaroo try despite Ashton's tackle

Great Britain won the 1959 Headingley Test and squared the series, when, from a late scrum near the Australian line, loose forward Johnny Whiteley dived over

Waterlogged Wembley, 1968

Some of the most famous names in the history of the code figured in the all-conquering St Helens team of the 60s. The brilliant Springbok winger Tom Van Vollenhoven is on the left of the seated front row, while in the centre is the mercurial and still actively involved Wigan coach, Alex Murphy

Bradford Northern were the outstanding cup side of the immediate post-war years. Ernest Ward is chaired with the cup after the 1949 12–0 victory over Halifax at Wembley

One of the great half backs of the years following the Second World War, Gerry Helme of Warrington, prepares to give help if required in a match against the Australians

Favourite for the title of greatest winger of all time is the Brown Bomber of Wigan, Billy Boston, and a Hull defender here feels the full weight of the Boston hand-off

When arguments rage about the finest wing threequarters ever, the name of Warrington's Brian Bevan is always on the short list. Here the lightning-fast, elusive 'Bev' takes a pass from his Other Nationalities colleague Tony Paskins, while England's Ted Cahill makes the tackle

The most prolific points scorer of all time, Neil Fox, was a remarkably nimble player for his size and weight as he demonstrates in a Test match against Australia

Colin Hutton played as a goal-kicking full back with Widnes and Hull, his last-minute goal winning a memorable Yorkshire Cup victory for Hull against Halifax. He later became manager of Great Britain, with John Whiteley as coach

*Left:* John Holmes, the Leeds half back, whose skilful passing of the ball has opened many defences on the Loiners' marches to trophy victories. Roy Dickinson looks on

Great Britain stand-off half David Topliss (*left*) won the Lance Todd trophy with Wakefield Trinity at Wembley, then joined Hull to steer the Airlie Birds to a challenge cup win over the same opponents, Widnes. In this Elland Road replay picture are Clive Sullivan MBE (*centre*), who left to coach Doncaster, and Paul Prendiville, who left the Boulevard for Leeds

Roger Millward was nursing a broken jaw when he raised the challenge cup in triumph after Hull Kingston Rovers' derby victory over Hull in 1980. Millward, now successfully coaching Rovers, is hoisted aloft by David Watkinson and David Hall (*left*)

Referee: G. Phillips (Widnes)

Unfortunately, the game did not live up to its billing or the crowd. Wigan scored first when Egan cross-kicked, Batten's attempted clearance kick was caught by Hilton, who scored, and Ted Ward kicked a touchline goal. Three minutes later a fumble by Ratcliffe saw Edwards touch down. With Wigan leading 5–3 the game became a tenacious struggle until a minute from the end when Wigan made the game safe as Barton ploughed over for a try. The Lance Todd trophy went to the giant Northern forward, Frank Whitcombe.

Northern's hopes of a consolation championship victory foundered at Maine Road with Warrington winning 15–5. Bevan, Powell and Pimblett got the Warrington tries, and Palin three goals, against a Case try and an Ernest Ward goal.

The success of Workington Town in the far north-west contributed towards a further Cumbrian admission in May 1948; Whitehaven joined the League with Jack Kitching, formerly of Bradford Northern and Great Britain, as manager.

The busy international season continued with the arrival of the Australians in late 1948 for their first post-war tour. Managers were Bill Buckley and E. J. Simmonds; captain was Colin Maxwell. The players were:

Backs: C. B. Churchill, V. J. Bulgin, R. Dimond, J. N. Graves, J. Horrigan, R. J. Lulham, C. M. Maxwell, P. McMahon, D. A. McRitchie, L. R. Pegg, W. H. Thompson, G. K. Froome, J. N. Hawke, B. Hopkins, W. P. O'Connell.

Forwards: W. Tyquin, L. G. Cowie, E. Brosnan, F. L. De Belin, A. Gibbs, D. Hall, N. R. Hand, R. F. Holland, F. E. Johnson, N. G. Mulligan, R. J. Rayner, K. B. Schubert.

The Kangaroos won four of their five club games before the first Test at Headingley on 9 October, seen by a crowd of more than 35,000 paying £8400. The match produced a feast of good rugby, with 44 points scored in a seesaw game, Great Britain finally getting home 23–21.

Hall and Froome scored tries for Australia in the first quarter, then brilliant rugby came from Britain with tries by Foster (2) and McCormick and a goal from Ward. In the second half McCormick and Valentine scored British tries to make it 17–6 but Australia rallied. Tries came from Froome, Graves and McMahon and two goals from Graves, but Pimblett grabbed two unimproved tries for Britain who hung on to win.

The second Test was at Swinton on 7 November. A crowd of 37,000 saw Australia fail to find form; Britain clinched yet another series by winning 16–7. Pimblett (2) and Lawrenson (2) touched down, and Ward kicked two goals, while Horrigan with a try and Graves, two goals, scored for a disappointing Australian side.

The third Test, postponed in December because of fog, was played at Bradford on 29 January. Great Britain made the expected clean sweep of the series, winning 23–9. The Australians were, as in the second Test, without their injured captain, Colin Maxwell, and fell away after leading 6–5 at half time. Ernest Ward, Curran (2), McCormick and Dicky Williams got the British tries, Ward kicking four goals.

## Record Wembley crowd

The post-war appeal of rugby league climbed steadily and the 1949 challenge-cup final at Wembley on 7 May brought a record attendance of 95,000. The teams were the consistent Bradford Northern, playing in their third consecutive final, and Halifax. Teams were:

*Bradford Northern*: Leake; Batten, E. Ward, Kitching, Edwards; Davies, D. Ward; Whitcombe, Darlison, Greaves, Foster, Tyler, Traill

*Halifax*: Chalkley; Daniels, Reid, Price, McDonald; Kenny, Kielty; Condon, Ackerley, Rothwell, Healy, Pansegrouw, Mawson

Referee: G. Phillips (Widnes)

The game was too one-sided to be a spectacle, with Northern overpowering Halifax. Winger Eric Batten played for most of the game with a cracked shoulder bone, but Northern kept the ball away from him and still won comfortably. Batten took Ward's cross kick to score and Trevor Foster got a second as Northern coasted home 12–0, Ward kicking three goals.

The spectator interest was nearly as great for the championship final at Maine Road between Huddersfield and Warrington on 14 May. The crowd was 75,194, paying £11,073.

The occasion provided a match worthy of the crowd, Huddersfield winning 13–12 after Warrington, down 13–0, had provided a breathtaking rally to pull back to within a point. Huddersfield tries came from Daly, Cooper and Devery, plus two goals from Devery, and in Warrington's great finish Francis and Jackson touched down and Bath (2) and Palin landed goals.

After the championship final Huddersfield and St Helens made a short 'missionary' tour of South Wales to promote an eight-team Welsh league to be launched in 1949–50. Yet another decision was to revive the Other Nationalities team in the international championship. The post-war boom was at its peak.

# 7

# Towards the World Cup

Despite its optimistic launch the Welsh league struggled against entrenched Rugby Union interest and prejudice and only two clubs survived to apply for admission to the Rugby League in 1950–51. In addition, two international matches, Wales *v*. France at Swansea and Wales *v*. Other Nationalities at Abertillery, made losses.

There was to be no respite from Test rugby in 1949–50. The second post-war tour of Australasia was scheduled for 1950. Managers were Tom Spedding (Belle Vue Rangers) and George Oldroyd (Dewsbury), with Ernest Ward of Bradford Northern as captain. The players selected were:

Backs: M. Ryan, J. Hilton, J. Cunliffe, E. J. Ashcroft, T. Bradshaw (Wigan), J. Ledgard (Leigh), A. H. Daniels (Halifax), R. Pollard (Dewsbury), L. Williams (Hunslet), E. Ward (Bradford N.), T. Danby (Salford), W. Horne (Barrow), R. Williams (Leeds), A. J. Pepperell (Workington T.).

Forwards: K. Gee, J. Egan (Wigan), D. Naughton, F. Higgins (Widnes), F. Osmond (Swinton), E. Gwyther, D. Phillips (Belle Vue R.), J. Featherstone, R. Ryan (Warrington), H. Street (Dewsbury), H. Murphy (Wakefield Trinity), K. Traill (Bradford N.). Wigan's record representation increased to eight when Williams withdrew for business reasons and Gordon Ratcliffe was included.

With eight players on tour Wigan displayed awesome reserve strength by reaching the final of, and winning, the championship. First, however, came the challenge cup, a derby match between Warrington and Widnes at Wembley. Another crowd topping 90,000 packed the stadium. Teams were:

*Warrington*: L. Jones; Bevan, Ryder, A. Naughton, Johnson; Knowelden, Helme; Fisher, Fishwick, Derbyshire, Bath, Lowe, Palin

*Widnes*: Bradley; Parks, Hutton, Sale, Malone; Fleming, Anderson; Rowbottom, Band, Leigh, J. Naughton, Wilcox, Reynolds

Referee: A. S. Dobson (Featherstone)

The battle between the old rivals was just a little too one-sided to be interesting, with Warrington overcoming a brave defence to win 19–0. Bath, Ryder and Knowelden scored the tries and Palin kicked five goals. The Lance Todd trophy went to the Warrington half-back, Gerry Helme.

## Amazing Wigan

The championship final brought together Wigan, minus eight tourists, and Huddersfield. Wigan played superlative rugby to win a resounding victory by 20 points to 2 before a 64,000 crowd at Maine Road. Silcock, Nordgren, Broome and Blan scored the Wigan tries and Ted Ward kicked four goals. Bawden replied with a solitary goal for Huddersfield.

During the summer of 1950 two new clubs joined the Rugby League. While Llanelli failed to reinforce their application, Cardiff was admitted, and in south Yorkshire a group of businessmen in Doncaster raised guaranteed capital of £10,000 and were granted admission. The annual meeting at Leeds in June raised the gate levy from 5 per cent to 10 per cent to help poorer clubs.

In Australia the tourists did well to win their first four games, and a typically big Sydney crowd saw the first Test on Monday, 12 June. The weather was dull, wet and squally, and poor ground conditions ruled out open play. Australia were awarded nineteen penalties against the four given to Great Britain, but the tourists performed prodigious feats in defence to win by 6 points to 4. Stars were the Wigan pair Ashcroft and Hilton, who twice broke through for Hilton to provide the finishing touches. Pidding kicked two goals for Australia.

The second Test was at Brisbane on 1 July, and again Australia were given a heavy advantage in penalties. In addition, Great Britain were handicapped by injuries and, although the tourists got the first try with a fine run by Danby, Australia took command and won 15–3 with tries from Graves, Cowie and Holman, and goals from Graves, Holland and Churchill. It was Australia's first Test victory against Britain in thirteen years.

## *Australian triumph*

Britain's injury misfortunes continued and for the third Test at Sydney on Saturday, 22 July, it had only fourteen fit men to choose from. The game was to end Britain's thirty years' stranglehold on the Ashes, as on another wet day and heavy ground Australia won a gruelling contest 5–2. At half time it was 2–2, with penalties from Churchill and Ward. In the second half the green-and-gold jerseys hammered away at the gallant British defence until Roberts finally forced his way over to tumultuous roars. The Sydney crowd invaded the pitch and chaired the Australian victors off the field, hardly surprising in view of the long, long wait for a series' victory.

A total of £43,000 in tour receipts was some consolation for the tourists. To this would be added the receipts from New Zealand where the disappointment was compounded by New Zealand winning both Tests, 16–10 at Christchurch and 20–15 at Auckland. The success of New Zealand brought a flurry of signings in Britain. Bradford Northern brought over Joe Phillips, a full-back, and N. Hastings, a winger; Leigh signed half-back G. Beatty and an Australian Rugby Union centre, Trevor Allan. In later deals Northern and Huddersfield secured New Zealand wingers J. K. McLean and Peter Henderson respectively, and Huddersfield brought over a South African centre Ian Clark. Not to be outdone, Rochdale Hornets brought over five young Australians, Reg and Ron Stanford, Duffy, Ellean and Kelly.

In 1950–51 another country unexpectedly, and briefly, joined the 13-a-side ranks: an amateur team from Italy toured in Britain. The Wembley final on Saturday, 5 May 1951, featured the all-conquering Wigan side and Barrow, and there was another capacity crowd of 95,000, with Matt Coates (Pudsey) as referee. Teams were:

*Barrow*: Stretch; Lewthwaite, Jackson, Goodwin, Castle; Horne, Toohey; Longman, McKinnell, Hartley, Grundy, Atkinson, McGregor

*Wigan*: Cunliffe; Hilton, Broome, Roughley, Nordgren; Mountford, Bradshaw; Gee, Curran, Barton, Slevin, Silcock, W. Blan

Unseasonal rain affected the pitch and ball, making both slippery; Barrow were paticularly affected. The only score of the first half was a Mountford penalty for Wigan. The first try came after sixty minutes when a Barrow defender slipped as he went to tackle Mountford, and the speedy half-back passed to Broome who put Hilton over. Another Mountford break gave a try to heavyweight prop Ken Gee, and Mountford kicked the goal. Not unnaturally, Mountford was voted by the press as Lance Todd trophy winner.

In the championship final at Maine Road the new Cumbrian club, Workington Town, won their first major trophy by beating an unlucky Warrington side 26–11. The fates were against Warrington for winger Johnson broke his leg and front-row-forward Derbyshire badly hurt an arm.

In 1951-52 New Zealand were the tourists, and Doncaster and Cardiff played their first games in senior company. Doncaster, under Gareth Price the former Leeds, Halifax and Wales centre, had an impressive opening, but Cardiff took beating after beating and was doomed from the outset.

The Kiwis were under the management of T. F. McKenzie and D. A. Wilkie, captain was M. Robertson, and with him were J. Forrest, J. Haig, D. Barchard, G. Davidson and C. McBride of the 1947 party. The remainder of the party consisted of:

D. White, A. Berryman, W. B. Hough, J. Edwards, C. Eastlake, T. Baxter, W. Sorenson, B. Robertson, A. Menzies, J. Good, C. Johnson, K. English, R. Crouch, W. McLenna, L. Blanchard, J. Curtain, G. J. Burgoyne, D. Richards-Jolley, A. J. Atkinson and M. Mulcare.

The tourists showed mixed form before the first Test at Odsal on Saturday, 6 October, and Great Britain won 21–5. The star of the win was the Workington winger, George Wilson, who ran in a hat-trick of tries. The tourists then won six games in a row and helped make history when they played under floodlights at Odsal, Bradford Northern beating the tourists 13–8 before a 30,000 crowd.

## Rough New Zealand luck

The tourists were in good heart for the second Test at Swinton and it was wretched bad luck that, after scoring five tries to four against

Great Britain they were beaten 20–19 with a last-minute penalty goal by Ledgard.

The third Test at Headingley produced another close and exciting game before Britain made a clean sweep, winning 16–12. The 1951 Kiwi team left for home without winning a single Test, but their fine performances had won renewed respect among British fans who awarded them the second Test as a moral victory.

At an international board conference at Lyons on 12 January 1952 it was agreed that exploratory moves would take place on the feasibility of a world cup. These moves were to culminate in the first world cup in 1954.

The 1951 challenge-cup final brought two new teams to Wembley. Gus Risman's Workington Town and Featherstone Rovers, from the small West Yorkshire mining town, were the combatants, with Mr C. F. Appleton (Warrington) as referee. Unfortunately, because of the relatively small populations in the areas of the competing teams, the attendance was 73,000 – still a good crowd by most standards – and receipts were more than £23,000. Teams were:

*Featherstone Rovers*: Miller; Batten, Tennant, Metcalfe, Mitchell; Cording, Evans; Welburn, Bradshaw, Daly, Hulme, Gant, Lambert

*Workington Town*: Risman; Lawrenson, Paskins, Gibson, Wilson; Pepperell, Thomas; Hayton, McKeating, Wareing, Mudge, Wilson, Ivison

Workington were favourites to win, but Rovers showed the grit and fighting qualities that had carried them through. The only try of the first half was by Lawrenson, the Town winger, who quickly played the ball to himself and touched down. Two goals from Risman against two from Miller made it 7–4 at half time. A spectacular try by Rovers' veteran winger Eric Batten made it 7–7, but then Mudge, Town's Australian forward, made a long run for a try and Lawrenson and Wilson added further tries. Rovers' Evans got a try, but the cup went to the Cumbrians 18–10 and the Lance Todd trophy to Billy Ivison, the crafty Town loose-forward.

The championship final brought together those two outstanding sides, Bradford Northern and Wigan, at Huddersfield. Dazzling Wigan won their fourth success in seven seasons. Silcock, Cunliffe and Ryan scored tries and Gee kicked two goals in a 13–6 win. Phillips kicked three goals for Northern and the crowd was 48,656.

At the annual meeting the end of the Cardiff experiment was announced. The Welsh side had been little more than a chopping block and clubs were weary of the long journey to South Wales.

Each season was bringing a Test series and in 1952–53 the Australians were back in Britain under the management of N. Robinson and D. MacLean. The players were:

Backs: C Churchill, R. W. Willey, N. Pidding, B. Carlson, T. A. Ryan, D. J. McGovern, F. Stanmore, K. Holman, H. Wells, D. J. Flannery, R. Duncan, N. Hazzard, G. Hawick, D. Donoghue, G. S. Geelan, K. McCaffery.

Forwards: D. Hall, T. L. Tyrrell, A. L. Collinson, A. Paul, K. Schubert, C. M. Gill, K. Kearney, J. Rooney, F. A. Ashton, B. Davies, A. Crocker, R. Bull.

Ken Kearney, the Australian hooker, was sent off in the match at St Helens and became the first Australian tourist to be suspended in Britain. The first Test was held at Headingley on 4 October and a 30,000 crowd saw a comfortable British win by 19 points to 6. Castle scored a brilliant try for Britain, and Ryder and Daniels also showed clean pairs of heels to the green-and-gold defenders. Horne kicked five goals and all Australia could muster were three goals from Pidding.

After some convincing victories against club sides Australia made six changes for the second Test at Swinton, bringing in Flannery, Stanmore, Donohue, Geelan, Collinson and Gill, while Britain called up D. Greenall (St Helens) at centre, T. McKinney (Salford) as hooker and D. Valentine (Huddersfield) as loose-forward, replacing Ryder, Ackerley and Ryan. Once again Australia were disappointing and superb passing by Great Britain brought five tries to Castle (2) Greenall (2) and Ward, with Ward kicking two goals and Horne dropping a goal. Geelan scored a try and Carlson a goal for Australia.

The Ashes had been regained easily and in the third Test the Kangaroos won a little consolation, winning by 27 points to 7. The match became ill-tempered and Hall, the Australian vice-captain, was sent off. In the best Australian performance of the tour Noel Pidding scored a try and six goals; other touch downs came from Ryan (2), Davies and Holman. Horne scored a try and Evans two goals for Britain.

## *World Cup boost*

The world cup came a step nearer when a French businessman and rugby enthusiast, Paul Barrière, offered to sponsor the competition for £25,000.

The 1952–53 season was an amazing one for St Helens who went through the season undefeated and reached the finals of both challenge cup and championship. The final at Wembley paired them with Huddersfield and the crowd was just under 90,000. Teams were:

*Huddersfield*: Hunter; Henderson, R. Pepperell, Devery, Cooper; Ramsden, Banks; Slevin, Curran, Bowden, Brown, Large, Valentine

*St Helens*: Moses; Llewellyn, Greenall, Gullick, McCormick; Honey, Langfield; Prescott, Blakemore, Parr, Parsons, Bretherton, Cale

Referee: G. S. Phillips (Widnes)

The teams were well matched and bristled with internationals, but it was a comparative 'unknown' who stole the honours and the Lance Todd trophy. He was the nineteen year-old Huddersfield stand-off-half Peter Ramsden who made his mark early on with a controversial 'sliding' try after he had beaten two men but had appeared to be tackled by Prescott. Devery kicked the goal. St Helens drew level with a sixty-yard try by Llewellyn to which Langfield added the goal. In the second half a fine combined move sent Langfield over for Saints to lead 8–5, but then Banks made a quick burst from a scrum and Cooper kicked the goal. A Langfield drop goal made it 10–10, but then Ramsden crowned his great day by beating three men for the winning try, goaled by Cooper.

St Helens gained consolation in the championship. In the semi-final they walloped Huddersfield 46–0, then beat Halifax 24–14 in the Maine Road final.

## *Short sprint by Bailey*

Leigh made world sporting headlines in 1953 by persuading the great West Indian sprinter E. MacDonald Bailey to sign for them. To say the least, the experiment was not a success. Bailey was obviously happier on the athletics track than on a rugby-league ground, and played just one game before a convenient injury ended his rugby career. In May 1953 a new club joined the League. Blackpool

Borough, supported by £6000 in seaside capital, joined under Chris Brockbank, the former Swinton player and Warrington manager. At the annual meeting the two-leg first-round challenge-cup ties were abolished.

The 1954 tourists to Australia made history by becoming the first touring team to travel by air. This was a decision hailed with delight all round, particularly by clubs who would otherwise expect to be denuded of players at vital trophy times. The managers were Hector Rawson (Hunslet) and Tom Hesketh (Wigan) and the players, selected after trials at Swinton and Headingley, were:

Backs: E. Cahill (Rochdale Hornets), J. Cunliffe, W. Boston, E. Ashcroft (Wigan), P. Jackson, F. Castle (Barrow), L. Jones (Leeds), T. O'Grady (Oldham), R. Price, G. Helme (Warrington), R. Williams, capt., A. Burnell (Hunslet).

Forwards: J. Henderson (Workington Town), A. Prescott (St Helens), T. Harris (Hull), T.McKinney (Salford), J. Bowden, B. Briggs, D. Valentine (Huddersfield), J. Wilkinson (Halifax), G. Gunney (Hunslet), C. Pawsey (Leigh), D. Silcock (Wigan), K. Traill (Bradford N.).

Saturday, 24 April 1954, was cup-final day at Wembley and it produced one of the dreariest finals in history, between Halifax and Warrington. Teams were:

*Halifax*: Griffiths; Daniels, Lynch, Todd, Bevan; Dean, Kielty; Thorley, Ackerley, Wilkinson, Fearnley, Schofield, Clarkson

*Warrington*: Frodsham; Bevan, Challinor, Stevens, McCormick; Price, Helme; D. Naughton, Wright, Lowe, Bath, Heathwood, Ryan

Referee: R. Gelder (Wakefield)

Despite the talent in each back division, defences were on top throughout and there were few exciting incidents. Griffiths kicked two goals to give Halifax a 4–0 lead, but two second-half goals from Bath ensured a replay that was to bring incredible scenes at Odsal Stadium in Bradford, scenes unequalled in the north before, or since.

## The invasion of Odsal

The match was played at Odsal on Wednesday, 5 May, and in between the teams reached the championship final, winning their semi-finals. No one could have foreseen the remarkable and almost frightening scenes at Odsal. During the day vehicles of every shape and horsepower poured towards Bradford. Shortly before the evening kick-off traffic queues stretched for miles around the ground and, inside the huge natural bowl of the former corporation refuse tip, an immense, seething crowd estimated at more than 100,000 spilled over the terraces and heights.

Half an hour before the kick-off spectators pushing to get inside were met by battered and frustrated fans pushing to get out of the mêlée. It was a minor miracle that there were no major disasters or riots and the game was able to start with clear touchlines.

The game was again closely fought and marginally more exciting then Wembley. Challinor scored a try for Warrington and a Griffiths goal made it 3–2 at half time. In the second half goals to Bath and Griffiths made it 5–4 and then came the thrill of the match. Helme, the brilliant little Warrington scrum-half, set off on a dazzling run from halfway, finally beating Griffiths at the left-hand corner to win the match and the Lance Todd trophy.

Three days later, at Maine Road, before a crowd of 36,519, Warrington completed the double against luckless Halifax. A try by Thorley and two goals from Griffiths put Halifax ahead, but four goals from Bath, including a dramatic late winner, won the game for Warrington.

The flying tourists did not make an impressive start in Australia, losing two and drawing one of their first five games. They caused raised eyebrows and criticism by engaging Ross McKinnon, a former Australian Test player, as 'adviser'. McKinnon, however, could not prevent a thumping defeat in the first Test at Sydney on Saturday, 12 June. With twenty minutes to go it was 12–12, but then the Australians surged into all-out attack and rattled up twenty-five points against a demoralized defence. Pidding scored a try and eight goals in the 37–12 win, and other tries came from McCaffery (2), Provan, O'Shea, Hall and Carlson. For Britain Silcock and Jackson scored tries and Jones three goals.

This defeat shook and stimulated Britain and they won six games in a row in Queensland before the second Test at Brisbane on 3 July. The tourists made five changes with O'Grady, Williams, Bowden, Pawsey and Boston replacing Cunliffe, Castle, Price, Wilkinson and Traill. The new spirit, and changes, worked and Britain won an entertaining Test 38–21 to square the series. Lewis Jones set up a Test record with ten goals, and Boston (2), Pawsey, Williams, Helme and Jackson scored tries. For Australia Carlson (2), Holman, Hall and Hazzard touched down and Pidding landed three goals.

## *Fierce brawl*

The euphoria of this win was shattered by the game with New South Wales and the third Test at Sydney on Saturday, 17 July. The New South Wales game ended in such a terrible, uncontrollable brawl that the referee abandoned the game. In the Test, before a noisy 60,000 crowd totally behind the Australians, Great Britain led 8–0, then Australia took the lead at 10–8. The game switched from end to end in the second half but Australia stayed in front to win 20–16. Wells, Watson, Pidding and Diversi scored tries for Australia, and Pidding scored four goals. For Britain the tries came from Williams (2), Valentine and Ashcroft, with two goals from Jones.

The Australians had won the series and the tourists set off for New Zealand knowing that the 1950 tourists had fared badly. Three tests were played. In the first the Lions swept to a 27–7 win, Boston getting four tries and Ashcroft two. In the second international at Greymouth, however, the Kiwis squared things at 20–14. White kicked seven goals for New Zealand and tries came from Butterfield and Mulcare. For Britain O'Grady and Wilkinson scored tries and Jones landed four goals.

The tourists toned up for the third, and deciding, Test by running up big scores against Canterbury and North Island. They successfully completed the tour by beating New Zealand 12–6 at Auckland on 14 August. Price and O'Grady got the tries and Jones scored three goals. The party returned to Australia briefly for a game against Southern Districts at Canberra. They won 66–21. Jones's fifteen goals gave him 127 for the tour, beating Sullivan's 1932 record of 110.

Close behind the tour came the first world cup, played in France in 1954. Many international players, jaded by the Australasian tour, pulled out of the Great Britain squad for a variety of reasons, and it was a 'scratch' British side full of unseasoned novice internationals who crossed the channel under the captaincy of Huddersfield's experienced Dave Valentine.

The party comprised:

J. Ledgard, F. Kitchen (Leigh), D. Rose, G. Brown (Leeds), P. Jackson (Barrow), M. Sullivan, W. Banks, R. Rylance, D. Valentine (Huddersfield), G. Helme, A. Naughton (Warrington), J. Thorley, A. Ackerley (Halifax), S. Smith (Hunslet), R. Coverdale, J. Whiteley (Hull), D. Robinson (Wakefield T.), B. Watts (York).

## *The underdogs' day*

This largely inexperienced squad was to take France and the first world cup by storm, surprising everybody, perhaps even themselves. In the fortnight of the competition France beat New Zealand 22–13 in Paris, and Great Britain shocked Australia 28–13 at Lyons. Great Britain and France drew 13–13 in Toulouse, while Australia beat New Zealand 35–15 in Marseilles. France beat Australia 15–5 at Nantes and Great Britain beat New Zealand 26–6 at Bordeaux. Play-off for the title was fixed for Paris on 13 November. This was the big moment for Valentine's 'scratch' team and they took the chance magnificently. With the 'old heads' Helme in the backs and Valentine in the pack marshalling the team, they beat France 16–12. Helme scored a brilliant solo try and stand-off Gordon Brown scored twice. Britain's other try came from David Rose; Ledgard kicked two goals. For France Cantoni and Contrastin touched down and Puig Aubert landed three goals. The no-hopers brought back the first world cup.

In 1954–55 Wales ceased to function in the home international championship due to a shortage of Welsh players. Welshmen were eligible for the Other Nationalities team which, ironically, was only to last for one more season.

The 1955 challenge-cup final was a north-west derby between Barrow and Workington Town. A somewhat 'parochial' final produced a crowd of only 67,000, low by Wembley standards. Teams were:

*Barrow*: Best; Lewthwaite, Jackson, Goodwin, Castle; Horne, Toohey; Belshaw, McKeating, Barton, Grundy, Parker, Healey

*Workington Town*: Vickers; Southward, Paskins, Gibson, Faulder; Wookey, Roper; Hayton, Lymer, Key, Mudge, Edgar, Ivison

Referee: R. Gelder (Wakefield)

The first half fell below expectations, both sides appearing to suffer from Wembley nerves. At half time it was 4–2 to Barrow, two goals for Horne against one from Paskins. In the second half Barrow put their attack together and Jack Grundy, a second-row-forward whose storming performance won the Lance Todd trophy, made a try for McKeating converted by Horne. Then Grundy started two more moves which brought tries to Castle and Goodwin. Workington, although handicapped by an injury to Roper, fought back and Faulder and Gibson scored tries. Horne kicked six goals for Barrow and Paskins three for Workington. Barrow's 21–12 victory was their first Wembley success.

The championship final at Maine Road on Saturday, 15 May, paired Oldham and Warrington. Heavy rain made conditions difficult and the scoring came late in the game. Bevan scored a try for Warrington then Pitchford slipped through to equal the scores; finally, the hefty boot of Bath scored again for Warrington with two penalties.

The 1955 annual meeting brought a sad loss with the resignation of Belle Vue Rangers who, as Broughton Rangers, had been one of the great teams of the early decades of Northern Union and Rugby League.

The tour merry-go-round continued with a visit from New Zealand, led by managers H. Tetley and C. Siddle. The tour began badly with a string of failures against club sides and New Zealand were in a state of low morale for the first Test at Swinton on 8 October. Great Britain won as expected, leading 10–6 and then running in fifteen points in an irresistible late spell. Sullivan (2), Boston, Grundy and Wilkinson scored tries and Jones kicked five goals. For the Kiwis Robertson and Maxwell scored tries.

The second Test was won by Britain as easily as the first. Stevenson, the Leeds half-back, ran seventy-five yards for a try, Sullivan got a hat-trick, and Prescott, Wilkinson and Watts touched down, Jones kicking three goals in a 27–12 win. Roberts and Menzies got late tries for New Zealand, and Haggie got three goals.

The third Test appeared a formality but the tourists found form at last against a Great Britain side which brought in Hollindrake (Keighley) on the wing, Davies (Oldham) in the centre and Schofield (Halifax) in the pack. The Kiwis won brilliantly 28–13 and, in a great team performance, six players scored tries, Blanchard, Roberts,

Percy, Bakalich, Butterfield and Maxwell, Creedy landing five goals. Jones, Sullivan and Brown were Britain's scorers, with two goals from Jones. It was a good end to a poor tour, with receipts down £2500 on 1951.

## *Unlucky Halifax; Saints alive*

The 1956 challenge-cup final brought together Halifax and St Helens, and the crowd was 80,000. Ronnie Gelder was the referee for the third year in succession. Teams were:

*Halifax*: Griffiths; Daniels, Lynch, Palmer, Freeman; Dean, Kielty; Wilkinson, Ackerley, Henderson, Fearnley, Pearce, Traill

*St Helens*: Moses; Llewellyn, Greenall, Howard, Carlton; Finnan, Rhodes; Prescott, McIntyre, Silcock, Parsons, Robinson, Karalius

Both sides were looking for Wembley victory after disappointments in previous years, and in a tense contest there was no score in the first half. In the second half Freeman, the Halifax winger, was injured and Carlton swept past him for a long-range try. Llewellyn and Prescott scored well-worked tries and Rhodes kicked two goals as the Saints won 13–2, Griffiths landing a goal for Halifax.

Halifax's combination of bad luck and inconsistency dogged them again in the championship final against Hull at Maine Road. With only a minute to go they were leading 9–8 with tries by Palmer, Daniels and Freeman against tries by Harris and Finn and a Hutton goal. In the last minute Hutton kicked a brilliant penalty goal from a wide position, and Halifax were beaten again.

The 1956 Australian tourists came for a shortened tour, with C. Connell and C. Fahy as managers, and the hooker Ken Kearney as captain. Six players had been on the previous tour, Churchill, Flannery, McGovern, Holman, Bull and Kearney. The tourists were:

Backs: C. Churchill, G. Clifford, D. Flannery, D. Adams, D. McGovern, I. Moir, A. Watson, T. Payne, R. Poole, K. O'Brien, R. Banks, I. Johnston, K. Holman, C. Connell.

Forwards: I. Doyle, T. Tyquin, N. Provan, K. O'Shea, B. Parcell, D. Furner, B. Davies, R. Bull, B. Orrock, W. Marsh, K. Kearney, E. Hammerton.

The Australian schedule included only nineteen games, and before the first Test at Wigan on 17 November the tourists won four and lost four of their eight games. The first Test was played in pouring rain with attendance and receipts badly affected. Although the Kangaroos got a flying start with a try by the fast winger Moir, Britain took a firm grip to win 21–10. Boston scored two tries and Davies, Sullivan and Grundy one each, Mortimer kicking three goals. Poole added a try and Holman two goals for Australia.

Before the second Test at Odsal on 1 December the tourists took a fearful drubbing at St Helens, losing 44–2. It was not surprising that only 23,000 saw the second Test, but those who stayed away missed a shock as Australia levelled the series. It was 7–7 at half time, but Australia went on to win 22–9 with tries from Holman, Banks, Davies and Bull and five goals from Clifford. Stevenson got a try and Mortimer three goals for Britain.

After more in-and-out club results, Australia squared up to Britain for the decider at Wigan on 15 December. The attendance again was moderate at 19,000 and the series ended in anti-climax as Britain won without difficulty. Little, Turner, Gunney, Sullivan and Boston ran in the tries and Davies kicked two goals. The tour had been a flop and Australia left for France still needing £8000 to cover expenses.

The British party to defend the world cup in Australia was announced on 1 April. This time it was a fully experienced squad, consisting of the following eighteen players: W. Boston, E. Ashton (Wigan), P. Jackson (Barrow), L. Jones, J. Stevenson (Leeds), R. Price (Warrington), M. Sullivan (Huddersfield), A. Prescott, T. McKinney, A. Rhodes, G. Moses (St Helens), T. Harris, J. Whiteley (Hull), S. Little, A. Davies, D. Turner (Oldham), G. Gunney (Hunslet), J. Grundy (Barrow).

Barrow and Leeds reached the final of the challenge cup at Wembley on 11 May. Frank Barton, the veteran Barrow and former Wigan forward, quit the game when he was surprisingly left out of Barrow's final line-up. Teams were:

*Barrow*: Ball; Lewthwaite, Jackson, Rea, Castle; Horne, Harris; Woosey, Redhead, Parker, Grundy, Wilson, Healey

*Leeds*: Quinn; Hodgkinson, McLellan, Jones, Broughton; Lendill, Stevenson; Hopper, Prior, Henderson, Robinson, Poole, Street

Referee: C. F. Appleton (Warrington)

The legendary Wembley nerves prevented this game being a great one, and Barrow slips contributed to a 9–7 Leeds victory. Leeds were the better side in the first half and led with a Quinn try against a Horne goal. In the second half Robinson scored a gift try for Leeds when he shouted 'Right, Jack' to the Barrow forward Jack Grundy and took the proffered pass to charge over. A Hodgkinson try made it 9–2 but then Jackson scored a try for Barrow, goaled by Horne. In the last seconds of the game the Barrow centre Rea broke away but, with Castle steaming up on his left, elected to kick, and the ball was fielded. The Lance Todd trophy went to Jeff Stevenson, the Leeds half-back.

The championship final at Odsal saw Oldham beat Hull in a dramatic finish. Oldham led 15–11 with minutes to go, with tries from Etty(2) and Ayres and three goals from Ganley against a Turner try and four goals from Hutton. Then Cowan made an interception in an Oldham passing movement and raced away to score. Hutton would have won the game with his kick but he failed to repeat his sensational effort against Halifax and the title went, deservedly, to Oldham.

The world cup began with Britain beating France 23–5 at Sydney, and Australia beating New Zealand 23–5 at Brisbane. On 17 June Great Britain met Australia and Britain, handicapped by injuries to Davies, Boston and Harris, was swept aside by Australia 31–6. Moir (2), McCaffery (2), Wells, Clay and O'Shea scored tries, and Carlson (4) and Davies the goals. Jones kicked three goals for Britain.

France beat New Zealand 14–10 at Brisbane, and Australia clinched the world cup when they hammered France 26–9 at Sydney. Great Britain lost to New Zealand 29–21, Australia beat the Rest 20–11 at Sydney, and the tournament was a great financial success.

## South African missionaries

On the way home from Australia, Great Britain and France engaged in missionary work in South Africa. They played exhibition matches in Benoni and Durban but the South African public did not take it too seriously nor, in all honesty, did the players. South Africa had opened up as a market for signings, however and St Helens made a sensational scoop signing, and a wonderful investment, when they brought Tom Van Vollenhoven, the brilliant Springbok winger to Knowsley Road.

Wigan signed full-back Fred Griffiths and half-back Tommy Gentles; Hunslet secured winger Ron Colin; Wakefield Trinity signed centres Jan Lotriet and Alan Skene and a forward Ivor Dorrington. St Helens followed up the Vollenhoven capture by bringing over Ted Brophy, a forward, and Jan Prinsloo, another fine winger. York signed winger Hugh Gillespie, Huddersfield swooped for another winger Athol Brown, and Leeds went for three backs, winger Wilf Rosenberg and the Deysel brothers.

During the season of 1957–58 Jim Sullivan's goal-kicking seasonal record of 204 was beaten. Bernard Ganley, the consistently accurate Oldham full-back, landed 219, helped largely by fine attacking rugby by Oldham. The Ruffyeds won the Lancashire cup but again failed in their bid for Wembley. The 1958 finalists were Wigan and Workington Town, who attracted only 66,000 to Wembley, paying £31,030. Teams were:

*Wigan*: Cunliffe; O'Grady, Ashton, Boston, Sullivan; Bolton, Thomas; Barton, Sayer, McTigue, Cherrington, Collier, Evans

*Workington Town*: McAvoy; Southward, O'Neill, Leatherbarrow, Wookey; Archer, Roper; Herbert, Eden, Key, Edgar, Thompson, Eve

Referee: R. Gelder (Wakefield)

The final provided an interesting contrast in styles. Wigan played their normal, attacking style, while Town blended a powerful, foraging pack to create openings for the backs. Town scored first when Edgar broke through to make a try for Southward, goaled by the winger, but Sullivan and the powerful Barton went over for tries for Wigan.

Cunliffe kicked the goals to both tries, and a penalty to Southward made it 10–7 to Wigan at half time. In the second half Town were weakened by injuries to Edgar and Archer, and McTigue finished off another good Wigan move. A Southward goal made it 13–9 and then came one of those great moments when games are won and lost in a single movement. Swift passing gave Workington's Southward an overlap, but across came the long-striding second-row-forward Cherrington to make a try-saving tackle on the line. It was Wigan's cup again. The Lance Todd trophy went to the beavering Rees Thomas, the Wigan scrum-half.

Workington's bad luck dogged them in the championship final in which they met Hull at Odsal on 17 May. Town got a typical Southward try made by Edgar, but then Cec Thompson, their hard-working forward, was taken off with a leg injury and shorthanded Town fell behind to four tries from Cooper, J. Whiteley, Scott and Finn, and five goals to Bateson. After a consistent season Town emerged with two sets of runner-up medals.

The 1958 annual meeting brought a play-the-ball change designed to open up play. The acting half-back had to pass the ball or concede a scrum.

Managers of the 1958 tour to Australia were Bennett Manson (Swinton) and Tom Mitchell (Workington Town), with Jim Brough (Workington Town) establishing a precedent by travelling with the team as coach. Alan Prescott (St Helens) was captain and players were:

Backs: G. Moses, F. Carlton, A. Murphy, A. Terry (St Helens), E. Fraser, J. Challinor (Warrington), I. Southward, W. Wookey, H. Archer (Workington Town), M. Sullivan, E. Ashton, D. Bolton (Wigan), P. Jackson (Barrow), A. Davies, F. Pitchford (Oldham).

Forwards: A. Prescott, V. Karalius (St Helens), B. McTigue (Wigan), B. Edgard (Workington T.), T. Harris, J. Whiteley (Hull), K. Jackson (Oldham), A. Ackerley (Halifax), R. Huddart (Whitehaven), M. Martyn (Leigh), D. Goodwin (Barrow).

# 8
# A Remarkable Tour

The 1958 tour was to prove the most fated and dramatic since the
'Rorke's Drift' tour of 1914. The British party was bedevilled from
early in the tour by internal off-the-field disagreements within the
management. It soon became apparent that feelings were strained,
with a clash between the hard-line disciplinary measures of Messrs
Manson and Brough and the freer methods of Tom Mitchell. Manson
and Brough believed some players indulged too heartily in the always
fulsome Australian hospitality, while Mitchell favoured more relaxed
discipline.

When the first Test was played on 14 June at Sydney the strains
were evident in the British display. Mistakes and fumbling gave away
points, Australia got easily on top and won 25–8. After this first Test
beating the British party held an inquest behind closed doors, and
the outcome was a decision to have special, tough, disciplined training
at the Queensland resort of Surfers' Paradise. As an aid to concentration Mr Manson pointed out that repetition of the first Test form
in the second Test would kill the tour and the players' hopes of a
bonus.

The Brisbane Exhibition Ground was too small to enclose all who
wanted to see the game and the gates were closed with 37,507 inside.
They were privileged to see an amazing game and a heart-stirring
performance by the British team against impossible odds, another
'Rorke's Drift'. In the early stages the British captain Alan Prescott
fell awkwardly and broke his arm. Soon afterwards the stand-off-half
David Bolton fractured his collar-bone and Fraser, Karalius and
Challinor all received knocks which normally would have meant

retirement. Amazingly, with Prescott playing on and tackling with one arm, Britain led 10–2 at the interval. At half time a doctor told Prescott not to turn out in the second half but the ginger-haired skipper, knowing defeat was inevitable if he did not resume, said 'I'll play on' and took pain-killing injections. In the second half the sight of Britain's twelve men being urged on by Prescott, his arm dangling by his side, roused the cheers of even the fiercely partisan Australian spectators.

The half-time lead had come from tries by Challinor and Sullivan and two goals from Fraser against a Clifford goal. Southward got a third try and Fraser's goal made the score, remarkably, 15–2. Australia hit back against eleven-and-a-half men and Marsh scored a try, goaled by Clifford, but Britain fought on magnificently, running the ball, and Southward raced away for another try, plus a goal from Fraser. At 20–7 the Australians stormed the tourists' line and Carlson and Dimond scored tries. Just as Britain seemed likely to crack, the youngest player on the field, the nineteen-year-old St Helens half-back Murphy, youngest player ever to tour Australia, corkscrewed his way through the Australian defence to score, and Fraser again banged over the goal. This try sealed the match for, although Holman got a late try, improved by Clifford, Britain won 25–18 and courage-ously squared the series. The victory was won at a cost as Prescott and Bolton had to fly home and others players were injured, but Great Britain were in great heart for the third and deciding Test at Sydney Cricket Ground on 19 July. For the third Test Jackson replaced Bolton and Terry took the place of Prescott, while a refereeing change brought in Jack Casey, of Queensland, instead of Darcy Lawler, an official much criticized by the British party. Another huge crowd, 68,230, saw the game, which produced almost as many sensations as the second.

Britain led 14–12 after a closely contested first half, with tries by Southward and Terry and four goals from Fraser, while Provan and Holman touched down for Australia, and Clifford scored three goals.

## Pandemonium

In the second half Mr Casey was given the bird by the crowd by awarding Britain two penalties, and then Murphy shot through for a try. Sullivan got a fourth try, with Fraser kicking the goal, and then came an incident which caused the crowd's frustrations to boil over. Moir, the Australian winger, was obstructed by Southward as he kicked ahead. Moir followed up and almost touched down, however, playing the advantage rule. Sullivan retrieved the situation and raced the full length of the field for a try as pandemonium erupted. Bottles, rolled-up newspapers, cans and fruit were hurled onto the field of play, and the British players helped cool things down by clowning, pretending to drink from bottles and peel oranges.

Sullivan's try crushed the Australians and Britain romped away with the game by 40 points to 17, Davies, Whiteley and Sullivan adding tries, and Fraser two more goals, while Hawick got a try and Clifford a goal for the humiliated Kangaroos. It was a record Test victory and a series triumph after the first Test débâcle.

It should have been a happy homecoming but eventually, after many inquests and much wrangling, an inquiry was held into the tour under the chairmanship of Mr F. Ridgway (Oldham), the council chairman. It took place on 15 December 1958, behind closed doors, and afterwards Mr Manson was criticized for certain actions militating against harmony on tour, Mr Mitchell for not revealing that he was unlikely to meet eye to eye with the coach, Jim Brough, and Mr Brough had part of his bonus impounded. In view of the successful outcome of the tour, Messrs Manson and Brough felt harshly treated.

## *Enter television*

The council was preoccupied at this time with another problem, television. Sport had entered the television era and there had been criticism of the decision to allow live coverage of games during the season 1958–59. The counter-claims were that television reduced attendances, alternatively, that it created nationwide interest in the game. The debate, and television coverage, continued.

In the close season Jim Sullivan, successful coach of Wigan and then St Helens, joined Rochdale Hornets, and Alan Prescott, his playing career over, took over at Saints.

The 1959 Wembley final brought a game between the cup holders Wigan and the championship holders Hull. A good crowd of 80,000 saw the game in perfect weather. It was Hull's first appearance at Wembley and their first final since 1923. Teams were:

*Hull*: Keegan; Cowan, Cooper, Saville, Watts; Matthews, Finn; Scott, Harris, J. Drake, Sykes, W. Drake, Whiteley

*Wigan*: Griffiths; Boston, Ashton, Holden, Sullivan; Bolton, Thomas; Bretherton, Sayer, Barton, Cherrington, McTigue, Evans

Referee: C. F. Appleton (Warrington)

The match proved disappointingly one-sided, particularly for Hull and their loyal but frustrated followers. Wigan played smoothly, with an assurance born of continued success, while Hull fumbled with Wembley jitters. Wigan won 30–13 with tries from Holden, Sullivan, Boston (2), Bolton and McTigue, and six goals from Griffiths. For Hull nothing went right and their only try, to add to five Keegan goals, came from Finn near the end. The Lance Todd trophy went to the strong and skilful Wigan forward, Brian McTigue.

The championship final the following week at Odsal brought a wonderfully entertaining game of rugby. A superb display of open handling and running by both teams produced a total of 66 points, St Helens winning 44–22 after Hunslet had swept to a 12–4 lead early in the game. The turning point was a spectacular try by Tom Van Vollenhoven, the South African winger, who ran seventy-five yards, beating man after man. St Helens dominated after this great effort and Prinsloo, Vollenhoven (2), Smith, Murphy and Huddart touched down, Rhodes landing ten goals. Gunney, Poole, Stockdill and Doyle scored tries for brave Hunslet, Langton landing four goals.

The 1959 Australian tourists arrived on 7 September 1959 under the management of Jack Argent and Ernest Keefer, with Clive Churchill as coach and Keith Barnes, who was born in Port Talbot, as captain. Players were:

Backs: K. Barnes, D. Chapman, E. Lumsden, B. Carlson, D. Parish, K. Irvine, R. Gasnier, H. Wells, R. Boden, B. Clay, J. Riley, T. Brown, B. Muir, R. Bugden, P. Burke.

Forwards: J. Raper, E. Rasmussen, R. Mossop, B. Hambly, J. Paterson, W. Wilson, G. Parcell, W. Delamere, D. Beattie, N. Kelly, I. Walsh.

The young and largely unknown tourists, only Carlson, Wells and Mossop being experienced, did reasonably well in their opening games and then beat the champions, St Helens, 15–2 at Knowsley

Road, just the tonic they needed before the first Test at Swinton on Saturday, 17 October 1959.

The game provided a rude shock to British confidence and threw the series wide open as Australia played brilliant rugby. The young centre Reg Gasnier gave an outstanding performance of incisive running. Gasnier crowned an electrifying display with a hat-trick, and his burly centre-partner Wells also crossed, Barnes kicking five goals in a 22–14 win for Australia. At one stage the Kangaroos led 20–4 and only a late burst brought British tries to Boston and Turner, Fraser completing four goals for Britain.

## A *close-run thing*

The delighted tourists followed up this decisive win with victory over France and more fine performances against club sides. Great Britain's selectors had cause to worry and there were changes for the second Test at Headingley on 31 November. J. Whiteley (Hull), D. Vines (Wakefield T.), D. Robinson (Leeds), N. Fox (Wakefield T.), F. Dyson (Huddersfield) and J. Stevenson (Leeds) replaced Huddart, Martyn, Terry, Murphy, Davies and Fraser. The second Test was a gripping, tense affair, Australia falling behind 6–2 at half time to tries by Robinson and Fox against a goal by Barnes. In the second half the tourists repeated their first Test form and Gasnier made openings for two tries by Carlson. Carlson, taking over as kicker from the injured Barnes, hit a post with one of the kicks at goal, and it proved a vital miss. With Australia leading 10–6 and only minutes to play, Britain launched a desperate late attack and, from a scrum near the line, Stevenson flipped a reverse pass to Whiteley who dived over. Fox's goal gave Britain a one-point victory and squared the series. For the vital third Test at Wigan Britain made changes through injury, G. Round (Wakefield T.) and J. Wilkinson (Halifax) replacing Dyson and Karalius. The game was a disappointment after the first two Tests, with Britain, coached by the secretary of the Rugby League, Bill Fallowfield, holding the ball in the forwards and closing up the game. The referee, Eric Clay, gave Australian infringements short shrift, and Neil Fox banged over six goals for Britain. Early on Fox had been awarded a try after an alleged knock-on, but despite these setbacks Australia fought back to 15–12 with tries from Raper and Carlson, and three goals from Barnes. Then Whiteley snapped up a dropped pass and sent Southward over for a clinching try at 18–12.

## Exit tap penalty

An important rule change was made for the 1959–60 season, designed to prevent teams from holding on to possession for long periods. The tap penalty was abolished, as also was the advantage rule at the scrum.

The closing days of the season saw Hull fight their way through to a second successive Wembley final. Their opponents were Wakefield Trinity, a new power in the land, and the Queen and Prince Philip gave the final a tremendous boost with the first royal patronage since 1949. The final was held at Wembley on 14 May 1960. Teams were:

*Hull*: Kershaw; Harrison, Cowan, Halafihi, Johnson; Broadhurst, Finn; Scott, Harris, Evans, Sutton, M. Smith, J. Whiteley

*Wakefield Trinity*: Round; F. Smith, Skene, Fox, Etty; Rollin, Holliday; Wilkinson, Oakes, Vines, Firth, Chamberlain, Turner

Referee: Eric Clay (Rothwell)

Hull sought to break their cup-final jinx but bad luck followed them to yet another final. So many key players were out with injuries that reserves and players close to retirement had to be pressed into service. Sam Evans and Tom Sutton were in the later stages of their careers, while Jack Kershaw and Mike Smith were A-teamers. The result, another hiding for Hull, was therefore predictable, and the star-spangled Trinity team overcame a brave but outclassed Hull by a Wembley record score of 38–5. At half time it was 7–5, but Hull tired in the second half as Trinity ran in some spectacular long-range tries. Harris was concussed but fought on bravely to win the Lance Todd trophy, while Whiteley and Cowan were also hurt. Neil Fox kicked seven goals and scored two tries, and other tries came from Skene (2), Rollin, Holliday and Smith.

Trinity sought the big double in the championship final at Odsal the following week. They made a great start against Wigan with a try by F. Smith, but then Fox was injured and Wigan took over to win decisively 27–3. Boston (2), Ashton (2) and Sayer scored tries and Griffiths kicked six goals.

## Italy setback

The infant Italian venture, with a handful of teams playing rugby league, suffered a setback in the close season, with Australia, France and New Zealand refusing to contribute to the cost of supporting the venture.

The big international event of 1960–61 was the third world cup, Australia defending the 1957 title. The Great Britain selectors chose the following team: E. Fraser, J. Challinor, R. Greenough (Warrington), E. Ashton, M. Sullivan, B. McTigue (Wigan), A. Davies (Oldham), A. Murphy, A. Rhodew, V. Karalius (St Helens), F. Myler (Widnes), J. Wilkinson, D. Turner (Wakefield T.), T. Harris, J. Whiteley (Hull), J. Shaw (Halifax), B. Shaw (Hunslet). The appointed referees were Eric Clay (Britain) and Edouard Martung (France).

The games began on 24 September, with atendances averaging the 20,000 required to cover expenses. Great Britain beat New Zealand 23–8 at Odsal and Australia scraped home 13–12 against France at Wigan. Great Britain hammered France 33–7 at Swinton on 1 October, while Australia beat New Zealand 21–15 at Headingley.

The 'final' between Great Britain and Australia was played on 8 October at Odsal. Attendances had been below par, television being blamed for the disappointing gates, and figures of 50,000 at Odsal and 10,000 at Wigan for France *v.* New Zealand were needed to reach break-even point. The attendances were 33,000 at Odsal but only a miserable 3000 at Central Park for the 'also-rans' third- and fourth-place game.

The Odsal game developed into an ugly brawl. Britain won 10–3 and regained the world cup. Sullivan and Boston got tries and Fraser kicked two goals, Carlson scoring a try for Australia. New Zealand beat France 9–0 at Swinton.

There was another crowd disappointment for the Northern Hemisphere *v.* Southern Hemisphere game on Monday, 10 October. Only 3908 turned up at Odsal for this 'exhibition' game, played in a light-hearted atmosphere and resulting in a win by Northern Hemisphere 33–27. The world cup had not proved a gigantic success, but receipts from television fees helped expenses to be covered.

In contrast to the poor world-cup attendances, the Wembley final of 1961 brought another tremendous crowd to the famous stadium, 95,000 for the St Helens *v.* Wigan derby game on 13 May.

It was a blazingly hot day, so hot that spectators stood in shirt sleeves, bathed in sweat, and in London the railway lines on the Piccadilly line buckled and caused delays. Teams were:

*St Helens*: Rhodes; Van Vollenhoven, Large, McGinn, Sullivan; Smith, Murphy; Terry, Dagnall, Watson, Vines, Huddart, Karalius

*Wigan*: Griffiths; Boston, Ashton, Bootle, Carlton; Bolton, Entwistle; Barton, Sayer, McTigue, Collier, Lyon, Evans

Referee: T. W. Watkinson (Manchester)

Despite the intense heat both teams produced a tough, well-contested game containing some fine rugby, and a brilliant clinching try by St Helens. The game seesawed dramatically until the last quarter, at which point the score was 5–4 to St Helens, a try by Murphy and a goal by Rhodes against two goals from Griffiths. Griffiths hit the St Helens upright with a penalty which would have given Wigan the lead, and this was the turning point. Large, the St Helens centre, broke through and after a bout of perfectly timed interpassing with Van Vollenhoven, Large sent the flying Springbok round to the posts for Rhodes to goal. Griffiths landed another goal but St Helens won 12–6.

The championship final the following Saturday at Odsal was won by Leeds who took the title for the first time. They easily beat a disappointing Warrington 25–10, an outstanding performance coming from Lewis Jones who capped his display with a solo try in the second half.

## Two divisions once more

In July, at a meeting of the council, it was agreed that two divisions would operate in 1962–63, the League being split on the basis of the 1961–62 placings. The 1961–62 tourists were New Zealand, bringing a young side lacking in Test experience. Managers were W. 'Snow' Telford and C. H. Siddle, and after an opening of mixed success and failure against club sides they played Great Britain in the first Test at Headingley on 30 September. The match provided a salutary jolt for British complacency for, although Britain went ahead with tries from Boston and Murphy and a goal from Rhodes, New Zealand began to throw the ball about with exhilarating abandon.

The British defence crumbled and New Zealand, after leading 14–8 at half time, won by the staggering score of 29–11. Edwards, Hadfield, Reidy, M. Cooke and Hammond, romped home with tries with Fagan kicking seven goals. It was a remarkable result and the Headingley crowd cheered the underdogs.

When the second Test took place at Odsal on 21 October Great Britain had made several changes, Fraser (Warrington), Fox (Wakefield T.) and Sullivan (St Helens) replacing Rhodes (St Helens), Hallas (Leeds) and O'Grady (Warrington). These changes proved to be shrewd moves as Britain squared the series 23–10 with a much more determined performance. Sullivan (2), Evans, Bolton and Ashton got the tries, and Fox scored three goals. For the Kiwis Roger Bailey scored two tries and Fagan two goals. At Swinton on 4 November Britain erased the memory of Headingley to win the Third Test and the series with a fine performance. Although the Kiwis took the lead with two goals from Reg Cooke, Sullivan (2), Herbert, Murphy, Fraser, Dagnall and Ashton touched down in a splendid attacking display, and Fox kicked seven goals. Edwards and Hadfield (2) scored tries for New Zealand to keep the game alive, and Cooke completed five goals in a 35–19 scoreline. The Kiwis gained consolation in France by winning one and drawing two of the international games there.

In Italy there was a setback when the Italian government refused to recognize the struggling rugby-league game. Good news, however, came from South Africa where two syndicates of wealthy businessmen announced their intention to launch organized rugby league in 1962. Invitations were sent to star Springboks like Tom Van Vollenhoven and Fred Griffiths inviting them to take out teams for exhibition matches. Wakefield Trinity made an exhibition tour, taking along several 'guest' players. In February 1962 several top South African rugby-union players signed up as professionals with the new organizations. They included Martin Pelser, Charlie Nimb, Hennie Van Zyl, Manetjie Gericke, and Natie Rens.

Encouraging news on the home front was provided by the League secretary, Bill Fallowfield, who said that gates were up 25 per cent.

## The unknown tourists

The touring team for Australasia was announced in March. There were several controversial choices of alleged 'unknowns', including Ken Noble (Huddersfield), Peter Small (Castleford) and Gary Cooper (Featherstone R.). Manager was S. Hadfield (Wakefield T.), assistant manager A. Walker (Rochdale Hornets) and trainer was Colin Hutton (Hull K. R.). The captain was Eric Ashton of Wigan. The party consisted of:

Backs: E. Fraser (Warrington), G. Round, N. Fox, H. Poynton (Wakefield T.), W. Boston, F. Carlton, E. Ashton, capt., D. Bolton (Wigan), M. Sullivan, A. Murphy (St Helens), I. Southward (Workington T.), G. Cooper, D. Fox (Featherstone R.), P. Small (Castleford).

Forwards: J. Wilkinson, D. Turner (Wakefield T.), B. McTigue, W. Sayer, R. Evans (Wigan), N. Herbert, B. Edgar (Workington T.), K. Noble (Huddersfield), J. Shaw (Halifax), R. Huddart (St Helens), J. Taylor (Hull K. R.), L. Gilfedder (Warrington).

The major trophies of 1961–62 produced some piquant situations. Four Yorkshire teams competed in the challenge-cup semi-finals and Huddersfield and Wakefield Trinity, yet again, reached the final. Then Huddersfield and Wakefield won through to the championship final.

There were 85,000 spectators at the Wembley final on Saturday, 12 May, as Trinity sought the third trophy in pursuit of all four. Trinity had already won the Yorkshire league and the Yorkshire cup. Teams were:

*Huddersfield*: Dyson; Breen, Booth, Haywood, Wicks; Deighton, Smales; Slevin, Close, Noble, Clark, Bowman, Ramsden

*Wakefield Trinity*: Round; Smith, Skene, Fox, Hirst; Poynton, Holliday; Wilkinson, Oakes, Firth, Williamson, Briggs, Turner

Referee: D. T. H. Davies (Manchester)

Wakefield, studded with internationals, were expected to make short work of Huddersfield, but Huddersfield's shrewd teamwork, dictated by their Scottish coach, Dave Valentine, kept play fairly tight. Trinity eventually won 12–6 after a hard tackling game; the match winner was the burly Neil Fox who landed three drop goals and scored a try. Hirst ran fifty yards for the other try, while, for Huddersfield, Smales and Ramsden scored tries.

The following Saturday, at a rainswept Odsal Stadium, battling Huddersfield put an end to Trinity's four-cup dream. A crowd of 37,000 saw a try and goal from Neil Fox put Trinity in the lead, but Huddersfield came back well and their tackling and harassing eventually wore down Trinity. Round was hustled off a pass by Ramsden and Wicks scored, Dyson goaling. In the second half Huddersfield kept the ball tight near the Trinity 25, and, in the closing minutes, after a third Dyson goal the scrum-half Smales scooted over for a try that brought delirious Huddersfield supporters swarming onto the pitch.

The 1962 tour brought its share of shocks and surprises, retention of the Ashes by Britain, and hammerings in New Zealand. The first Test at Sydney on 9 June was easily and unexpectedly won by Britain, 37–12. Sullivan (2), Ashton (2), Turner, Huddart and Boston got the tries, and Neil Fox kicked five goals.

Britain made sure of the series by winning the second Test at Brisbane on 30 June, 17–10. Great Britain were denied a clean sweep in the third Test at Sydney, however, on 14 July. Australia were given considerable assistance in their 18–17 win by the referee who sent off Turner and Sullivan and gave Irvine the benefit of considerable 'forward pass' doubt for Australia's winning late try.

An injury-hit touring team went to New Zealand without the skipper, Eric Ashton, who was flown home with a leg injury. The tourists were heavily beaten in both Tests, 19–0 and 27–8, both matches being played at Auckland. In the second Test Boston and Edgar had to play despite injuries. The final humiliation was a 46–13 beating by Auckland, and it was a jaded party which called on South Africa on the journey home to play three exhibition games.

Two new competitions were played at the start of the 1962–63 season, the Eastern and Western Divisional championships, with Yorkshire clubs playing in the former and Lancashire and Cumbrian clubs in the latter. The new competitions did not prove crowd-pullers and only moderate interest was shown as Workington beat Widnes in the play-off for the Western championship at Wigan and Hull K. R. beat Huddersfield at Headingley.

After the opening weeks of the new, two-division scheme, crowds proved good at the top clubs, less than good among unsuccessful clubs. In the second division, clubs at the bottom suffered considerable drops in gate money without first-division opposition, though successful teams like Hunslet, Keighley and Whitehaven did well.

## Springbok tour

On the South African front it was stated that a Springbok touring team would tour Australia in the summer of 1963, and would include players with English clubs. An international board meeting at Auckland recommended that South Africa be invited to take part in a world-cup tournament in 1965, Mr Fallowfield adding the prophetic rider 'provided the game has developed to a sufficiently high standard in South Africa'.

Great Britain played two internationals against France during the season. The first, in Perpignan, saw the French referee Edouard Martung penalize Britain out of the game, awarding numerous penalties to the French while allowing France to lie offside and inflict all kinds of mayhem on the British players. France led 17–2 until M. Martung relented late in the game, and Britain fought back to 17–12 with tries from Ashton and Fox and two more Fox goals. Britain won cruel revenge on 3 April at Wigan, trouncing the French 42–4. Try scorers were Stopford (2), Smales (2), Bolton, Fox, Ashton and Boston with nine goals from Fox.

Grounds were frozen from Boxing Day 1962 until well into February; the country experienced the most vicious cold weather for many years and the league season was thus extended to 31 May. Widnes used a locally made chemical to soften their pitch, and played several games, but the long-term effects of the chemical were regarded dubiously at Naughton Park.

After a backlog of fixtures had been completed, the challenge-cup final at Wembley was played on its traditional Saturday in early May. Finalists were Wakefield Trinity, playing their third consecutive final, and the consistent Wigan. Teams were:

*Wakefield Trinity*: Round; Greenwood, Brooke, Fox, Coetzer; Poynton, Holliday; Wilkinson, Kosanovic, Sampson, Vines, Turner, Pearman

*Wigan*: Bolton; Boston, Ashton, Davies, Carlton; McLeod, Pitchford; Barton, Sayer, McTigue, Collier, Lyon, Evans

Referee: D. T. H. Davies (Manchester)

The match was another triumph for Ken Traill's brilliant Trinity side, though injuries again handicapped its opponents. David Bolton was concussed; this proved a vital factor as a bemused Bolton threw a loose pass which was intercepted by Poynton for a runaway try. Trinity won 25–10 with a typical display of open rugby, Sampson, Coetzer (2), Poynton and Brooke getting the tries and Fox five goals. Carlton and Pitchford touched down for Wigan, Ashton landing two goals.

On 19 May Swinton, another attractive running side, clinched the first-division championship by beating their closest rivals, Widnes. Tragically, the club chairman, Bill Scholes, collapsed and died while watching the match. Relegated from division one were Bramley and Oldham, while Hunslet and Keighley were promoted. The first season of the revived two-division system received a mixed verdict. Gates had held up among top teams but had declined catastrophically in some division-two centres.

## Demoralized 'Boks'

South Africa toured Australia in 1963. They won a 'country' game against southern New South Wales, 41–2, but were then demoralized by several thumping defeats, Queensland winning 33–16. In Test matches Australia beat the Springboks 34–6 at Brisbane and 54–21 at Sydney.

The 1963–64 season demonstrated the manner in which television was becoming a major influence within the game. It was announced that the challenge-cup semi-finals would be played on separate Saturdays in order that BBC and ITV could screen one game each.

In September the Australian tourists arrived, the managers being J. Lynch and A. Sparks. The first Test was scheduled for Wembley Stadium, in midweek under floodlights, the BBC screening part of the game. This first Test, designed in part as a propaganda exercise for the south of England, was played on Wednesday, 16 October, and the attendance was a dismal 14,000, a figure which hardly justified the taking of the game to Wembley. Teams were:

*Great Britain*: Gowers (Swinton); Burgess (Barrow), Ashton (Wigan), Fox (Wakefield Trinity), Field (Batley); Bolton (Wigan), Murphy (St. Helens); Tembey (St Helens), Sayer (Wigan), Tyson (Hull K. R.), Measures (Widnes), Bowman (Huddersfield), Karalius (St. Helens)

*Australia*: K. Thornett; Irvine, Langlands, Gasnier, Dimond; Harrison, Muir; Gallagher, Walsh, Kelly, R. Thornett, Hambly, Raper

Referee: D. T. H. Davies (Manchester)

There were heavy showers during the day and the ball was slippery. Britain's handling was much worse than that of the Kangaroos and, when Bolton was injured and Ashton moved to stand-off-half with Bowman in the centre, shorthanded Britain fell to pieces. Australia won 28–2 with a fine display of rugby, Gasnier getting a typical hat-trick, and Langlands, Irvine and Ken Thornett also touching down, with five goals from Langlands. Fox kicked a penalty goal for outplayed Britain. Australia were working hard for a first-ever series' win in Britain.

A crowd of 30,000 saw the second Test at Swinton. Britain brought in Sullivan (York), Stopford (Swinton), Myler (Widnes), W. Robinson (Leigh), McIntyre (Oldham), Watson (St Helens) and Morgan (Swinton) to replace Burgess, Field, Bolton, Tembey, Sayer, Tyson and Bowman.

## Injury fiasco

No one could have anticipated the outcome of this game which brought crushing defeat for Britain. The game started promisingly for the home team, with an early try by Stopford, but the British team then suffered two literally crippling blows. Ashton and Myler both received heavy tackles, and in the second half Great Britain was reduced to eleven men. There was to be no Rorke's Drift or Brisbane '58 this time, and the Australians gleefully and ruthlessly seized on their good fortune to run up a record Test-match total of fifty points. This match was a watershed in the campaign, later successful, for substitutes in rugby league.

The Australian tries came from Irvine (3), Langlands (2), Gasnier (2), Dimond (2), Kelly, R. Thornett and Harrison, with seven goals from Langlands. Great Britain's token reply came from Stopford and Measures (tries) and three goals from Fox in a 50–12 slaughter.

With a historic series' win safely under their belts the Australians could afford to sit back and, not surprisingly, the third Test was an anti-climax, with a victory for Great Britain. Even this was small consolation for Britain, however, since the match was scarred by fights and brawls and two Australians, Muir and Hambly, were sent off, along with Britain's Watson.

The match was played at Headingley and Bill Fallowfield was persuaded to stay on as team manager after offering to resign. Geoff Smith (York), Keith Holden (Warrington), Alan Buckley (Swinton), Frank Collier (Wigan), John Ward (Castleford), Ken Roberts (Halifax) and Don Fox (Featherstone R.) came into a much-changed side. Despite its rather unsatisfactory nature the win for Britain was welcome and debutants Smith, Don Fox and Ward got tries, Stopford scoring the fourth, Don Fox kicking two goals. The attendance was 20,000. The Australians went to France where they won the Test series 2–1 after losing the first game.

Distress signals were flying over Odsal where once-great Bradford Northern were losing large sums of money, with gates below the 1000 mark. Northern's directors announced that the game at Oldham on 14 December would not be fullfilled. The management committee called for public meetings to ascertain whether new directors would come forward to take over. On 10 January Northern officially gave up membership of the Rugby League.

## Two divisions fails again

There were two further unhappy events. January brought the death of Harry Sunderland, the former Australian tour manager who had settled in England and become a popular rugby-league journalist and commentator. Then, in February, it was agreed that the two-division scheme would be abandoned after having been launched with such optimism in 1962. The inventive and lively Swinton side won the first-division championship, and Oldham galloped away with division two in which Bradford Northern's results were expunged.

Hull Kingston Rovers and Widnes reached the final of the 1964 challenge cup, before a crowd of 85,000. Hull K. R. figured in a remarkable semi-final with Oldham before getting to Wembley, and much sympathy was given to Oldham. After a 5–5 draw at Headingley Oldham and Hull K. R. replayed in midweek at Swinton. With the scores tied 14–14 after eighty minutes Oldham went ahead with a try in extra time, but then the light, without benefit of floodlights, became so bad that the referee, Dennis Davies, abandoned the game. The following Monday at Fartown, Huddersfield, Rovers took advantage of their escape, winning 12–2 against luckless Oldham. The teams for Wembley's traditional May final were:

*Hull K. R.*: Kellett; Paul, Major, Elliott, Blackmore; Burwell, Bunting; Tyson, Flanagan, Mennell, Palmer, Clark, Poole

*Widnes*: Randall; Chisnall, Briers, Myler, Thompson; Lowe, Smith; Hurstfield, Kemel, Collier, Karalius, Measures

Referee: R. L. Thomas (Oldham)

Rovers' free-scoring ability was blunted from the start by the Widnes tackling, and perhaps by Wembley nerves. At half time it was 2–0 to Widnes, Randall having kicked a goal, and in the second half Widnes opened up with Karalius and Collier leading the assaults, and tries coming from Briers, Collier and Myler, with another goal from Randall. Burwell scored a fine individual try for Rovers and Kellett landed a goal, Widnes triumphing 13–5.

Great Britain and France played home-and-away games at Perpignan and Leigh during the 1963–64 season. Britain did the double, winning 11–5 in France, getting a better deal from the French referee and, resoundingly, 39–0 in the return, Neil Fox landing nine goals to add to seven tries.

# 9
# Enter Substitutes: a World Cup Setback

During the summer of 1964 France toured Australia and New Zealand with dismally unsuccessful results. The president of the Australian Board of Control, Bill Buckley, said that because of the poor form of the French the 1965 world cup in Australasia should be postponed. Despite misgivings by Great Britain the tournament was shelved, to return in 1968.

A major, and necessary, rule change came as the result of Britain's humiliation at the hands of Australia when reduced to eleven men at Swinton. For the 1964–65 season two substitutes were to be allowed, before and during the interval. Eventually, substitution was allowed at any time.

Splendid news came from Bradford where public meetings had elicited terrific support for Northern. Two popular former players, Joe Phillips and Trevor Foster, headed a new board of directors. The revival of Northern became a Cinderella story as crowds of 10,000 poured into Odsal and a re-shaped team began to win matches on the way to a dramatic success in the Yorkshire cup.

The return to one-division football brought innovations in a top-sixteen championship play-off and a short-lived and badly supported bottom-fourteen 'sop' tournament. Swinton and St Helens installed good quality floodlights and another minor revolution was on its way.

International competition in 1964–65 involved home-and-away games between Great Britain and France, plus the first under-24 game between the countries. In the first full international at Perpignan, France, smarting under the Australian snub, won 18–8, Britain's only real contribution being a brilliant long-range try by

Berwyn Jones, the Olympic sprinter who had successfully turned professional with Wakefield Trinity. The return match was won by Great Britain 17–7 at Swinton, but in unpleasant circumstances. The referee Dennis Davies sent off the French forward Bescos, but he refused to go. Mr Davies went to his dressing room, followed by an arguing and gesticulating French team. Eventually Arthur Walker, chairman of the Rugby League, went down to the dressing rooms and persuaded everyone to go back 'for the sake of international rugby league'.

Rather more encouraging, in terms of spectator appeal, was the challenge-cup final at Wembley on Saturday, 8 May. It was a memorably thrilling final, rivalling the Warrington *v.* Huddersfield game of revered memory. The crowd was 92,000 for a great match. Teams were:

*Hunslet*: Langton; Griffiths, Shelton, Preece, Lee; Gabbitas, Marchant; Hartley, Prior, Eyre, Gunney, Ramsey, F. Ward

*Wigan*: Ashby; Boston, Ashton, Holden, Lake; Hill, Parr; Gardiner, Clarke, McTigue, Stephens, Evans, Gilfedder

Referee: J. Manley (Warrington)

Gilfedder promptly put Wigan ahead with a prodigious penalty goal from halfway, but Langton quickly equalized. Wigan went into a 12–4 lead with Holden and Lake getting tries and Gilfedder two more goals against a goal by Langton. Hunslet came back with a brilliant try by Shelton and Langton's goal made it 12–9. The game continued with flowing rugby at each end, but Wigan's finishing was clinical, and they went to 20–9 with Gilfedder and Lake tries and an Ashton goal to Gilfedder's try. Hunslet seemed beaten but Griffiths scored a wonderful long-range try, Langton landed two goals, and at 20–16 Hunslet were in with a chance. Time ran out for them after a magnificent game, so good that the Lance Todd trophy was shared between Hunslet's Brian Gabbitas and Wigan's Ray Ashby.

St Helens headed the League table but were beaten in the top-16 play-off by Halifax, Burnett (2) and Jackson getting the Halifax tries and James three goals against a Killeen try and two goals from the same South African winger.

## A poor tour

The New Zealanders arrived for the 1965 winter tour having shared a series 1–1 with Australia, winning 7–5 at Auckland. It was, however, a disappointing tour in every respect. The Kiwis were beaten in half their games, lost two and drew one of the Tests, and attracted only moderate crowds. The respective Test-match attendances were 8497, 15,849 and 7919, and much of the blame was placed upon live television.

In the first Test at Swinton on 25 September an uninspiring game ended with victory for Great Britain by 7 points to 2. Smales got a try and Holliday two goals, Tait kicking a goal in reply. The Second Test at Odsal on 23 October followed a similar pattern, Great Britain winning comfortably by 15–9 with tries from Burgess, Shelton and Stopford and three goals from Holliday, while New Zealand's points came from a try by W. T. Schultz and Fagan's three goals. The third Test at Wigan salvaged a little pride for New Zealand. They were the livelier side in a 9–9 draw. Burgess scored the home try, Gowers landing three goals, against a Tait try and three goals from Fagan.

Although television was severely criticized for its alleged effect on attendances, the BBC enterprisingly introduced a new trophy competition, the Floodlit Trophy, which was to prove both popular and well contested. The matches were played on midweek evenings and televized live.

October 1965 brought the climax of the Bradford Northern revival. In the Yorkshire cup final, amid tremendous crowd enthusiasm, they won 17–8 against Hunslet in a gripping and fluctuating match. Early on Hunslet missed a lot of chances and when Brooke scored a brilliant eighty-yard individual try for Northern it turned the game, and Northern went on to crown its fairy-tale revival with a trophy. Australian winger Lionel Williamson added two tries and Clawson kicked four goals. For Hunslet Lee and Thompson scored tries and Langton kicked a goal.

## St Helens' four cups

The honours of 1965–66 went, however, to St Helens. It won the Lancashire league, the league leaders' trophy, the challenge cup and championship, though their challenge-cup win was clouded by third-round controversy. In the game with Hull K. R. at Knowsley Road the Saints trailed 10–7 in injury time. Mr Clay, the referee, allowed up to five minutes of added time and with Rovers' players and fans pleading for the final whistle Murphy, the canny St Helens half-back, followed up a kick and, in a mêlée of bodies near the Rovers' dead-ball line, was awarded a touch down.

The referee was surrounded by Rovers players but, after consulting a touch judge, he confirmed his decision and, when the goal was kicked, St Helens went through. An inquiry was called for at council level into Mr Clay's handling of this incident and the game but, sadly for Rovers, the only outcome was an implied censure on their officials for publicly abusing the referee. St Helens marched on to Wembley but there was further controversy in the semi-final when Mick Sullivan, playing for Dewsbury, was rendered unconscious and carried from the field.

After all this the Wembley final on 21 May brought a record attendance of nearly 100,000 and record receipts. It was another great derby battle between St Helens and Wigan, but the game was a disappointment after all the publicity and anticipation. Teams were:

*St Helens*: Barrow; Van Vollenhoven, Murphy, Benyon, Killeen; Harvey, Bishop; Halsall, Sayer, Watson, Warlow, French, Mantle

*Wigan*: Ashby; Boston, D. Stephens, Ashton, Lake; Hill, Parr; Gardiner, Woosey, McTigue, A. Stephens, Gilfedder, Major

Referee: H. Hunt (Culcheth)

Wigan were handicapped from the start without their regular hooker, Clarke, who was injured. Woosey, a prop-forward, filled the hooking spot but was well beaten by the experienced Sayer. In addition, St Helens used a lot of tactical offside play, knowing they would win scrum possession, and the result was the stifling of Wigan's attack. St Helens won crushingly 21–2, Killeen getting five goals and a try, Mantle and Bishop tries, and Murphy a dropped goal against a penalty goal by Gilfedder. St Helens's tactics aroused considerable criticism and their persistent offside running led to a rule change whereby a penalty could be kicked into touch, with a tap from the point at which the ball entered touch, rather than a scrum.

St Helens completed their quartet of triumphs without controversy or ill feeling when they hammered Halifax in the championship final at Swinton, the score being a conclusive 35–12.

## French without tears

After all the traumas, it was a good year for France. They compounded the New Zealand gloom by winning in all three Tests in France, and then gained a double over Great Britain. The score at Perpignan was 18–13, but the most impressive victory was a dull but competent beating of the home side 8–4 at Wigan. France had cocked a snook at their contemptuous dismissal by the Australians from the proposed 1965 world cup. A desirable innovation during these games was the appointment of an English official, Eric Clay, in France, and a French referee, Edouard Martung, at Wigan.

Australasia was the venue for the summer's major tour by Great Britain, the tourists trying to avenge the beatings of 1963. One absentee was Alex Murphy who cried off for 'business reasons' after being overlooked as captain in favour of Harry Poole of Leeds. Managers were Wilf Spaven (Hull K. R.) and J. Errock (Oldham), and the squad was:

Backs: K. Gowers, A. Buckley (Swinton), A. Keegan (Hull), W. Burgess (Barrow), B. Jones (Wakefield T.), G. Shelton (Hunslet), F. Myler (Widnes), I. Brooke (Bradford N.), G. Wrigglesworth (Leeds), A. Hardisty (Castleford), W. Aspinall (Warrington), C. Dooler (Featherstone R.), T. Bishop (St Helens).

Forwards: K. Roberts (Halifax), B. Edgar (Workington T.), F. Flanagan (Hull K. R.), C. Clarke (Wigan), C. Watson, J. Mantle (St Helens), G. Crewdson (Keighley), W. Ramsey (Hunslet), W. Bryant (Castleford), T. Fogerty (Halifax), D. Robinson (Swinton), H. Poole (Leeds).

The tour was to be littered with refereeing controversies as the tourists, from first to last, and in particular during the second and third Test matches, complained of biased treatment from Australian officials. Despite mixed success in the early games, and many altercations involving referees' interpretations, Britain won the first Test 17–13 at Sydney on 25 June. The captain Harry Poole was unfit to play and Robinson took his place. Barnes kept Australia in the game with a series of penalties but Britain, playing the better rugby, scored tries through Watson, Hardisty and Burgess, with goals from Keegan (2) and Bishop. Banks got a late try for Australia, and Barnes five goals.

The referee for this game was J. Bradley. When the Australian Board of Control nominated Col Pearce for the second Test at Brisbane the tourists accepted that a strict Australian 'interpretation of the rules' would be the order of the day. This proved correct as Australia won a bruising, brawling match, and Ramsey, the British forward, was sent off early in the second half. At one stage Britain hung on to lead 4–2 but, late in the game, Mr Pearce awarded two simple penalties to Australia and Barnes kicked them to give Australia a victory of 6–4, squaring the series.

The third Test decider was at Sydney, with Mr Pearce again the referee and a big crowd of 65,000. Australia produced a good attacking performance to win 19–14, but again the match left a nasty taste. The British player, Watson, was sent off and one of Irvine's three tries appeared to come from a blatant knock-on. Lynch and King also crossed and Johns kicked two goals. Britain attempted to keep in touch but eventually fell away. Hardisty scored two tries and Gowers four goals. The Kangaroos retained the Ashes.

The tourists went to New Zealand and won both Tests comfortably, although again there were refereeing difficulties. In the second Test at Auckland referee John Percival's penalty count was 24–8 to New Zealand. The Lions did well to win 22–14 after winning the first Test, 25–8, also at Auckland.

## Sunday rugby vote

Rugby League played its part in precipitating a social and sporting revolution in December 1966. At a special general meeting of club representatives approval was given for clubs to stage games on Sundays.

In addition the experimental play-the-ball rule which had been given a trial in floodlit tournaments, was ratified for all competitions. This called for a scrum after four consecutive tackles had been completed, unless the attacking side kicked or otherwise gave away possession.

The internationals between Great Britain and France took place at Carcassonne on 22 January 1967, and at Wigan on 4 March. Strangely, Great Britain won in France, 16–13, Clive Sullivan racing half the length of the field for a try, and France won 23–13, in a game in which Bryant broke a leg and Hardisty was also injured.

It was west Yorkshire's year in the battle for major honours in 1967. Wakefield Trinity beat St Helens in the championship, winning 21–9 in a replay at Swinton after a 7–7 draw at Headingley. In the challenge cup Featherstone Rovers won the cup for the first time, beating a disappointing Barrow at Wembley. Teams were:

*Barrow*: Tees; Burgess, Challinor, Hughes, Murrray; Brophy, G. Smith; Hopwood, Redhead, Kelland, Sanderson, Delooze, Watson

*Featherstone R.*: Wrigglesworth; Thomas, Cotton, Jordan, Greatorex; M. Smith, Dooler; Tonks, Harris, Dixon, Morgan, Thompson, Smales

Referee: E. Clay (Ossett)

Barrow started promisingly enough with a clever try by Brophy and two goals from Delooze giving them a 7–2 lead, Smales landing a goal for Rovers. Barrow, however, faded and Smales (2) and Thomas added tries, with a goal from Smales and a dropped goal from Dooler. Barrow got a last-minute consolation try by Watson and a goal from Tees, but Rovers returned to their tiny pit village victorious by 17 points to 12.

Several amendments to the rules were made at the annual meeting at Leeds. The two notable ones were that, after an unsuccessful drop goal attempt, play would re-start on the '25', and when a penalty try was awarded the kick at goal would be from underneath the posts.

When the Australian tourists arrived in 1967 they were seeking to become the first Australian side to win three successive series against Great Britain. Managers were Jack Drewes and Harry Schmidt and the tourists made an unimpressive start with several defeats against club sides. The first Test was at Headingley on 21 October. This was not a propitious sign for the tourists who had not won in eight Tests at Leeds. Teams were:

*Great Britain*: Keegan (Hull); Young (Hull K. R.), Price (Rochdale H.), Brooke (Wakefield T.), Burgess (Barrow); Millward (Hull K. R.), Bishop (St Helens); Holliday (Hull K. R.), Flanagan (Hull K. R.), Watson (St. Helens), Mantle (St. Helens), Irving (Oldham), Robinson (Swinton)

*Australia*: Johns; McDonald, Gasnier, Langlands, King; Gleeson, Smith; Gallagher, Kelly, Manteit, Lynch, Rasmussen, Raper

Referee: F. G. Lindop (Wakefield)

The Headingley hoodoo dogged Australia once again, for injuries reduced the effectiveness of Gasnier and Raper and Britain won 16–11. Young and Millward touched down for Britain and Millward landed four goals, Bishop dropping a goal. For Australia, who lost Manteit, sent off in the second half, Langlands had a fine individual game with a try and four goals.

The Rugby League made another experimental propaganda gesture for the second Test, holding it at London's White City under lights on Friday, 3 November. Australia had McDonald at centre for the injured Gasnier, and Coote and Gallagher replaced Manteit and Raper in the pack. On the British side Neil Fox replaced Price and Foster (Hull K. R.) replaced Robinson. There was an alarm for Britain during the day as Burgess cried off with a leg injury. Jordan (Featherstone R.) could not be located, so Wigan's Bill Francis, answering a telephone SOS, drove 200 miles to play on the wing. A crowd approaching 20,000 saw Australia square the series 17–11, though the tourists only took the lead seventeen minutes from the end after Britain had twice led 7–2 and 9–7. Bishop scored a try and Fox four goals for Britain, while Langlands, King and Coote touched down for the Kangaroos and Langlands landed four goals.

## Kangaroo hat-trick

Australia's ambition to make it a series' hat-trick came to fruition at Swinton on 9 December. Price, Jordan and Millward came into the British back division, with Rob Valentine of Huddersfield getting a cap in the forwards. Johnny Raper came back to give guile and experience to the Australian pack. Australia won 11–3 with Coote, substitute Branson and King running in the tries and a goal from Langlands. Millward made a good break to create a try for Price, but that was a flash of rare brilliance to arouse a crowd of 12,515. In France the Australians met anti-climax, losing two and drawing one of the three Tests.

Worse was to come for the Australians since, after allegations of rowdyism and orgies of destruction by the tourists at the Ilkley Moor

Hotel, the Australian players were reprimanded and their bonuses reduced.

In mid-December the first Sunday games were played. On 16 December Bradford Northern played York, Featherstone R. entertained Salford and Leigh met Dewsbury. There were above average crowds, with 10,000 at Bradford.

The internationals between Great Britain and France brought a double for Britain, turning form upside down in view of the fact that France had beaten the Australians. In Paris on 11 February Britain won 22–13; the double was achieved with a 19–8 win at Bradford on 2 March.

The domestic season in Britain ended with the most dramatic and bizarre cup final ever seen at Wembley, a remarkable and, for one player, unhappy finale. Leeds and Wakefield Trinity were the finalists and the events were, alternately, tragi-comic and purely farcical. The attendance was 90,000 and the unfortunate referee was J. P. Hebblethwaite. Teams were:

*Leeds*: Risman; Smith, Hynes, Watson, Atkinson; Shoebottom, Seabourne; Clark, Crosby, K. Eyre, Ramsey, A. Eyre, Batten

*Wakefield Trinity*: Cooper; Hirst, Coetzer, Brooke, Batty; Poynton, Owen; Jeanes, Shepherd, D. Fox, Haigh, McLeon, Hawley

Although the sun shone at the start of the game there had been a prodigious downpour beforehand, soaking both ground and spectators. The ground was slippery and players slithered about like Dumbo on the ice rink. Trinity went ahead when Atkinson, moving across to tackle Hirst, slipped and the winger scored. Don Fox landed two goals for Wakefield and Risman two for Leeds to make it 7–4 at half time. During half time there was another monstrous deluge and the pitch became so waterlogged that abandonment seemed certain. Mr Hebblethwaite, however, not wishing to be the first referee to abandon a Wembley final, played on, and the result was aquatic farce. Leeds went into an 11–7 lead when Atkinson kicked ahead and, as everyone slithered, he won an 'obstruction' try. Risman kicked the goal and added a penalty.

## The Don Fox moment

Then came the amazing finish which is recorded for ever in television archives and in the memories of all who saw it. It is acutely engraved on the memory of Don Fox, the Trinity forward and goal-kicker, for the saddest of reasons. Straight from the kick-off from Risman's penalty Hirst gathered and kicked ahead. Defenders splashed and floundered as Hirst got his toe to the ball and kicked on, sent the ball over the line, and dived for the touchdown in a cloud of spray. It was 11–10 and the match hinged on Don Fox's goal kick, a simple one near the posts. Fox placed the ball, stepped back a pace or two, moved forward, slipped and sliced the ball wide. He buried his head in his hands and Leeds defenders danced the highland fling. It was small consolation for the inconsolable, unlucky Fox that he was awarded the Lance Todd trophy.

Further consolation for Trinity was the fact that they had already won the championship, beating Hull K. R. 17–10 at Headingley on 4 May.

Attention switched to Australia and New Zealand where the first world cup for eight years was to be held. The British party, captained by Bev Risman was:

D. Edwards (Castleford), C. Young, C. Sullivan, A. Burwell, R. Millward, P. Flanagan (Hull K. R.), I. Brooke, R. Haigh, (Wakefield Trinity), M. Clark, J. Atkinson, M. Shoebottom (Leeds), T. Bishop, C. Watson, J. Warlow (St Helens), K. Ashcroft (Leigh), R. French (Widnes), A. Morgan (Featherstone R.), C. Renilson (Halifax). Managers were Bill Fallowfield and Colin Hutton.

The Great Britain side reacted bitterly to the handling of their first game, against Australia at Sydney. The New Zealand referee John Percival applied the rules mercilessly against Britain, frequently awarding 'double' penalties, alleging that the Lions were slow getting back ten yards from penalties. Simms, the Australian full-back, had a field day, kicking eight goals in Australia's 25–10 win, with Smith, Raper and Coote scoring tries. Brooke and Sullivan touched down for Britain and Risman kicked two goals.

Worse was to come for Britain for, against France at Auckland, torrential rain reduced the pitch to a swamp and France won 7–2, Ledru getting a try and Garrigues and Capdouze goals against a

Risman goal. Australia won every game against Britain, France and New Zealand, and in the final Australia met France at Sydney. A crowd of 54,290 saw the expected easy win for the home country by 20 points to 2. Britain ended with a hollow consolation win, 38–14 against New Zealand at Sydney.

The revival of the Welsh international side came at Salford on Thursday, 7 November. It was the first Wales team since 1953 and it was a successful revival, Wales beating England 24–17. Dixon, Watkins (Salford), Rees (St Helens) and Sullivan (Hull) got the Welsh tries and Price (Bradford Northern) kicked six goals. For England Atkinson, Taylor, Smith (2) and Watson touched down, and Jefferson landed one goal.

A Great Britain side, with the Welshmen playing alongside the English, comfortably accounted for France at St Helens on 30 November. The score was 34–10, Burgess scoring a hat-trick and Gemmell two tries. The return game was at Toulouse early in 1969, France turning the tables 13–9.

The 1969 challenge-cup final produced teams which were making their first appearance at Wembley since the 1930s. Castleford and Salford met on 17 May before a capacity 100,000 crowd. On the Salford side was a former England international rugby-union player Mike Coulman, and for 'Cas' a former star union winger Alan Lowndes. Teams were:

*Castleford*: Edwards; Briggs, Howe, Thomas, Lowndes; Hardisty, Hepworth; Hartley, Dickinson, Ward, Redfearn, Lockwood, Reilly

*Salford*: Gwilliam; Burgess, Whitehead, Heskeith, Jackson; Watkins, Brennan; Ogden, Dickens, Bott, Coulman, Dixon, Hill

Referee: D. S. Brown (Preston)

Salford's hopes of outpacing Castleford on the flanks were destroyed when Burgess suffered a hard tackle early on. Castleford's close marking stifled Salford's attempts to open up and Salford's points came from three Hill goals. Howe and Hardisty got tries for Castleford and Redfearn landed a goal. Hepworth got the clinching try for Castleford in an 11–6 win, and Malcolm Reilly (Castleford) took the Lance Todd trophy.

Castleford went in search of the big double in the championship final but their hopes were dashed with just four minutes to go. They were leading 14–11 when Shoebottom broke through for Leeds,

Risman kicked ahead, and the ball bounced nicely for Atkinson to gather and run round to the posts, Risman adding the winning goal.

The substitute rule was enhanced in July. It was decided that a substitute could be allowed at any stage in the game, not merely after the interval.

## *Triangular tournament*

The three-cornered European tournament between England, France and a revived Wales team was played in 1969–70, but was not over-successful. Attendances were small, television being made the scapegoat once again, and the matches varied between high-scoring exhibitions and low-scoring yawns. Matches were played home and away. England beat Wales 40–23 and 26–7, both matches being played at Leeds. England and France drew 11–11 at Wigan, France beating England 14–9 at Toulouse. To complicate matters Wales beat France by a surprising 15–11 at Perpignan, then France beat Wales 8–2 at Salford, leaving England the rather unconvincing winners on points aggregate. There was one nasty incident, referee Dickie Thomas being attacked by French fans after the Wales shock.

Clubs made several big money signings from Wales. Wigan brought north the winger Keri Jones and Barrow paid £14,000 for Keith Jarrett, the big, long-striding centre and goal-kicker of Newport and Wales. Leigh paid £6000 to secure the signature of Stuart Ferguson, Swansea and Welsh trials' full-back.

The 1970 challenge-cup final brought back Castleford, the previous year's winners, and the ever-consistent Wigan. Teams were:

*Castleford*: Edwards; Briggs, Thomas, Stanton, Lowndes; Hardisty, Hepworth; Hartley, Dickinson, Redfearn, Kirkbride, Lockwood, Reilly. Substitute: Hargrave

*Wigan*: Tyrer; Jones, Francis, Rowe, O'Loughlin; D. Hill, Parr; Ashcroft, Burdell, Hogan, Ashurst, Robinson, Laughton. Substitute: C. Hill

Referee: F. G. Lindop (Wakefield).

An unpleasant incident occurred in the eighteenth minute when the Wigan full-back Tyrer was flattened by a late, high tackle from Hepworth and was carried off, robbing Wigan of their goal kicker.

Francis took over as kicker but missed a couple of kicks at

Featherstone Rovers, Salford and Great Britain threequarter lines have each in turn benefited from the quicksilver bursts and accurate passing of one of Britain's best post-war scrum halves, Steve Nash, who carried on playing for Salford despite an injured eye and medical advice to quit

The Leigh flier and TV Superstar Des Drummond, saved the last series for Great Britain against New Zealand with a spectacular late try at Headingley

Allan Agar served six clubs well as a player, principally Hull Kingston Rovers. His greatest-ever moment was coaching Featherstone Rovers to a remarkable and totally unexpected challenge cup final win over Hull in 1983, an achievement which won him the coveted title 'Man of Steel' from his fellow professionals

The early try that set Featherstone Rovers on their way to the Wembley upset of the odds-on favourites Hull. David Hobbs dives over despite a despairing tackle by Bridges

The towering influences on the Widnes team that swept the board with trophies in the 70s. Duggie Laughton, loose forward and coach, is backed by the formidable figure of the giant prop forward, Jim Mills

The Hull Kingston Rovers and England front row forward Roy Holdstock made an unwanted piece of history when he was suspended by the disciplinary committee on the evidence of a TV video camera, which caught an off-the-ball tackle on Andy Gregory, the Widnes scrum half. *Right:* Ellery Hanley, rising star of Bradford Northern and 1984 Australasian tourist

Trevor Skerrett, the strong-tackling Hull and former Wakefield Trinity forward, was appointed captain of the 1984 tour to Australia, but then had to withdraw with a serious knee injury

Wigan's left-winger Henderson Gill in control despite a tackle from behind, while Eric Hughes (3), Widnes, looks on during the 1984 State Express Challenge Cup final at Wembley

important stages. Castleford got the only try of a poor game when Reilly, Kirkbride and Hepworth sent over Lowndes and Redfearn landed two penalties. Tyrer kicked a penalty for Wigan before his enforced departure.

The Yorkshire club was involved in more controversy, this time of a more favourable nature, during the championship semi-final with St Helens. After the teams had drawn at Castleford the replay was fixed for Monday, five days before Wembley. Castleford therefore fielded an A-team at St Helens which did extraordinarily well to lead 12–10 with seven minutes to go. St Helens, bristling with internationals, lifted their game desperately to win with two late tries, but it was a close-run thing. St Helens went on to win the championship comfortably, Myler starring in the 24–12 victory over Leeds at Odsal.

During the summer of 1970 Great Britain went on another Australasian tour, arriving as the underdogs under manager Jack Harding and his assistant John Whiteley. The party was: T. Price, A. Fisher (Bradford Northern), R. Dutton (Widnes), J. Atkinson, A. Smith, S. Hynes, M. Shoebottom, B. Seabourne (Leeds), R. Millward (Hull K. R.), F. Myler, capt., C. Watson (St Helens), C. Sullivan (Hull), K. Hepworth, A. Hardisty, (Castleford), J. Ward (Salford), D. Chisnall (Leigh), P. Flanagan, P. Lowe (Hull K. R.), D. Hartley, M. Reilly, D. Edwards (Castleford), D. Robinson, D. Laughton (Wigan), J. Thompson (Featherstone R.), R. Irving (Oldham).

The tourists swept through all their opening matches but were rudely shattered in the first Test at Brisbane on 6 June. Australia thrashed Britain 37–15. Langlands kicked nine goals and tries came from Morgan (2), King (2) and McDonald. Britain's token efforts, which never seriously threatened Australia, were tries from Watson, Flanagan and Laughton, with three goals from Price. There were problems off the field as Malcolm Reilly, the Castleford forward, was involved in two incidents alleging assault. Mr Harding fined Reilly £75 after Australian feelings had been placated with difficulty.

Things brightened for Britain in the second Test at Brisbane on 20 June. Playing with greater spirit and determination, Great Britain found Australia in complacent mood and won 28–7 before a crowd of 60,692. Australia missed the injured Langlands and could only manage one try, scored by King, and goals by McDonald and

Hawthorne. For Britain the outstanding player was Millward who scored two tries, kicked six goals from six attempts, and dropped a goal for a record-equalling individual tally of twenty points. Atkinson and Fisher also scored tries and Hynes a dropped goal. The one blemish was that Hynes was sent off.

After a very rough game against Wagga Wagga at Riverina, after which Mr Harding alleged that Riverina's players had set out deliberately to injure the tourists, the third Test was played at Sydney on 4 July. Despite everything that the Australians could throw at them, including the award of frequent penalty kicks to Australians, Great Britain won magnificently 21–17. McKean, aided and abetted by the many penalty decisions, kicked seven goals, and McCarthy got a late disputed try for the Kangaroos. Great Britain played fast, flowing football and scored tries through Hartley, Atkinson (2), Hynes and Millward, with Millward landing two goals. In addition to the fine individual play of Millward, Myler was widely praised for his captaincy and leadership.

In New Zealand all three Tests were won, at Auckland twice and Christchurch. A slight cloud was cast over a successful tour when it was revealed that several British stars, including Reilly, had been offered big sums to play in Australia.

## World Cup brawl

There was only a brief respite from international rugby for the world-cup tournament was played in Britain from 22 October to 7 November 1970. Attendances were mostly poor and again television was blamed. Specimen attendances were 3900 at Hull for France *v.* New Zealand and 6215 for Australia *v.* France. Even Great Britain *v.* Australia in the play-off only brought 18,776 to Headingley. Great Britain won all three preliminary games, but Australia only qualified on points' difference after winning only one game, 47–11 against New Zealand before 9586 at Wigan. France and New Zealand also won once.

The final was unfortunate for Britain in every way. Not merely did they lose, they lost in a brawling, punching, fighting match that brought no credit to the code. Players fought out personal rivalries, perhaps echoes of the 1970 tour, and there were many ugly scenes. Cootes and Williamson scored tries for Australia, with three goals from Simms. Atkinson got a late try for Great Britain, Dutton kicked a penalty and Hynes dropped a goal.

# 10

# Sponsorship, Two Divisions and Six Tackles

When France beat Great Britain 16–8 at Toulouse in February 1971 a French referee officiated, British officials having decided to revert to home referees because French referees' control of games in England had not always been of the desired quality.

The 1971 challenge-cup final brought the first appearance of Leigh in a final for fifty years. Leigh's driving force was the combative, fiery and cunning Alex Murphy, now player-coach. He exuded confidence before the game, a confidence assisted by the absence from the Leeds side, through injury, of Shoebottom, Smith and Batten. Teams were:

*Leeds*: Holmes; Langley, Hynes, Cowan, Atkinson; Wainwright, Seabourne; Burke, Fisher, Barnard, Hick, Haigh, Ramsey. Substitutes: Dyl, Cookson

*Leigh*: Eckersley; Ferguson, Dorrington, Collins, Walsh; Barrow, Murphy; Watts, Ashcroft, Fiddler, Grimes, Clarkson, Smethurst. Substitutes: L. Chisnall, Lester

*Referee*: W. Thompson (Huddersfield)

Alex Murphy's confidence was totally justified as injury-hit Leeds never found a balance and Leigh swept through to a 24–7 victory. Although Leigh only scored two tries they were always comfortably in front. Murphy out-generalled Leeds so much that Hynes became frustrated and, in an incident which is still argued about, was sent off the field for an alleged foul on Murphy, a charge he denies to this day. Dorrington and Eckersley, the latter capable of a brilliant weaving run, got the tries, goals coming from five place kicks from Ferguson and dropped goals from Murphy (2), Fiddler and Eckersley. Ferguson thus became the third British player to score in every game in a season. For Leeds Wainwright scored a try and Holmes kicked two goals.

The championship final brought a piece of desperately bad luck for Wigan who played St Helens in the final at Swinton. With seconds to go they led 12–11 but then Walsh, the Saints centre, tried a dropped-goal attempt which swerved yards wide, only to bounce favourably back into the arms of the centre, Benyon, who dived for a try which Coslett goaled.

## Sponsorship

Sponsorship in rugby league arrived as a major force in 1971–72. There had been some small sponsorships previously, but the first major injection of funds was £11,000 from the John Player organization for a trophy bearing their name, a competition which has become one of the big trophy events of the season.

A major report shook up the 13-a-side game in 1971. The Caine Report, commissioned by the League from a Manchester public-relations company, John Caine Associates, presented both a preliminary survey of trends in the game and a fuller document entitled 'The Future'. The first report cited the problems of lack of good communications and criticized the presentation of the game on television. The second, major, report suggested a change to Sunday rugby league; the formation of two or more divisions; the introduction of a six-tackle rule, and the publication of a regular magazine. Although the Caine Report was not received with universal acclaim, most of its recommendations were accepted in whole or in part. Eddie Waring, the BBC commentator, issued a spirited defence of televized rugby league, saying that he had received no complaints from sources within the game in nearly twenty years of commentaries; television, he said, had helped introduce the game to new audiences in the midlands and south.

The Test series brought another shake-up for Britain as New Zealand clinched the first-ever triumph by a full Kiwi team in England (the 1907–1908 party had won a series but their team had included several Australians).

In the first Test at Salford on 25 September, New Zealand won 18–13, a surprising result in that several club matches had been lost before the Test. Williams, Whitaker, P. Orchard and R. Orchard scored the tourists' tries, Tatana landing three goals. Tries for Great Britain were scored by Benyon, Ashurst and Hesketh, with two goals from Whitehead. The second Test at Castleford confirmed the Kiwis' form, though the match aroused controversy. Great Britain's players claimed they got the rough edge of the decisions made by referee Derek Brown. Britain led 11–0 at one stage, but New Zealand fought back to 11–10. At this point Walsh and Benyon had touch downs disallowed for failing to ground the ball properly, while P. Orchard was given a try despite claims that he had stepped into touch. To make matters worse for Britain, Haigh broke an arm.

New Zealand won 17–14, P. Orchard (2) and Tatana getting tries and Tatana four goals. For Britain Coulman, Walsh, Millward and Sullivan scored tries, but Watkins could only land one goal. The third Test at Headingley on 6 November brought minor consolation for Britain in a 12–3 win, Atkinson got two tries and Holmes three goals, Greengrass touching down for the Kiwis. If the results were bad for Britain, the attendances were equally disappointing, totalling 3764, 4108, and 5479. The triumphant Kiwis went over to France and won two and drew one of their games.

In the challenge cup Leeds reached the final for the second successive year, facing St Helens in an attractive inter-county match, played on 13 May before a Wembley attendance of 90,000. Teams were:

*Leeds*: Holmes; Smith, Hynes, Dyl, Atkinson; Hardisty, Hepworth; Clawson, Fisher, Ramsey, Cookson, Haigh, Batten. Substitutes: Langley, D. Ward

*St Helens*: Pimblett; Jones, Benyon, Walsh, Wilson; Kelly, Heaton; Rees, Greenall, Stephens, Mantle, Chisnall, Coslett. Substitutes: Whittle, Earl

Referee: E. Lawrinson (Warrington)

For the second successive year Leeds frustrated and disappointed their followers. A particularly unhappy time was had by forward Terry Clawson who missed several kicks at goal, one from near the posts. St Helens, skilful and composed, ran in tries from Rees and Jones, with Coslett landing five goals. Cookson got a try for Leeds while Clawson, despite his misses, also kicked five goals.

Leeds won consolation in the championship final at Swinton and Clawson's pride was restored, along with that of the Leeds team, when Leeds beat St Helens 9–5. Clawson landed three goals, including a touchline conversion of a try by Atkinson.

The Great Britain *v.* France Test matches, regarded as trials for the proposed 1972 world cup in France, resulted in a double for ·Britain, 10–9 at Toulouse and a sweeping 45–10 at Bradford.

## *The hooter blows*

During the season of 1972–73 the six-tackle rule replaced the four-tackle rule. Another major development was the Australia-type system of having timekeepers at matches, a hooter ending the game. The new system removes this responsibility from referees and avoids contentious arguments, each side now having a timekeeper on duty.

The 1972 world cup was played in France in October and November and, after failure at the last game in 1970, Great Britain stood behind Australia in the ante-post betting. As in the first tournament in France in 1954, however, the British party turned up trumps with some fine attacking displays. In the first game at Perpignan, Great Britain won a pulsating match against Australia by 27 points to 21. In a great finish, after Australia had led 21–17, Great Britain came back with tries by O'Neill and Stephenson. The French referee, M. Teissère, awarded Britain a seven-point try after Atkinson had been fouled running round to the posts. In addition to Clawson's goal he gave Britain a penalty, kicked by Clawson.

France beat New Zealand 20–9, Britain beat France at Grenoble 13–4, and Australia beat New Zealand 9–5 in Paris. The Lions hammered New Zealand 53–19 at Pau, Holmes setting up a world individual record with ten goals and two tries. Australia qualified for the final, beating France comfortably at Toulouse, although there was an amazing incident. Australia appeared to score a perfectly good try by Branighan. Mick Naughton, the Widnes referee, allowed the try, then saw the French touch judge waving his flag, apparently for Branighan having put his foot in touch. There was a long altercation between Mr Naughton, the French officials, and Australian players, until finally Australia's captain, Graeme Langlands, reluctantly accepted the fact that the try was disallowed. Justice was done when Australia romped away with the game 31–9. Great Britain won the world cup on points difference when the Lyons final was drawn 10–10 after a bruising, bitter battle.

The outstanding feature of the game for Britain was a ninety-yard try-scoring dash by Sullivan. O'Neill and Beetson scored tries for Australia, Branighan kicking two goals, but Clawson landed a penalty for Great Britain. The scores were tied when Stephenson backed up a Lockwood break to touch down and Clawson goaled.

In December a team of Australian schoolboys made a pioneer tour of Britain. The Australian High Schools' tour proved a rampaging triumph as they won a twelve match programme without being seriously extended, recording 402 points against 17.

## Another two-division attempt

The two-division argument raged again and, on 16 February 1973, yet another special general meeting was convened to discuss proposals. This time the vote was in favour of a further two-division experiment (sixteen teams in the first division and fourteen in the second), a four up and four down promotion and relegation system.

The 1973 challenge-cup final was a Yorkshire affair after four clubs east of the Pennines, Bradford Northern, Dewsbury, Featherstone Rovers and Castleford, reached the semi-finals. Northern and Rovers won through and, although the attendance at Wembley in May was 74,000, well below capacity, the receipts were a world record at £125,000. Teams were:

*Bradford Northern*: Tees; Lamb, Stockwell, Watson, Redfearn; Blacker, Seabourne; Hogan, Dunn, Earl, Joyce, Pattinson, Fearnley. Substitutes: Long, Treasure

*Featherstone Rovers*: C. Kellett; Coventry, M. Smith, Newlove, K. Kellett; Mason, Nash; Tonks, Bridges, Farrar, Thompson, Rhodes, Stone. Substitutes: Hartley, Hollis.

Referee: M. Naughton (Widnes)

This was a final for records. It produced the highest total of points and a record-breaking goal-kicking performance from Cyril Kellett, the Rovers full-back. As a contest it was over in twenty minutes, with Featherstone running up a quick seventeen points against a nervous and fumbling Northern. Newlove touched down twice, Farrar got a third try and Kellett landed four goals. For Northern Tees kicked three goals but there was no serious threat to the Rovers line.

The second half was much more balanced and keenly contested, but a Rovers victory was never in doubt. Smith and Hartley added tries, Kellett completed his record nine goals and Nash dropped a goal. For Northern, looking to restore pride, Redfearn and Fearnley scored tries and Tees kicked another goal in a 33–14 scoreline.

The championship final at Odsal produced one of those major turn-ups which are the life-blood of any spectator sport. Unfancied Dewsbury took on Leeds and, after being slaughtered by Leeds in the Yorkshire cup, Dewsbury upset the odds by winning 22–13. Mick Stephenson, the hooker, was the inspiration, scoring a decisive try and leading by example, while Nigel Stephenson scored a try and five goals. It was also unfortunate for Leeds that Alan Hardisty was sent off for the first time in a distinguished and non-controversial career.

It was quite a season for records, with David Watkins, the Salford and former Welsh Rugby Union half-back and captain, setting up a new world seasonal goal-kicking record by landing 221 and beating Bernard Ganley's 219.

The return of two divisions created an attendance pattern similar to 1962. Top first-division games drew good crowds, while bottom second-division sides had poor attendances.

One club bravely, but barely, surviving was Hunslet. The Parkside ground had been sold by previous directors but a nucleus of players, led by the long-serving forward Geoff Gunney and backed by some keen Yorkshire businessmen, opened up as New Hunslet at Leeds Greyhound Stadium.

The arrival of the Australian touring party caused some consternation at headquarters. Anxious to have their tour over and finished by Christmas, the Kangaroos had left their precise time of arrival in some doubt, and hasty arrangements had to be made to receive them on Monday, 24 September. There were more controversies to come as the manager Charlie Gibson complained that fixtures had been badly arranged, some games conflicting with nearby attractive League fixtures. Furthermore, the tourists insisted that the first game should again be at Wembley rather than at Wigan, claiming that the Australian population of London would turn up in force. The plan misfired and, when the match was played at Wembley on 3 November, with television coverage, the crowd was only around 10,000.

Great Britain upset the odds by winning 21–12. Lowe, the big Hull K. R. forward, had an outstanding game and scored two tries. Hooker Clarke and second-row-forward Lockwood also went over the Kangaroos' line in a great pack performance. Clawson kicked four goals and Nash landed an international one-point dropped goal. For a shaken Australia Branighan and Fulton were the try scorers and Langlands kicked three goals.

The Kangaroos made six changes for the second Test, Eadie replacing the injured points' machine, Langlands, at full-back. On a wild, wet and windy day, Australia adapted well to the unfamiliar conditions and squared the series at 14–6. Lockwood, the British forward, got his marching orders. McCarthy scored a try for Australia, Eadie kicked five goals and Fulton dropped a goal. The attendance at Headingley was 16,000.

## Ice cold in Warrington

The third, deciding, Test was played at Warrington and brought further controversy. The ground was frozen rock solid and it was felt the match should not be played on such a surface. The tourists, however, were anxious to keep to their tight itinerary and, after much discussion, it was agreed that the game would be played, despite grave misgivings among the British party. These were amply justified when, before a 10,000 crowd Australia won 15–5. Australia were set on their way to five tries by an interception try by Fulton. Clawson, the British goal-kicker, had to play in borrowed boots, having left his own behind. For Britain Millward scored a try and Clawson one goal. Australia had won back the Ashes but it had been an unsatisfactory tour.

Australia was also winning the signatures of the best English players, and star names who accepted appetising contracts included Mick Stephenson (Dewsbury), Doug Laughton (Widnes), Bill Ashurst (Wigan), Phil Lowe (Hull K. R.) and Alan Hardisty (Leeds).

In 1973–74 there was a new competition, the Captain Morgan trophy, destined to last just one season. The televised BBC 2 Floodlit

Trophy, an established success, brought a welcome new winner. Bramley, the small Yorkshire club in the shadow of the West Riding giants, beat Widnes at Naughton Park to win their first-ever trophy.

Big-money signings helped stimulate interest. Rugby Union international backs Keith Fielding of England, and John Bevan of Wales, joined Salford and Warrington respectively and became free-scoring wingers in the 13–a-side game. Indeed, Fielding's forty-nine tries in his first season helped Salford win the first-division championship, and John Bevan's twenty-two tries helped Warrington towards a four-trophy haul.

In January 1974 Jim Challinor was appointed coach to the Great Britain side, with Reg Parker as team manager, and, because of the impending tour, the matches against France assumed the mantle of Test trials. At Grenoble on Sunday, 20 January, Great Britain won 24–5, Fielding scoring a hat-trick. In the return game at Wigan in February, Great Britain won even more easily, 29 points to nil. Charlton (2), Redfearn (2), Laughton, Willicombe and Gray scored tries, with two goals from Clawson and one each from Gray and Watkins.

In the major competitions of 1973–74 Warrington swept the board under the controversial and dynamic leadership of Alex Murphy. Brought to Wilderspool by a wealthy industrialist chairman Ossie Davies, Murphy led Warrington to the Captain Morgan, John Player, challenge-cup and championship finals. Murphy's tactics were effective and not always attractive; Warrington's challenge-cup victory over Featherstone Rovers at Wembley created considerable argument and raging discussions. Teams were:

*Featherstone Rovers*: Box; Dyas, Smith, Hartley, Bray; Newlove, Nash; Tonks, Bridges, Harris, Thompson, Rhodes, Bell

*Warrington*: Whitehead; M. Philbin, Noonan, Whittle, Bevan; Murphy, Gordon; Brady, Ashcroft, Chisnall, Wright, Nicholas, Philbin

Referee: S. Shepherd (Oldham)

Rovers were seeking their second consecutive challenge-cup win, and at half time they led 9–8, scoring the only try of the first half while Murphy was off the field injured. Murphy returned for the second half, replacing Gordon, and almost immediately Warrington got to grips with the game, Ashcroft and Nicholas going over for tries, Whitehead kicking three goals and Murphy dropping two.

## *A rough house*

Warrington won 24–9 but the match became so rough in the second half that Tonks and Bridges of Featherstone were carried off, there were several brawls and Nicholas (Warrington) and Thompson (Featherstone) were also hurt. Several days after the game letters were still pouring into League headquarters in Leeds deploring unsavoury incidents witnessed live and on television, and David Watkins, the captain of Salford, attacked Murphy for his concentration on achieving victory at the expense of open rugby. This elicited the reply from Murphy that rugby league was not a game for girls and that he would only choose 'fancy' players like Watkins if the games were 'tig and pass'. A week after Wembley, in a game which produced many more thrills and much more open football, Warrington had won four trophies by beating St Helens 13–12 in the championship final. The match was played at Wigan before 18,000 spectators. Warrington led 13–7 with twenty minutes to go, having scored tries from Mike Philbin, Brady and Noonan, plus two goals from Whitehead, against a try from Wilson and two goals from Coslett. Then Wilson got a second try, goaled by Coslett to make the score 13–12, and there was a cliff-hanging twenty minutes before the whistle blew and Murphy was hoisted shoulder high by the Warrington supporters.

The final act of the 1973–74 season was the departure of the tourists to Australasia, minus Laughton who had previously joined the emigration exodus, Fielding, who dropped out for business reasons, and Nicholas, injured in the cup final.

The party which flew out in an attempt to regain the Ashes consisted of:

Backs: K. Willicombe (Wigan), C. Hesketh, capt., P. Charlton, D. Watkins, K. Gill (Salford), D. Eckersley (St Helens), J. Butler (Rochdale Hornets), D. Redfearn (Bradford Northern), J. Bevan (Warrington), J. Atkinson, L. Dyl (Leeds), R. Millward (Hull K. R.), A. Bates (Dewsbury), S. Nash (Featherstone Rovers).

Forwards: T. Clawson (Oldham), J. Gray (Wigan), J. Mills

(Widnes), G. Nicholls, E. Chisnall (St Helens), J. Bridges, J. Bates, J. Thompson (Featherstone R.), K. Ashcroft (Warrington), C. Dixon (Salford), P. Rose (Hull K. R.), S. Norton (Castleford).

The end of the season saw the retirement of William (Bill) Fallowfield after twenty-eight years as secretary of the Rugby League, a career maintaining the remarkable longevity of tenure of office. He was replaced by David Oxley (like Bill Fallowfield an M.A.) from the Duke of York Military School in Dover.

## Unlucky tour

The tour was dogged by bad luck, John Bates and John Atkinson having to return home. Maurice Richards and Bill Ramsey flew out to join the tourists; Bates's career was ended by the serious head injury sustained against Northern Division at Tamworth. David Eckersley also flew home and was not replaced. The injury situation eventually became so bad that the coach Jim Challinor had to play in games in New Zealand.

In the Tests Great Britain fought back splendidly to square the series with a 16–11 victory at Sydney, the injured Gray, with three goals and a dropped goal, the hero of a great fight back. Britain continued to hit back, after losing the first Test 12–6 at Brisbane. Great Britain's misfortunes came to a climax in the final Test at Sydney on 20 July, the Australian referee Keith Page giving Australia a spate of penalties in vital positions in the second half. Even so, it was close at 22–18, Langlands crowning a great career by completing more than 100 points in Tests against Great Britain. The British tour manager, Reg Parker, gave a telling postscript to the tour when he said: 'After this we will have neutral referees in world championships.'

# 11
# Widnes Triumphs: Great Britain Disasters

The Australian disappointments were compounded by failure in New Zealand in the first Test, played on an Auckland mudheap in miserable conditions, on 27 July. Great Britain lost 13–8, Bevan and Nash getting tries and Clawson a goal. Some pride was restored at Christchurch, however, on 4 August, Britain winning 17–8 with tries from David Redfearn, Dyl and Hesketh and four goals from Gray. The tour ended on a happy and successful note with a resounding British victory by 20 points to nil in the third Test at Auckland on 10 August. The tries came from Bevan (2), Dyl and Hesketh, and Gray kicked four goals.

At the League's annual meeting in June 1974, attempts to introduce a rule whereby a try would be worth four points were defeated. Nine years were to elapse before this move would succeed. The value of a drop goal however, was reduced from two points to one, giving more leeway between a try and a dropped goal. Loose-forwards were to pack properly in the scrums, and the defending scrum-half was ordered to retire to the base of the scrum.

The reduction in value of the dropped goal cut down the number of matches won on a spate of drop goals, while still allowing for enterprise in closely fought matches.

## Widnes emerge

The challenge-cup final played at Wembley on 10 May 1975 began a remarkable sequence of trophy successes by Widnes who undoubtedly became the pot-hunting team of the decade. They met their old rivals

Warrington before a crowd of 87,000, gate receipts being more than £140,000. The day was notable for the introduction of a schoolboys' curtain-raiser, the under-11s of Widnes beating Wigan under-11s on a proud day for schoolboy rugby league. The score was 8–0, but the Wigan boys soon forgot their disappointment in the thrill of appearing at the game's Mecca before a huge and enthusiastic crowd. The teams for the senior final were:

*Warrington*: Whitehead; M. Philbin, Noonan, Reynolds, Bevan; Whittle, Gordon; Chisnall, Ashcroft, Wanbon, Conroy, Martyn, B. Philbin. Substitutes: Briggs, Nicholas

*Widnes*: Dutton; Prescott, George, Aspey, O'Neill; Hughes, Bowden; Mills, Elwell, Sheridan, Foran, Adams, Laughton. Substitutes: T. Karalius, Nelson

Referee: P. Geraghty (York)

Warrington made a splendid start when Bevan, showing typical speed and enterprise, followed up an Ashcroft kick and touched down, Whitehead kicking the goal. Widnes fought their way back with two penalty goals from Dutton and took a grip on the game when, after several close shaves near the Warrington line, George created a big gap and the mammoth front-row-forward Mills romped over unattended for a try. Dutton kicked a goal, then added a penalty and Widnes led 11–5 at half time. The quality of play declined in the second half, with defences largely on top. Whitehead landed a penalty goal for Warrington but Dutton kicked a penalty and dropped a goal in a 14–5 Widnes win.

## The premiership

The first of the new-style top eight premiership finals took place at Wigan on Saturday, 17 May, between Leeds and the champions St Helens. Leeds, themselves a remarkable trophy-hunting team, won convincingly by 26 points to 11. Mason, Hynes, Atkinson (2) and Smith scored the Leeds tries, Holmes kicking two goals and Marshall three, while Hynes added a drop goal. The St Helens points came from tries by Jones, Mathias and Heaton and a goal from Coslett.

1975 was a busy, though not totally successful, year for international rugby league. In the resumed European championship England beat France 11–9 at Perpignan and won the championship by beating Wales 12–8 at Salford. At Swansea Wales beat France 21–8.

Far more important in concept was the 1975 world championship. This was an ambitious and experimental venture in which England, Wales, Australia, France and New Zealand played home-and-away matches in all countries and in northern and southern hemispheres.

It was a bewildering and long-drawn-out hotchpotch of fixtures, and crowds varied between 33,858 for Australia *v*. England at Sydney to 1581 at Bordeaux for France *v*. England. The long series of twenty matches stretched at intervals over nine months and parts of two seasons. It was unwieldy and did not inspire great enthusiasm. Australia were the eventual winner, winning six and drawing one of their eight matches. England won five games, Wales three, New Zealand two and France one, the French win being recorded at Toulouse with Wales as the victims.

The 1975–76 season brought the beginnings of a remarkable transformation in a club's fortunes. Hull became the first side from the second division to reach the final of the John Player trophy which had, since 1972, been a successful sponsored tournament. Although Hull were beaten by the formidable Widnes team, 19–13, a momentum had begun that was to take Hull to the pinnacle of rugby league in the late seventies and early eighties.

The 1976 challenge-cup final at Wembley on 8 May was played in scorching temperatures approaching 100 degrees F. The crowd was 90,000 and receipts topped £190,000, a record for the event. Widnes were there again, and their opponents were their neighbours and close rivals St Helens. Teams were:

*St Helens*: Pimblett; Jones, Cunningham, Noonan, Mathias; Benyon, Heaton; Mantle, A. Karalius, Coslet, Nicholls, E. Chisnall, Hull. Substitutes: Glynn, James

*Widnes*: Dutton; Prescott, Hughes, George, Jenkins; Eckersley, Bowden; Nelson, Elwell, Wood, Foran, Adams, Laughton. Substitutes: D. O'Neill, Sheridan

Referee: R. Moore (Wakefield)

The match was billed in advance as a battle between the young lions in the Widnes pack and the experienced old heads in the St Helens pack. In the event, the experience of such as Mantle, Coslett and Nicholls proved too much for the younger Nelson, Wood and company, and St Helens eventually won comfortably by 20 points to 5. At half time Widnes were well in the game, St Helens leading 6–4 through a try by Cunningham, goaled by Pimblett, and a Pimblett dropped goal against two penalties from Dutton. In the second half St Helens took a firm grip on the game, Widnes faded disappointingly after an early Elwell drop goal, and Heaton and Glynn (twice) crossed the Chemics' line. Pimblett added two more goals and a dropped goal and carried off the Lance Todd trophy.

A fortnight later, at Swinton, before an 18,000 crowd, St Helens crowned a great season by beating Salford in the premiership final. It was a fiercely fought game, full of ruthless tackling and crunching forward play, Saints again staying the pace best and racing away with the match in the closing stages. At half time Salford had a fragile 1–0 lead through a Watkins dropped goal. Pimblett kicked a penalty then Watkins landed his second dropped goal. A Glynn try put St Helens in front. Late tries were added by Chisnall and Karalius, Pimblett landing two further goals in a 15–2 success.

## More controversy

The 1977 world cup was played in Australia and New Zealand, between 29 May and 25 June, and led to another dramatic and controversial confrontation between Australia and Great Britain in the play-off final. Australia beat New Zealand 27–12 at Auckland, France 21–9 at Sydney, and Great Britain 19–5 at Brisbane. Great Britain beat France 23–4 at Auckland and New Zealand at Christchurch, and qualified to meet Australia in the play-off by finishing second.

The match was played at Sydney on 25 June before a crowd of 24,400.

Great Britain could have won the decider but for their own mistakes. Elwell gave them plenty of possession but only two tries resulted, and two mistakes by the full-back George Fairbairn gave tries to Australia. McMahon got the first Kangaroo try, Cronin goaling, but a splendid try by the forceful Pitchford and a Fairbairn goal made it 5–5. Then came Fairbairn's first error, a loose pass giving Gartner a try, and goals from Cronin and Fairbairn made it 10–7 at half time. In the second half another Fairbairn slip, this time a fumble near his own line, enabled Kolc to pick up and score, and it was 13–7. Great Britain fought back well and Millward and the magnificent Pitchford set up a try for the substitute Gill. Firbairn kicked the goal and it was 13–12 for the remaining minutes.


## A Yank at rugby league

The expansion of the game internationally appeared to be on the verge of a major breakthrough in 1977 when a very large, well-built and personable American from Wisconsin, Mike Mayer, declared his readiness to launch rugby league in the United States.

Mayer, a former American college footballer, launched an association called the United States Rugby League, of which he was president. Convinced that a tough, exciting, physical-contact sport like rugby league would be received well in America, he flew to Britain to sell his idea to the League. League officials, wary of putting money into such an ambitious and unproven venture, gave encouragement through moral support and assistance with publicity and organization, but no promises of cash.

Refusing to be dismayed, Mayer organized a press conference in the famous Gallagher's Restaurant in New York on 15 August 1978. Mayer wanted wealthy businessmen in the States to take out stadium franchises on the lines of American football, baseball and basketball, and asked a friend and partner, Jim Taylor, a former gridiron star, to be League commissioner. Mayer organized a coaching session near Chicago for Americans who wanted to try the new code, and Britain's Albert Fearnley and Australia's Doug Nye went out to coach.

Adopting a more positive stance, the Rugby League offered to send the England and Wales teams to America to play exhibitions, but Mayer could not find backers to raise the £50,000 guarantee. Since then the United States Rugby League has drifted into the doldrums, no major sponsors emerging despite Mayer's ardent advocacy.

Widnes reached Wembley again in 1978. Their opponents were Leeds and, once again, despite their upset against St Helens twelve months previously, Widnes were favourites. The referee was J. V. Moss of Manchester and the teams were:

*Leeds*: B. Murrell; A. Smith, Hague, Dyl, Atkinson; Holmes, Dick;

Harrison, Ward, Pitchford, Eccles, Cookson, Fearnley. Substitutes: Dickinson, D. Smith

*Widnes*: Dutton; Wright, Aspey, Eckersley, O'Neill; Hughes, Bowden; Ramsey, Elwell, Mills, Dearden, Adams, Laughton. Substitutes: Foran, George

Despite an apparent air of invincibility in cup competitions, Widnes were overturned, Leeds taking charge in the second half just as St Helens had done. Widnes started confidently, Aspey scoring a fine individual try and Dutton kicking two goals against a penalty goal from Dick. The turning point was a high kick by Holmes which Wright misjudged as it dropped. Atkinson swept on to the ball, as it eluded Wright, and scored. This gave Leeds renewed confidence and Dyl slipped through speedily, after a scrum, to make it 8–7. Then Dick sold an outrageous dummy to go under the posts and kicked the goal to make it 13–7. Dick added a dropped goal and a penalty as Leeds won 16–7.

The championship final on 28 May 1977 was another triumph for St Helens who beat Warrington in a thrilling, high-scoring game at Swinton. St Helens won 32–20 with tries from Pimblett, Benyon, Mathias, Cunningham, Ken Gwilliam and James, and seven goals from Pimblett. Warrington's points came from tries by Alan Gwilliam, Philbin, Weavill and Gordon and four goals from Hesford.

The European championship, suspended in 1975–76 because of the world cup, was resumed in 1977. It was a disappointing tournament for England who lost both games, and a good one for France who beat England and Wales. At Leeds, in a match in which England failed to function as an attacking force, Wales tackled well to win 6–2. A much more open game in Carcassonne saw France beat England 28–5, despite the fact that England made wholesale changes, particularly in the pack, where Coulman, Ward, Farrar, Lowe, Rose and Norton were a mass replacement for Hogan, Bridges, Thompson, Grayshon, Les Gorley and Laughton. France, who had the advantage of playing both their games at home, beat Wales 13–2 at Toulouse.

## Wales trounced

England's honour was restored with victory in the 1978 European championship, though their victory over Wales at St Helens was a dreadful humiliation for the Welsh side after they had handsomely beaten France 29–7 in an impressive display at Widnes in January. The two closing games of a disjointed tournament were played in May, England beating France at Toulouse 13–11. The match against Wales was played in broiling summer sunshine, Wales appeared to have no real heart for the fight and England scored fourteen tries through Wright (4), Atkinson (2), Hughes (2), Norton, Dyl, Casey, Nash, Pimblett, and Millward. Pimblett kicked nine goals. Willicombe, Sullivan and Clive Jones touched down for an outclassed Wales and Watkins and Woods kicked goals. The margin of victory again caused misgivings to be expressed about the ultimate survival of the Welsh international side, and the European championship was eventually wound up in 1981.

In October 1977 the amateur team, Cawoods, won their way into the annals of the game when they beat Halifax 9–8 in the John Player trophy. This was a great season for BARLA, the British Amateur Rugby League Association, an organization which had made giant strides since its official recognition in 1974. In May and June 1978 a BARLA open-age touring team became the first to visit the new international rugby-league territory of Papua New Guinea, together with Australia and New Zealand. Matches were played at Rabaul, Lae, Mount Hagen and Port Moresby, 14,100 seeing Great Britain win the first-ever international match between Great Britain and Papua New Guinea by 28–7 at Port Moresby.

The 1978 challenge-cup final produced one of the most dramatic finishes in the history of the competition. A capacity attendance of 96,000 paid £330,000 to see a game which brought an amazing comeback from a quick 10 points deficit, and a piece of cruel ill-luck in the dying seconds. Leeds returned to Wembley, St Helens, the 1976 winners, being their opponents. Teams were:

*Leeds*: Oulton; D. Smith, Hague, Dyl, Atkinson; Holmes, Sanderson; Harrison, Ward, Pitchford, Cookson, Eccles, Crane. Substitutes: Dick, Dickinson

*St Helens*: Pimblett; Jones, Noonan, Glynn, Mathias; Francis, K Gwilliam; D. Chisnall, Liptrot, James, Nicholls, Cunningham, Pinner.

Referee: W. H. Thompson (Huddersfield)

Leeds started shakily in defence and St Helens were cock-a-hoop as they grabbed two quick tries. Liptrot touched down as Leeds defenders made a mess of a kick ahead, and Francis waltzed around some weak tackling to score a second try. Pimblett landed two goals, and Leeds were 10–0 down. Leeds, however, refused to submit, and that fine finisher Atkinson weaved his way over for a splendid try. A goal each from Pimblett and the Leeds full-back Oulton made the score 12–5 to St Helens, and the Saints seemed well set to hold on for victory despite Leeds's revival.

Then began the sensations. Cookson, the Leeds second-row-forward, took a pass ten yards from the line and bulldozed his way over the line with irresistible force. David Smith took a long, wide pass to go over for another try. Then the Leeds fans went wild as Ward dropped two goals, Holmes dropped a goal with his left foot while falling in a tackle, and Leeds led 14–12.

Saints gathered themselves for one final, desperate effort, and with literally the last move of the game they could have won. Quick passing to the right caught the Leeds defence overstretched and the St Helens centre Noonan had only to take a sharp pass and dive over himself or send Jones in at the corner. He dropped the ball, the match ended, and Leeds jumped for joy while poor Noonan and his St Helens colleagues trudged wearily off the field. Like Don Fox's tragically famous kick at goal, Noonan's dropped pass snatched defeat from the jaws of victory; there was universal sympathy for the player – other than in the Leeds dressing room!

Bradford Northern won the premiership at Swinton before a 16,813 crowd, beating Widnes 17–8. After a good start, Widnes faded and Northern finished well on top. Barends, Roe, Haigh and David Redfearn scored the tries, Mumby kicked two goals and Wolford dropped a goal. Aspey scored two tries for Widnes and Woods kicked a goal.

Australia came to Britain in 1978 as holders of the Ashes. The managers were Peter Moore and Jim Caldwell; the captain was Bobby Fulton who had spent a period as a player with Warrington. The first Test was at Wigan on 21 October and resulted in a scrambled victory by Australia after a Bevan kick and chase try had put Britain in a 9–7 lead. For threequarters of a rough game, in which the scrum-halves Nash and Raudonikis were sent off, no tries were scored, Fairbairn landing three penalties and Cronin kicking three

for Australia with a drop goal from Fulton. After Bevan's try had
nosed Great Britain ahead, quick Kangaroo passing sent Boustead
in at the corner. Fulton clinched victory by 15–9 when he squirmed
over the line despite British defenders' claims that he was held short.
Cronin kicked the goal.

Faced with the necessity of winning the second Test at Bradford
to save both the Ashes and Britain's reputation, the British coach
Peter Fox instilled grim determination into his team for the match
on 5 November. It was a rough, tough encounter, a typical Test
match between the Lions and the Kangaroos, but Britain played
splendidly for threequarters of the game and hung on as Australia
staged a dramatic revival. Two tries by Wright and six goals from
an on-form Fairbairn gave Great Britain a comfortable 18–4 lead,
but two late tries brought Australia too close for comfort at 18–14 as
the game ended.

## An anti-climax

The third Test was, for Great Britain, a disappointing anti-climax,
the home team failing to repeat the Bradford performance, and a
young and fast Australian side romping home at Headingley on 18
November by 23 points to 6. Australian taunts about the British
'Dad's Army' pack, its over 30s being Mills, Fisher, Farrar and
Nicholls, seemed cruelly justified as Britain were outpaced and,
without the injured Lockwood, lacked guile up front. Boyd, Gerard,
Peponis and Raudonikis got the tries, Cronin five goals and Fulton
a dropped goal. One bright spot of the series for Britain came from
the attendance figures. The crowds at the three games totalled 17,644
at Wigan, 26,447 at Odsal and 29,267 at Headingley, the best
aggregate of crowd totals in Britain since 1959.

The Australians' runaway success in the third Test had unfortunate
repercussions for Peter Fox, the Bradford Northern coach who had
engineered the second Test victory. After a long and sometimes
stormy selection meeting he was outvoted as coach for the 1979 tour
of Australasia, Eric Ashton, the St Helens coach, getting the final
vote.

The challenge-cup final at Wembley in May 1979 produced a
disappointing game and yet another victory for Widnes, who beat

Wakefield Trinity by 12 points to 3 before a crowd of 94,218 paying £383,157. Although the Lance Todd trophy went to the brilliant Trinity stand-off-half, David Topliss, Widnes were in command for most of the game and Trinity players mostly played well below their normal form. Wright and Hughes scored the Widnes tries, Burke kicked two goals and Elwell and Eckersley each dropped goals. Fletcher gave Trinity a brief moment of hope with a try in the corner and Trinity made occasional bursts, prompted by the untiring Topliss, but Widnes never looked in serious danger of defeat.

Preparations and departures for the 1979 Australasian tour cast shadows over the premiership final, held late in May after the first party of tourists had flown to Australia. Northern, with four tourists in Mumby, Alan Redfearn, Grayshon and Casey, seemed more affected by tour calls than Leeds, who came storming through from a low position in the final table to win the match at Huddersfield by 24 points to 2. Dick had a remarkable game for Leeds, scored seven goals and a dropped goal for 15 points, and Alan Smith, David Smith and a tourist Ward scored tries. Ferres kicked a solitary goal for Northern. The attendance was 19,486.

Harry Womersley and Dick Gemmell were the managers of the 1979 touring party, Doug Laughton of Widnes being the captain. They left Britain for Mackay in Queensland on 21 May, to begin the most injury-prone and unsuccessful tour ever of Australia. Injuries and poor performances on the field made the 1979 tour one to forget, or to regard as a catalyst in improving standards in British rugby league.

Nevertheless, despite losing the Tests in a 3–0 whitewash, the tourists lost only one game outside the internationals and beat New Zealand by two Tests to one. These facts were clouded by heavy and convincing Australian victories in the Tests. The party was bigger than usual, thirty players instead of twenty-six, and two specialist wingers, Wright of Widnes and Bevan of Warrington had to withdraw because of injury. The party consisted of:

Backs: D. Barends, K. Mumby, A. Redfearn (Bradford Northern), S. Evans (Featherstone Rovers), P. Glynn, R. Mathias (St Helens), Holmes (Leeds), E. Hughes (Widnes), J. Joyner, G. Stephens (Castleford), R. Millward, M. Smith (Hull Kingston Rovers), S. Nash (Salford) and J. Woods (Leigh).

Forwards: M. Adams, D. Laughton, J. Mills (Widnes), L. Casey, J. Grayshon (Bradford Northern), P. Hogan, D. Watkinson, B. Lockwood (Hull K. R.), M. James, G. Liptrot, G. Nicholls (St Helens), T. Martyn (Warrington), S. Norton, C. Stone (Hull), T. Skerrett (Wakefield Trinity), D. Ward (Leeds).

During the ill-fated tour of Australia Mills, Martyn and Millward were flown home with injuries, to be replaced by J. Burke (Wakefield Trinity), G. Fairbairn (Wigan) and D. Topliss (Wakefield T.). The captain, Doug Laughton, and Steve Nash also returned home but were not replaced, Nicholls taking over the captaincy late in the tour.

## Tour disasters

After a series of moderate performances 'up country' in Queensland, Great Britain faced Australia at Lang Park, Brisbane, for the first Test on 16 June. Victory was not anticipated after unimpressive performances elsewhere, but no one in the British party expected the débâcle of a 35–0 defeat before a 23,000 crowd. Great Britain's cause was not helped by typical Australian pre-match press comment about 'strong-arm' tactics by the Lions. The match was won and lost at an early stage when the Brisbane referee Eddie Ward gave penalty after penalty to Australia, allowing Cronin to have a field day with kicks at goal. While Kangaroo mistakes were given the benefit of the referee's doubt, Britain's errors were punished and the match was won and lost before the half-time whistle blew.

Cronin eventually kicked ten goals in eleven attempts, and Boustead and Price scored two tries each, Corowa getting the other. It was Britain's worst defeat on Australian soil and made the restoration of British reputation and morale a major task for the managers and coach.

The second Test at Sydney Cricket Ground on Saturday, 30 July, produced a better performance by Britain in defeat, and a better scoreline, 24–16. The tourists' defence, however, was again too easily riddled by the fast Australian attacks, and Britain conceded four tries to two. Australia had won the game at half time, when they led 17–4, and Cronin again reaped a rich harvest, with two tries and six goals in his eighteen-point haul. Joyner and Hughes scored second-half tries for Great Britain, just to prove that the Lions could still attack, and Woods completed five goals.

This narrowing of the Test gap, and a fine win over New South Wales, gave Britain good heart for the third Test at Sydney on 14 July. The series had already been lost but Britain were anxious to avoid a total series' defeat in Australian Test matches. In the event, the match was almost as big a disaster as the first game, Australia winning 28–2 and Norton being sent off for fighting. As the tourists' coach Eric Ashton said, after the game, 'We went from bad to worse.' Australian tries came from Eadie, Price, Boyd and Reddy, and the prolific Cronin landed another eight goals as he completed a record series' total of fifty-four points. Fairbairn kicked a solitary penalty goal for Great Britain.

It was a deflated and dejected party which flew off to New Zealand where some consolation was drawn from the 2–1 series' victory. Great Britain won the first Test 16–8 at Auckland, and the second 22–7 at Christchurch, losing the third 18–11 on the return to Auckland. To add the final cruel twist to an unfortunate tour, a first-ever loss of £35,000 was later reported.

Australia had seemed light years ahead in pace and skill, and inevitably there was much public and private breast-beating on the return of the touring party. There were calls from all sides for a dramatic reconstruction and reappraisal of the standard of the game in Britain.

Snow, ice and fog played havoc with the fixtures in the midwinter of 1979. Snows fell shortly after Christmas and then froze on the grounds and, as match programme after match programme was postponed, an extension of the season became inevitable. The first-division season, normally scheduled to end in April, was extended to 13 May.

## *Differential penalty*

The 1979–80 season brought a major rule change, designed to cut down on the spate of penalty goals resulting from scrum offences. The differential penalty was introduced for 'technical' offences like foot up and improper scrummaging, as opposed to foul play and offside. The differential penalty did not allow a kick at goal but called for a tap from the mark.

The 1979–80 challenge-cup final, played on 3 May 1980, produced a dream fixture, a Humberside local derby between Hull and Hull Kingston Rovers. The meeting at Wembley was an inevitable sell-out from the moment the semi-final rounds were completed, and the city of Kingston-upon-Hull became a ghost town on that famous Saturday afternoon. A capacity attendance of 95,000 produced receipts of £448,202 and, although there were police and League misgivings about possible confrontations and fights between the rival fans, no trouble whatever ensued, the safety barriers were not needed and the behaviour of the crowd won universal admiration. There was not a single unsavoury crowd incident and, at the end of the game, fans bedecked in red-and-white of Rovers and black-and-white of Hull locked arms together to walk through Wembley. Families were seen bearing both sets of colours and there was a carnival atmosphere throughout.

On the field of play the derby-match tensions militated against a fast, open game, but the tension created its own excitement. Hubbard, the big Rovers winger, and Millward, the captain, were to have remarkable mixed fortunes. They both played leading roles and both were injured, Millward suffering a broken jaw and playing on despite the pain. Teams were:

*Hull*: Woods; Bray, Walters, Wilby, Prendiville; Newlove, Pickerill; Tindall, Wileman, Stone, Birdsall, Lloyd, Norton. Substitutes: Hancock, Farrar

*Hull K. R.*: Hall; Hubbard, M. Smith, Hartley, Sullivan; Millward, Agar; Holdstock, Watkinson, Lockwood, Lowe, Rose, Casey. Substitutes: Hogan, Millington

Referee: F. Lindop (Wakefield)

Rovers broke through early with a dashing try by Hubbard from a neat pass by Lockwood, and were never headed thereafter. While Hubbard kicked three goals for Rovers, Lloyd was off-form for Hull and landed only one goal from several attempts. Millward, despite suffering a broken jaw in a tackle, landed a fine drop goal. Even a well-worked try by Wilby failed to lift Hull's game as Rovers won by 10 points to 5. Hubbard suffered a late injury and had to hobble to the royal box on crutches to receive his winner's medal, while

Millward's jaw fracture, one of several received by the player in quick succession, precipitated his retirement.

In the premiership final Widnes picked up yet another major trophy, beating their doughty rivals Bradford Northern by 19 points to 5 before a crowd of 10,215 at Swinton, and thus avenging defeat two years earlier. The highlight was a try by the Widnes winger Bentley who showed great pace to beat the Northern cover to a pinpoint kick-through by his centre Aspey. Wright, Aspey, Elwell and Gorley also touched down, Burke kicked a goal, and Eckersley and Elwell dropped goals for Widnes in a performance which won tributes even from Northern's coach Peter Fox. David Redfearn scored a try and Mumby a goal for Bradford.

## *The Narbonne riot*

England retained the European championship in 1980, after holding it in 1979 by beating Wales 15–7 and France 12–6. On 29 February they beat Wales 26–9 at Craven Park, then came the fireworks. There was a remarkable occurrence in the France *v.* England European championship game at Narbonne on 16 March. What in political circles would be called a major diplomatic breakdown between the countries followed a riot which saw the referee, Billy Thompson, imprisoned in the dressing room for his own safety for two hours after the match.

England won the match 4–2 but Mr Thompson incensed the French spectators by disallowing a late try for a forward pass. When the final whistle blew the English referee had to sprint for his life to the dressing room where he was enclosed for two hours in the custodial protection of the gendarmerie before being smuggled out of the ground under escort, along with senior British officials Bill Oxley and Joe Seddon. So angry were the British officials, both with the crowd reaction and the violent behaviour of the French team, that at a Rugby League council meeting no dates of the following season's fixtures with France were considered until representatives of both countries had met to discuss the problem of violence on and off the field in France.

Eventually, during the auspicious and exciting weekend in which Fulham entered the Rugby League, officials of Great Britain and

France met in London and thrashed out a three-point charter. This established immediate dismissals for acts of extreme violence; the provision of a referee and one touch judge by the visiting country, and a four-man joint disciplinary committee to sit immediately after games.

By 1980 sponsorship was playing a major part in rugby league. Indeed, as the secretary-general David Oxley was quick to point out, sponsorship was proving a life-saver to many clubs. The successful John Player trophy sponsorship had been followed by highly lucrative, and equally successful, major sponsorships by Slalom Lager in the championship and premiership, and by State Express in the challenge cup. In addition, both county cups were sponsored; the Yorkshire sponsorship varied but Burtonwood Brewery was a steady sponsor in Lancashire. In July Featherstone Rovers announced the first major club sponsorship with a local packaging company, LinPac.

One major competition which ended its life and association with the 13-a-side game was the popular and prestigious BBC 2 Floodlit trophy, withdrawn because of the BBC's financial cutbacks after the 1979–80 final in which Hull beat Hull K. R. 13–3 before a full house at the Boulevard. Thus ended a fifteen-year association and a regular midweek date for armchair fans.

## Pompey votes against

The successful arrival of Fulham on the scene led to a spate of enquiries from clubs and organizations, including a senior football club, Portsmouth. The Fratton Park club took the unusual step in December of asking their supporters to vote on the establishment of rugby league at Pompey. More than 9000 voted and the result was an overwhelming 9–1 vote against the idea, an unexpected setback, but, in view of Portsmouth's geographical location, not without its compensations.

The New Zealand touring team arrived in Britain to play a highly concentrated, high-speed tour encompassing fourteen matches in seven weeks during October and November. Great Britain were anxious to beat the Kiwis convincingly to prove that the shattering lessons of the 1979 summer tour had been learned, but the tour was a shock to the British team as they struggled to square the series 1–1 with one match drawn.

The Kiwis did not have a particularly successful tour outside the Test matches. Of their fourteen games they won seven, lost six and drew one. They fought tooth and nail in the Tests, however, and made a good start in the first international at Wigan on 8 October, drawing 14–14 with a late penalty. The Kiwis faced a Great Britain side considerably changed from the 1979 disasters; there were seven new caps under the new management team of Colin Hutton and coach John Whiteley. They were Bentley, Camilleri, Hartley, Dick, Holdstock, Les Gorley and Pinner.

After an early bad-tempered mêlée had been quelled by the referee Billy Thompson, Fairbairn kicked two penalties for Britain. New Zealand replied with two quick tries from Ah Kuoi and Coll, Smith landing two goals to give New Zealand a 10–4 lead. A try by Camilleri, goaled by Fairbairn, made it 10–9 at half time.

The Kiwi lead was increased by a Smith penalty, but Mike Smith touched down for Great Britain and Fairbairn's goal made it 14–12. Five minutes from the end Smith landed a goal to tie the scores. The attendance was 7031.

The second Test was played before 10,946 spectators at Odsal on 2 November, and Great Britain received a further jolt, losing 12–8 against a Kiwi team bursting with confidence and enthusiasm after their draw in the first international. New Zealand were badly beaten in the scrums by Elwell, but Britain made little of their ample possession, whereas New Zealand made the most of every opportunity and half chance. Great Britain kept in touch with the tourists only by virtue of four Fairbairn penalties, but O'Donnell and O'Hara scored tries for New Zealand and Smith kicked three goals.

## Bulldog Drummond

A further boost to the tourists' confidence was a win by 18 points to 14 against Great Britain's under-24s at Fulham. Thus the stage was set for the third Test at Headingley on 15 November, Britain desperately needing a win not merely to tie the series, but to retain self-respect in international rugby league after the traumas in Australia. The attendance of 8210 was disappointing, perhaps indicative of the disenchantment with Britain's international failings. The home team had to struggle again, and relied on two tries by Leigh's fast, strong and elusive coloured winger Des Drummond to win by 10 points to 2. Drummond had an excellent game, saving a certain try with a tackle on Dickison, and clinching the game with his second try late in the game. It was a brilliant individual effort, Drummond twisting, turning, ducking and weaving past half-a-dozen defenders in a confined space near the New Zealand line. New Zealand missed several kicks at goal through Smith and Edkins, and British face was temporarily saved.

In November 1980 independent television, through the Granada and Yorkshire companies, expressed interest in ending the BBC's monopoly of coverage of rugby league, which had existed throughout the late sixties and the seventies. Agreement was reached and, early in 1981, 'RL Action', a programme combining match highlights, interviews, statistics and news reports, was launched on northern ITV channels to general and widespread acclaim, though supporters would have preferred an earlier time of viewing than late Monday evenings. A sadder event in television was the decision of Eddie Waring, the BBC commentator and nationally known personality, to retire.

Hull followed up the successful Kiwi tour, and enhanced their own growing stature within the game, by despatching director Dick Gemmell to New Zealand where he enterprisingly secured the signatures of three star backs, Gary Kemble, James Leuluai and Dane O'Hara.

A necessary development in international rugby league was prompted by the England *v.* France game at Headingley in February 1981; referee Guy Cattaneo of France proved to be the principal architect of a 5–1 French victory which provoked continuous booing from the crowd.

M. Cattaneo allowed France to run offside and commit offences with impunity, but penalized Britain every time a promising move threatened. At half time the British secretary-general had 'a polite but serious discussion about rule interpretation' with M. Cattaneo, but to no avail, and France's totally unsatisfactory victory led to successful calls for neutral referees. Later in the season the ailing

European championship was ended and plans were laid for Great Britain *v.* France Test matches in 1981–82.

In an exciting, though controversial and busy, end to the championship season, Warrington found themselves playing eight games in nineteen days to hold a lead at the top of the table. It was too much and, on Easter Monday 1981, Warrington lost with a crippled team at Leigh while Bradford Northern, who had found top gear with a magnificent late run, beat Hull at Odsal to take the championship at the final hurdle. Warrington's plight at Leigh was so bad that their goal-kicking full-back Hesford was strapped up and limping, others were carrying injuries, and Eccles had to have the plaster taken from his leg before he could hobble onto the field.

The 1981 challenge-cup final brought together two outstandingly successful sides, Hull Kingston Rovers and Widnes. The match took place at Wembley on 2 May and a crowd of 92,496 paid £591,117. Teams were:

*Hull K. R.*: Hall; Hubbard, Smith, Hogan, Muscroft; Hartley, Harkin; Holdstock, Watkinson, Crooks, Lowe, Burton, Casey. Substitutes: Millington, Proctor

*Widnes*: Burke; Wright, George, Cunningham, Bentley; Hughes, Gregory; M. O'Neill, Elwell, Lockwood, L. Gorley, Prescott, Adams. Substitutes: J. Myler, Shaw.

There was a pre-match drama for Widnes as their brilliant young scrum-half Andy Gregory suffered raging toothache on Friday night and had to have an extraction early on Saturday. The minor operation did him a remarkable amount of good for Gregory had a tremendous game. His superb individual try, a bobbing and weaving and sidestepping effort early in the second half, helped sink Rovers and clinch an 18–9 Widnes win against a disappointing Robins side. Burke scored a fine early try for Widnes, picking up a good bounce from his own kick ahead, and he went on to win the Lance Todd trophy, landing four goals in addition to his try. George also touched down for Widnes and the captain Adams dropped a goal. Burton got a consolation try for Rovers and Hubbard kicked three goals.

Rovers won ample consolation in the premiership final, yet another major Humberside derby with Hull. A capacity attendance of 30,000 at Headingley saw Rovers win 11–7, with three tries from Hogan,

Hartley and Smith and a goal from Hubbard against a try by Crane and two goals from Woods.

## Mood of optimism

The 1980s had opened with rugby league in Britain in bouyant mood, despite lack of success internationally. David Howes, the League's public-relations officer, said in a published statement: 'In the latter part of the 1970s the code received a massive injection of confidence from the public and private enterprise. The 1980s have opened with 360,000 more people watching the game than four years ago and sponsorship running at nearly a quarter of a million pounds this season.' To add to the confidence, Cardiff City and Carlisle entered the lists in 1981–82 following Fulham's great opening season, and enquiries were being received from places as diverse as Milton Keynes, London White City, Glasgow Rangers, Heart of Midlothian, Colchester, Reading, Nottingham Forest, Crystal Palace, Charlton Athletic, Bolton Wanderers and Bristol.

Nevertheless, there was a running dispute, with many acrimonious meetings, between the League and the British Amateur Rugby League Association which had also made massive strides in the 1970s. The issue was the growth of colts' teams attached to League clubs. BARLA objected to these on the grounds that there was a direct clash between the colts' league and amateur under-17 competitions.

Happily, after many prolonged meetings and much correspondence, a truce was declared in the latter months of 1982. Colts' leagues and amateur leagues have survived and thrived happily together despite the early misgivings.

# 12
# Scrum Blitz; Players Union

The early months of the 1981–82 season were traumatic ones for referees and hookers. A directive was given to referees to clean up untidy scrummaging, a constant blot on the game's image, and a great time-waster and creator of frustrations. Referees were instructed by the League to take a hard line on scrum offences, and the result was a veritable spate of sendings-off of hookers. In the first month of the season fourteen hookers were given marching orders and, at one disciplinary committee meeting, in September, ten hookers appeared. In the Yorkshire cup semi-final at Craven Park, Hull, the referee Stan Wall dismissed both hookers, Rovers' Watkinson and Northern's Handforth. Gary Hale took over as Bradford's replacement hooker, and he, too, was sent off. Like all such crash campaigns the scrum purge eventually settled back into normality but, for a time, hookers complained that, if they so much as moved an eyebrow before the ball was put in, they were liable to be penalized.

In December 1981 a new trade union, the Rugby League Professional Players Association, was formed. For several years players had talked of a professional association to further and protect their interests, and the new venture was a bold and well-planned one. The RLPPA was to be a branch of APEX, the Association of Professional, Executive, Clerical and Computer staff, and was thus affiliated to the TUC through APEX. The Association, with Gary Hetherington, the Huddersfield forward, as first chairman, promptly went into action to recruit members and to put forward its first major act of negotiation. This was a demand for a precise and generous injury insurance scheme, an attempt to standardize compensation procedures and make them binding. The format for such a scheme was eventually thrashed out in talks between the League and the Association.

The Great Britain *v.* France Test matches, both played within a fortnight in December 1981, produced games which defied logic. In the first game at Hull on 6 December, before a crowd of 13,173 on a cool but bright afternoon, Great Britain trounced France with an exhilarating display. The score was 37–0 and the outstanding performers were the two coloured wingers, Des Drummond and Henderson Gill, who scored five tries between them. Gill got a spectacular hat-trick on the left and Drummond, hero of the New Zealand series, ran in for two tries. Hartley and Woods also touched down, Woods kicked seven goals and Fairbairn one. A fortnight later there was an amazing reversal of form and result. France, making many changes, produced a much more spirited display before a wildly partisan 6500 crowd at Marseilles, and scored four tries to nil to win 19–2. The exchanges got a bit rough at times and Les Gorley and Jacques Guigues were sent off by the Australian referee Greg Hartley who threatened at half time to abandon the game if the niggling persisted. Hartley's performance in both Tests proved the value of the decision to appoint neutral referees following the Cattaneo fiasco at Headingley.

## *Freeze-up*

There was yet another freeze-up after Christmas and so many games were postponed that the first-division season was extended by ten days and the second-division season by a fortnight. The weather was so bad, and postponements so irritating, that Bradford Northern proposed, without success, a two-month break in the middle of the season. Yet again a major trophy brought a Humberside derby final and the seesaw scorelines continued, Hull emerging victorious at Headingley on 23 January before 25,165 spectators. Hull's victory in the John Player Trophy final was marred by the sending-off in the second half of their captain Charlie Stone, but they held out well against Rovers' attacks and scored the only try in a 12–4 win, a great individual effort by the hooker Wileman.

It was to be a great season for Hull, the big spenders of the League who were setting up attendance records with their consistent five-figure crowds at the cock-a-hoop Boulevard. The challenge-cup final brought together Hull and the trophy titans Widnes, and produced a Houdini-like comeback by Hull at Wembley and a magnificent replay at Elland Road football ground.

The first game was at Wembley on 1 May 1982; there was an attendance of 92,147 paying £684,500 and the result was a 14–14 draw after Widnes had seemed to be cruising to yet another trophy with a 14–6 lead. Teams were:

*Hull*: Kemble; O'Hara, Day, Evans, Prendiville; Topliss, Harkin; Skerrett, Wileman, Stone, Crane, Lloyd, Norton. Substitutes: Crooks

*Widnes*: Burke; Wright, O'Loughlin, Cunningham, Basnett; Hughes, Gregory; M. O'Neill, Elwell, Lockwood, L. Gorley, Prescott, Adams. Substitutes: T. Myler, S. O'Neill

Referee: F. Lindop (Wakefield)

Hull were seeking to end their Wembley jinx which had seen them compete in three finals without success. Indeed, in nine challenge-cup finals since 1908, they had recorded just one victory, in 1914. This year Widnes appeared well on the way to an easy win as a magnificent long-range interception try by Wright, added to two tries from the Lance Todd trophy winner Eddie Cunningham, goals from Gregory and Burke and an Elwell dropped goal, gave them a seemingly uncatchable 14–6 lead. Hull, however, lifted their game and scored two late tries to draw level. Lloyd had kept Hull on the scoreboard with three goals, and Norton slipped through a gap to touch down, Lloyd's goal making it 14–11. Hull redoubled their efforts and O'Hara took Crooks's pass to score. Lloyd could have won the game with his kick at goal, but pulled it wide, and the stage was set for a superbly thrilling replay at Elland Road.

This took place on Wednesday, 19 May, a crowd of 41,171 providing an electric atmosphere that rivalled Wembley. The match was given added piquancy by the fact that, four days earlier, Widnes had comprehensively mastered Hull 23–8 in the premiership final before a 12,000 crowd at Headingley. As if to emphasize their determination not to do a repeat of Wembley, Widnes scored five tries to one and were never in danger of defeat. Basnett, Wright, Hughes, Burke and Adams were the scorers and Burke kicked four goals, against a try, two goals and a dropped goal by Crooks for Hull.

## Elland Road spectacular

Consequently, few expected Hull to win so splendidly and decisively as they did at Elland Road. Hull made several changes, bringing in three experienced veterans in international winger Clive Sullivan, hooker Tony Duke and half-back Tony Dean. With the crowd in a continual ferment of excitement, Burke gave Widnes an early lead with a penalty, but fast attacking by Hull gave tries from Kemble and Topliss, with a goal from Crooks. It was 8–2 at half time; Widnes briefly got back into the game with a penalty by Burke and a try to Wright from O'Loughlin's pass. Burke's kick hit the upright and it was 8–7. Topliss backed up his skilful mentor Norton, however, to reach over at the posts, and Crooks kicked the goal. A goal from Burke kept Widnes apparently in the contest, but Crooks clinched victory for Hull by racing under the posts through a tiring Widnes defence and kicking the goal. It was Hull's cup again after nearly seventy years, but a Wembley triumph had again eluded them. For Steve Evans, the Hull centre, a winner's medal meant a unique achievement. He had appeared for Featherstone Rovers in a preliminary round and had been cleared to play for Hull because his appearance had not been in the competition proper. The laws governing the competition were later firmly amended to ensure that this could not happen again.

On the international front the management team of Colin Hutton and John Whiteley conducted several training sessions and seminars to prepare for the visit of the Kangaroos in the autumn of 1982.

The squad system was used to its fullest extent by Hutton and Whiteley, and players carrying injuries or missing training and fitness sessions were ruthlessly axed. The managers were determined that the humiliations of 1979 would not be repeated.

## The Bradford walk-off

The premiership first round in May 1982 produced one of the most unpleasant matches, and one of the most remarkable scenes, in the history of the game. The game between Hull Kingston Rovers and Bradford Northern began bad temperedly and steadily deteriorated as the referee, Robin Whitfield, tried desperately by every means at his disposal to restore order. Punches were thrown, brawls erupted and head-high tackles became the norm as the two teams lost control. Both sets of directors and players laid the blame at their opponents' door but, whoever started the fracas, the result was a series of sendings-off, penalty after penalty, and, ultimately, the Northern players, led by the captain Jeff Grayshon, walked off the field.

The first four players went off in pairs. John Millington (Hull K. R.) and Gary van Bellen (Bradford Northern) went after an early skirmish, to be followed to the dressing room by Steve Hartley (Hull K. R.) and his opposite number Dean Carroll. Penalties and warnings flowed from Mr Whitfield's whistle but the niggling continued and Ian Ellis (Northern) became the fifth player to leave the field at the referee's request.

The situation boiled over in the fifty-sixth minute when Grayshon was sent off, appeared to hurl the ball at the referee and called the rest of the Northern team to follow him down the tunnel. They marched off to the dressing room, the door was locked and the game was abandoned. The Rugby League council, faced with an obvious rebellion against the authority of a referee, plus a complete breakdown of discipline, banned Northern from the 1982–83 challenge cup, John Player trophy and premiership, censured the chairman Ronnie Firth and the players, imposed a four-figure fine and suspended Grayshon until the end of September.

The punishment was either hailed as justified, or criticized as too draconian, depending on the point of view and the degree of support for Northern's drastic and anarchic action. In the event, the banning of Northern from all cup tournaments was later substituted for a suspended sentence; the club was fined £3000, its gate share, and the chairman Ronnie Firth was banned from holding the chairmanship. It could hardly be described as excessive punishment in the final analysis.

The preparations for the Australian tour of Britain provided for an international 'exhibition' match between Great Britain and France at – of all places – Venice. The match was not particularly successful, either as a propaganda exercise in Italy or as a Test warm-up, with Great Britain losing 8–7 before a sparse crowd. There were also 'competitive' games between Great Britain squad sides and Hull K.

R., Widnes and Leeds, none of which gave great help or encouragement to Messrs Hutton and Whiteley.

The tourists arrived in Britain in October and, before the first
match at Craven Park, Hull, the manager Frank Farrington said that
the team intended to make history by winning all fifteen matches in
Britain. It was to prove no idle boast, but rather an accurate
prophecy, as the brilliant Kangaroos swept through home ranks like
a bush fire, making a mockery of Britain's summer preparations and
training camps, and cruelly emphasizing the huge disparity in playing
and fitness standards between the countries. Although what was
virtually the tourists' 'second team' had to struggle to beat Wigan
13–9 in the second game of the tour, the rampant and spectacularly
exciting Kangaroos swept through all other opposition before the first
Test at Boothferry Park, Hull, on Saturday, 30 October. Showing
lightning pace, and complete command of the rugby-league basic
skills of passing, backing up and tackling, Australia beat Hull K. R.
30–13, Barrow 29–2, St Helens 32–0, Leeds 31–4 and Wales 37–7 at
Ninian Park, Cardiff.

## Britain outclassed

The first Test proved an even worse disaster for Britain than the
35–0 humiliation in Brisbane in 1979. Before a crowd of 26,771 at
Boothferry Park, Great Britain scored first, with a second-minute
penalty from Lee Crooks, but thereafter the Lions' roar was first
muted, then silenced. Meninga, the tall, long-striding Aboriginal
centre, scored a try for Australia and Boyd, the aggressive front-row-
forward, scored a second, Meninga kicking two goals to give the
tourists a 10–4 half-time lead. In the second half the Kangaroos
unleashed an avalanche of fast attacks to which the slow-footed
British defence had no answer. Six more tries came from Grothe,
Price, Boustead, Kenny, Pearce and Reddy, and Meninga completed
eight goals, the highest individual total in an international between
the two countries in Britain. It was a rout, 40 points to 4, and, to
coin the polite euphemism, Great Britain 'went back to the drawing
board'.

On marched the tourists, walloping Leigh 44–4 but facing a harder
game at Bradford before beating Northern 13–6. Ominously for

Britain, tries were proving almost impossible to score against the ferocious, lethal tackling of the Australians. Hull K. R. had scored two in the first match but only four more were recorded before the second Test at Central Park, Wigan, on 20 November, with no team managing more than a single try. The crowd at Wigan was 23,216; it witnessed yet another superb attacking performance by Australia, who won 27–6. Mumby kicked three goals for a Great Britain team containing only six players from the first Test squad, but Australia swept in for five tries from Price, Sterling, Grothe, Meninga, and Rogers, with six more goals from Meninga.

Widnes, one of the best British club sides, were beaten by 19 points to 6, conceding five tries and replying only with three goals from Burke. Then came the third Test at Headingley on 28 November 28.

The Leeds attendance was 17,318, a reasonable one considering Great Britain's performances in the first two Tests, and, although the final score, 32–8 to Australia, indicated another thrashing, Britain put up a creditable, fighting show for much of the game before crumbling in the later stages. Indeed, for fifty minutes there were hopes of a possible home victory, Great Britain only trailing by 6–5 after Steve Evans had crashed over in the left-hand corner to give the home fans the chance to cheer the first British try of the series. The French referee, Julien Rascagnères, sent off the young British forward Lee Crooks, who had kicked a penalty and dropped a goal, and in the last half hour Australia cut loose with six tries as the home defence collapsed. The tries came from Ribot, the team captain Krilich, Boustead, Rogers, Pearce and Kenny, and Kenny kicked seven goals. It was a rousing end to a brilliantly exciting tour and British fans, while sharing the prevailing gloom about Britain's international status, saluted the greatest touring team to visit this country.

As with 1978 and 1979 there were many inquests and heart-searching inquiries into Britain's disastrous performances, and yet more calls for greater dedication, fitness and attention to basic skills at all levels. With the tour to Australia and New Zealand due in 1984, there was precious little time.

On the purely domestic front the season opened with a threat of strike action from the newly formed Rugby League Professional Players Association. The threat came in pursuit of a new and improved injury insurance scheme for players, and negotiations with the League were successfully concluded before the need for such drastic action, which might not have won unanimous support from players, became seriously evident. There was a brief, and somewhat peculiar, attempt to add to the League's new clubs when Hull F. C. offered to back Hull White Star and their rivals Hull K. R. countered with Hull Kingston Raiders, both teams to be formed from within the existing clubs but with separate management. Not surprisingly, the plans were not encouraged at official level.

## *The sin bin*

A major rule change was introduced on 1 January 1983 with the arrival of the sin bin in British rugby league. It had been used for the Tests with Australia, but now its use entered the full league programme. Referees were given authority to send players off the field for five or ten minutes, depending on the severity of the offence, and controversy soon developed. Criticisms of the sin-bin rule were that referees tended to take an easy option rather than dismissing miscreants for good, and that there was no 'totting-up' system of points to ensure that persistent sin-bin offenders ultimately received suspensions. This latter weakness was corrected during the 1983–84 season when it was decreed that a points system would be introduced, one point for five minutes, two points for ten, with suspension at six points.

In the season's tournaments Wigan revived memories of former glory by bringing the John Player trophy back to Central Park. They beat Leeds convincingly 19–4, at Elland Road, Leeds, Gill and Juliff scoring tries. Whitfield kicked three goals and dropped a goal. Dick landed two goals for Leeds.

The biggest upset of the season, and one of the most unexpected results in the history of the challenge cup, came with the Wembley final on 7 May, 1983. Featherstone Rovers, the amazing little club from a West Yorkshire colliery village, had a disastrous season in the League, avoided relegation by just one point, and were in desperate financial difficulties. In traditional manner, however, they fought their way to Wembley taking with them the scalps of Batley, Salford, St Helens and Bradford Northern.

Rovers opponents were the formidable and internationally star-studded Hull side, who romped past Blackpool Borough, Huyton, Warrington and Castleford to reach the final.

## David and Goliath

The final between the brilliant attacking machine of Hull, backed by their enormous following, and homespun Featherstone seemed so ridiculously one-sided in prospect that the match was written off as a contest. The Featherstone chairman Bob Ashby called publicly for all neutrals in the crowd to shout for Featherstone to give them some support against the Humberside uproar. The below-average attendance of 84,969, paying £655,510, reflected the widespread belief that Hull only had to walk onto the Wembley turf to retain the cup. What actually happened came straight out of the best ripping yarns for schoolboys. Teams were:

*Featherstone Rovers*: N. Barker; J. Marsden, S. Quinn, J. Gilbert, K. Kellett; A. Banks, T. Hudson; M. Gibbins, R. Handscombe, S. Hankins, D. Hobbs, T. Slatter, P. Smith. Substitutes: P. Lyman, G. Siddall

*Hull*: G. Kemble; D. O'Hara, S. Evans, J. Leuluai, P. Prendiville; D. Topliss, K. Harkin; T. Skerrett, K. Bridges, C. Stone, P. Rose, L. Crooks, S. Norton. Substitutes: T. Day, M. Crane

Hull, who had already won the Slalom Lager championship in swashbuckling style, were shaken out of their complacency within 7 minutes as the big second-row-forward David Hobbs took a pass from Hudson close to the line and crashed over. Quinn kicked a goal and Hull trailed 5–0. Hull suffered a severe blow which affected the team's rhythm when Harkin, the scrum-half, was kicked as he dived on a loose ball near a scrum. Both Day and Crane were pressed into service as utility scrum-halves, but the service from behind the Hull scrum was erratic and Topliss lost the platform for his skilful breaks and crisp passes. Despite performing in fits and starts like a car engine working on three cylinders, however, Hull worked their way into a 12–5 lead and the crowd settled back to greet the inevitable win. Lee Crooks was awarded a penalty try early in the second half when he was obstructed diving for a touch down, Leuluai scored a fine try from a flash of the Hull attacking play, and Crooks kicked three goals.

It seemed all over bar the shouting of the Hull followers, a cheering mass of black-and-white on the Wembley terraces. Featherstone were in no mood to capitulate, however. Quinn landed a penalty and then, to the delight of the small band of Rovers fans and the neutrals who had ranged themselves behind the underdogs, quick passing and another strong burst by Hobbs produced a second try, and Quinn's goal levelled the score. Another replay seemed certain but then came the moment that produced a remarkable result against all the odds, predictions and form. Rovers were attacking near the Hull 25-yard line when a touch judge raced onto the field and told Mr Whitfield that Stone, the Hull and former Featherstone forward, had butted the Rovers' forward Smith. The referee awarded the penalty and Quinn sent the kick through the posts. Hull had no time to reply and, at the end of the game, there was pandemonium among the Featherstone contingent and sporting applause from the chastened Hull supporters who had seen their side fail yet again to beat the Wembley jinx. It was a great achievement for Featherstone; David Hobbs was awarded the Lance Todd trophy while the coach Allan Agar was later named coach of the year in the prestigious Man of Steel awards.

The premiership final brought further misery to Hull. The inevitable Widnes once again mastered the Airlie Birds, winning 22–10 in a superbly exciting and open game before nearly 18,000 spectators at Headingley. Basnett (2), Myler and Gregory scored the tries and Lydon kicked five goals for Widnes, while Topliss and O'Hara touched down for Hull and Crooks kicked two goals.

The close season of 1983 produced a host of talking points and a welter of anticipation as new international rules were pondered and digested for the 1983–84 season. All were designed to make rugby league faster, more attacking and therefore more attractive.

In October a major step was taken at international board level. The ban on transfers between Australia and Great Britain was lifted, opening the floodgates for top Australians to sign or 'guest' on short-term contracts in Britain.

## *Major rules revolution*

English clubs were quick to seize the possibilities, and the two outstanding captures were the Australian stand-off-half and captain Wally Lewis by Wakefield Trinity, and his partner Peter Sterling by Hull.

The new international rules made significant changes. The four-point try, sought by many clubs at a succession of annual meetings, became a reality. At scrums, the non-offending side was given the loose head and the feed with, in the case of a mutual infringement, the attacking side having head and ball.

There was a drastic change in the six-tackle rule. At the completion of the sixth tackle the ball had to be handed over to the opposing side by placing the ball on the ground. This change was designed to encourage tactical kicking and inventive moves on the final tackle. Other new rules required the scrum-half to put the ball into the scrum straight, holding the ball point to point, rather than in a downward direction; the loose-forward had to pack down in the scrum; and, at the play-the-ball, players had to remain onside until the ball was passed clear of the acting half-backs. Finally, at the kick-off, if the ball was kicked directly out of play the game would be resumed by a penalty kick from the centre spot. Previously, play would have resumed with a 25-yard-line tap.

It took several weeks for the new rules to settle down and there was much frenetic kicking and passing at the start of the season. The need for fitness and pace was obvious and there were certainly signs of faster flowing rugby, with fewer scrums. Tackling came into its own as a rugby-league art, and the fact that the hard, traditional game need not disappear was demonstrated by those doughty foes, Widnes and Bradford Northern, who fought out a rugged John Player Special trophy match with a final scoreline of 2–1 to Widnes.

The Great Britain under-24 squad won a resounding victory by 48 points to 1 at Watersheddings, Oldham, on 4 December completing yet another double against the hapless France under-24 team, and making it thirteen wins in a row against the French. Shortly after this thumpingly decisive victory, at a council meeting in Leeds, a major innovation was announced for the 1984 tour to Australasia.

It was agreed that, for the first time ever, a 'fitness consultant' would be taken along with the management team. The choice fell upon Rod McKenzie, senior lecturer in physical education at Carnegie College, Leeds. McKenzie, whose fitness courses at Carnegie had long been a feature of British preparation, joined manager Dick Gemmell, coach Frank Myler, physiotherapist Ronnie Barritt and business manager Roland Davis, whose appointment was made from several candidates in January 1984. Davis, finance officer of the League for four years, was appointed specifically to handle the financial affairs of the tour.

December brought an edict from the council which shook the complacency of many leading coaches. To bring British clubs in line with Australia, it was announced that all professional coaches must qualify through the game's national coaching scheme in time for the 1986–87 season. Top coaches affected included the Great Britain coach Frank Myler, Roger Millward (Hull KR), Vince Karalius (Widnes), Arthur Bunting (Hull) and Derek Turner (Wakefield Trinity). In all, thirteen club coaches were stated to be 'unqualified' in the terms of the edict.

The League's spokesman, David Howes, said that the decision, to be implemented and supervised by the director of coaching, Phil Larder, would 'see an end to the situation where a player can retire one day and take over as a club coach the next'. Coaches who had had a minimum of five years as a coach at senior level could qualify by attending a course in May 1984.

## The Oldham brawl

If the Bradford Northern infamous 'walk-off' against Hull KR had caused dismay at headquarters, an incident on 8 January brought total consternation. In the fifty-ninth minute of the Oldham *v.* Leigh game at Watersheddings the referee John Mean, of Leyland, abandoned the game because of persistent brawling by the players. Mr Mean refused to restart the game or to emerge from his dressing room to talk to reporters about the incidents, which saw players of both sides slugging it out as a scrum broke up in fighting. A policeman who attempted to intervene was himself manhandled; angry spectators demanded their money back, and Leigh officials were particularly incensed at the abandonment since their team was leading 26–14 at the time of the brawl.

The management committee of the League met at Leeds on Wednesday, 18 January, to consider the matter, to decide whether the game had been brought into disrepute, and to impose punishment. In attendance were Mr Mean and his touch judges, and also called, though not all interviewed, were officials of Oldham and Leeds, the coaches Peter Smethurst and Tommy Bishop; players included Wilkinson, Pyke, Varley and Woods, all from Leigh.

After a meeting lasting more than four hours David Oxley, the League's secretary-general, read out a four-point judgement. It stated that the match was void and would be replayed; that the competing clubs would each be fined a record sum of £1000, subject to appeal; that 'certain players' might be called to answer allegations on their conduct during the brawls; and that the referee could have used 'other options' rather than abandoning the game. None of the contending parties seemed happy with, or clear about, the judgement.

In January there were two further major club sponsorships. Widnes signed a £47,000 deal over three and a half years with a leisure company, and Leeds renewed a lucrative McEwan Younger contract.

As preliminary rounds were played in the challenge cup, the sponsors, State Express, announced that, as part of a rationalisation scheme, they were pulling out of the major sponsorship which had provided more than £500,000 in six seasons. The search for a big new sponsorship began.

The first of the two Test matches against France, played as superior tour trials, took place at Avignon on Sunday, 29 January. It was a hard, scrappy, unattractive game, with few moments of inspiration, and after a dismally shapeless first half Great Britain got on top in the second to score tries through a Goodway interception and gallop, and a fine break by Foy. Crooks landed three goals, and Britain came away with victory and full credit for unyielding defence.

The return game was at Headingley on Friday, 17 February. Only one Widnes player, John Basnett, was in the British squad after the Widnes coaching staff of Vince Karalius and Harry Dawson told the 10-man Widnes 'delegation' to train at Naughton Park rather than with the squad. Only Basnett chose to train with Myler, and the rest were not considered for the international match. Great Britain completed the double 10–0, but it was another disappointing game, Britain's points in a dreary encounter coming from five penalty goals by Hobbs.

The final tour party of 30 was announced in mid-April. John Woods, the Leigh utility back, pulled out of the tour for 'family and business reasons', David Hall (Hull K.R.) withdrew for business reasons, Steve Evans (Hull) for family reasons, Chris Arkwright (St Helens) with knee trouble which emerged sadly after he had been named as a tour replacement, and skipper-elect, Trevor Skerrett (Hull), fought a losing battle against knee ligament and cartilage trouble. Len Casey, the Hull K.R. captain, received a massive cumulative suspension following the alleged pushing of a touch judge in the Good Friday Hull *v*. Hull K.R. game, and he, too, missed out. The eventual squad was: R. Ashton (Oldham), M. Burke (Widnes), G. Clark (Hull K.R.), D. Drummond (Leigh), D. Foy (Oldham), S. Donlan (Leigh), R. Duane (Warrington), A. Gregory (Widnes), E. Hanley (Bradford N.), N. Holding (St Helens), J. Joyner (Castleford), J. Lydon (Widnes), K. Mumby (Bradford N.), G. Schofield (Hull), M. Smith (Hull K.R.), M. Adams (Widnes), K. Beardmore (Castleford), C. Burton (Hull K.R.), B. Case (Wigan), L. Crooks (Hull), A. Goodway (Oldham), D. Hobbs (Featherstone R.), B. Noble (Bradford N.), capt., M. O'Neill (Widnes), H. Pinner (St Helens), W. Proctor (Hull), Keith Rayne (Leeds), M. Worrall, T. Flanagan (Oldham).

Hull Kingston Rovers crowned their splendid season by becoming the first team to pull off the Slalom Lager-sponsored double. After clinching the title, they beat a brave and skilful, but ultimately outpaced, Castleford, 18–10 at Headingley before 12,000 spectators, producing yet again an outstanding premiership final.

The 1983 Wembley final was played on 5 May before a crowd of just over 80,000, paying £686,171. Perennial Widnes were appearing in their seventh final in 10 seasons. Their opponents, Wigan, were playing in their first challenge cup final since 1970, backed by a tidal wave of enthusiasm with a supporting army variously assessed at between 25,000 and 35,000. Both teams were making their twelfth appearance at Wembley, and the match brought into verbal and physical confrontation two tough and outspoken former club and international team-mates, Vince Karalius and Alex Murphy. The teams were:

Widnes: M. Burke; S. Wright, E. Hughes, J. Lydon, J. Basnett; K. O'Loughlin, A. Gregory; K. Tamati, K. Elwell, S. O'Neill, L. Gorley, M. O'Neill, M. Adams. Substitutes: D. Hulme, F. Whitfield.
*Wigan*: S. Edwards; D. Ramsdale, D. Stephenson, C. Whitfield, H. Gill; M. Cannon, G. Stephens; K. Helmsley, H. Tamati, B. Case, G. West, M. Scott, J. Pendlebury. Substitutes: W. Elvin, B. Juliff

The referee, Billy Thompson was officiating at his final game before retiring at the age of 50, and he was inundated with good luck telegrams before the game.

The Wigan squad had a strong Antipodean flavour, with Graeme West and Howie Tamati representing New Zealand, and Mark Cannon, Kerry Hemsley and Wayne Elvin providing the Australian element. Alex Murphy went to the extreme of having Hemsley flown back from Sydney to play in the final, despite a late challenge from Glyn Shaw. It was not, in the final analysis, a successful gamble, since Widnes won comfortably 19–6 and were rarely extended by a disappointing Wigan side who, virtually without exception, failed to rise to the occasion.

Widnes called upon the vast depths of Wembley experience of Burke, Hughes, Elwell, Adams and Wright, with Hughes, Elwell and Adams equalling the record of four winning medals, and breaking the record number of Wembley final appearances with seven. They could also call upon the brilliant 20-year-old emerging star Joe Lydon, who followed up a superb individual try in the semi-final against Leeds with two spectacular long range efforts which knocked the heart out of Wigan. O'Loughlin scored the third Widnes try, Burke kicked three goals and Steve O'Neill dropped a goal. Whitfield kicked a penalty and Hemsley got a late consolation try for a dejected and well-beaten Wigan. Inevitably, Lydon's roof-raising efforts won him the Lance Todd trophy.

In the 1983–84 trophy finals there were shocks for the perennial pot-hunters Widnes. The club was beaten by Barrow in the Lancashire cup, giving Barrow their first major success in twenty-nine years. Then, in January, they met their bogey team Leeds in the John Player Special trophy final at Central Park, Wigan. Leeds, after a disastrous start to the season, had replaced their coach Robin Dewhurst with Maurice Bamford; he completed a remarkable revival of the Headingley club when Leeds won its ninth consecutive game 18–10 on a wild, storm-lashed afternoon. The growing influence and presence of Antipodean players were emphasized by Leeds; the Australians Laurie, man of the match, and Webb were outstanding, the New Zealand centre Dean Bell also playing a key role.

The touring team won all six games before the first Test at Sydney on Saturday, 9 June, but as in 1979 they were dogged by injuries. A major pack reshuffle, caused by injury to Keith Rayne forced Goodway into the front row, and the young Oldham back Des Foy was pressed into service at stand-off half in the absence of Myler, Donlan and Joyner.

The result was, as feared and expected, a 25-8 win by Australia, but the score flattered Australia and did not do full justice to the tourists. Midway through the second half Britain pulled back from 12-2 to 12-8 with a try by Schofield, made by a splendid Drummond break, and the goal from Burke. Then, as if overawed by the prospect of winning, the Lions fell apart in defence and conceded two more tries. One unfortunate contributory factor to defeat was an early knee injury to the scrum half Neil Holding, which ruled him out of the second Test.

There was an air of inevitability about the result of the second Test, played at Lang Park, Brisbane, on Tuesday, 26 June before 31,000 people. Australia won 18-6 after a tough, bruising and occasionally bitter battle, and the series yet again went to the Kangaroos. Such had been the supremacy of Australia in the previous three series, that a closely fought 12-point margin, with Britain getting the best try of the match, seemed to be regarded as a moral victory in the British camp. Certainly, the Lions tackled well for most of the game, and earned the displeasure of the otherwise tolerant New Zealand referee Ray Shrimpton, by giving Wally Lewis special off-the-ball treatment.

Meninga, who signed for St. Helens after the game, Pearce and the Leeds-bound Grothe scored tries for Australia, and Meninga kicked three goals. Schofield scored a brilliant try for Britain after superb inter-passing with Drummond and Goodway, and Burke, while missing one easy penalty, kicked a touchline goal. It was regarded as an honourable defeat by a touring team with internal doubts of their own ability to win.

The bravery of the Great Britain side was epitomized by the captain, Brian Noble, who suffered a broken nose when Lewis reacted to his treatment with a late and very blatant elbow.

Australia duly completed their third consecutive whitewash of Great Britain by winning the third Test 20–7 at Sydney, though again Britain acquitted themselves well and at one stage led 7–2.

# 13
# Amateur Rugby League: a Ten-Year Success Story

In 1983 the British Amateur Rugby League Association (BARLA) celebrated a decade of unbroken growth and astounding success. A straggling patchwork quilt of local amateur leagues, welded under one banner, became one of the great success stories of our time, sharing with, and contributing to, the rugby-league boom.

The amateur game was struggling when, in 1973, a group of enthusiasts met at Greenside Workingmen's Club in Huddersfield, giving the Yorkshire town the honour of being progenitor of rugby league at both professional and amateur levels. Secretaries of the local leagues in Lancashire, Yorkshire and Cumbria pooled their strengths and organizational ability behind Maurice Oldroyd, who became national administrator, secretary Tom Keaveney, chairman Jack Clayton, and vice-chairman Bob Beal.

At first BARLA was regarded as a maverick, rebel body by the Rugby League, unrecognized by the Government, Sports Council or Central Council of Physical Recreation. The bank balance was £25. Hard work, hard-headed organization of the local leagues, sensible stewardship of fees, social receipts and other monies, and, above all, immense pioneering enthusiasm based on a central Huddersfield headquarters enabled BARLA first to consolidate amateur rugby league, then to make tremendous progress.

BARLA has increased its membership by nearly 18,000 players and more than 700 teams since 1973, from just over 150 teams to approaching 900. Within these figures youth teams have increased by 400 and 10,000 players.

BARLA's great triumph, outside the spreading boundaries of its own game, has been to achieve, by friendly persuasion and years of patient negotiation, a quiet revolution in the relationship between Union and League. One by one barriers have fallen (though some remain), and a major breakthrough is the agreement that amateur players can play union one season, league the next. At schools and colleges there is no longer any restriction.

There are school and amateur teams in a thriving London league, in Newcastle, Sunderland, Scarborough, Hamilton, Scunthorpe, Chesterfield, Rotherham, Carlisle, Milton Keynes, Edinburgh, Bexley Heath, Southampton, Bristol, Swansea, Cardiff and Aberavon.

University and college rugby league have boomed in all northern universities and in Swansea, Cardiff, Nottingham, Birmingham, Loughborough, Wolverhampton and Warwick. The Rugby League Varsity match, Oxford *v.* Cambridge, is now an annual event. In addition, BUSCARLA, the British Upper Schools and Colleges Amateur Rugby League Association, another burgeoning success, was recently formed.

The expansion of amateur rugby league has been such that, in 1981, Dickie Jeeps, chairman of the Sports Council, said BARLA was 'the sporting success story of the seventies'.

History-making tours have been made under BARLA's banner: an under-18 tour to Australasia in 1977; the 1978 British tour to Papua New Guinea, Australia and New Zealand; Papua New Guinea's pioneer tour to Britain in 1979; the first visit to Britain of the New Zealand Maoris in 1983, following closely on the heels of the 'Young Lions' tour to New Zealand during which the British team won seven out of eight games.

In the New Year's Honours List of 1984 Bob Beal, a founder member and chairman of BARLA, and president since 1978, was awarded the OBE.

Playing standards have improved dramatically, coaches proliferating under the guidance of the National Coaching Scheme administered by Phil Larder. During the decade several amateur teams entered the first round of the Rugby League challenge cup and, before big attendances, came close to humbling senior opposition. It was a severe blow to the ebullient growth of the amateur game when the arrival of new teams into the second division of the Rugby League resulted in the ending of the entry of amateur teams into the challenge cup.

This decision has aroused a major outcry from all quarters asking for the restoration of amateur-team entry into the cup, with some professional bodies throwing in their weight behind the amateur cause.

As its membership of teams and players has increased weekly, the British Amateur Rugby League Association has overcome its early struggles and the traumas of bitter, but now resolved, argument with the Rugby League over colts' rugby. There is no greater success story within the game.

# Appendix

## Rugby League Champions (1902–1984)

| YEAR | WINNERS | RUNNERS-UP |
|------|---------|------------|
| 1901–02 | Broughton R. | Salford |
| 1902–03 | Halifax | Salford |
| 1903–04 | Bradford | Salford |
| 1904–05 | Oldham | Bradford |
| 1905–06 | Leigh | Hunslet |
| 1906–07 | Halifax | Oldham |
| 1907–08 | Hunslet | Oldham |
| 1908–09 | Wigan | Oldham |
| 1909–10 | Oldham | Wigan |
| 1910–11 | Oldham | Wigan |
| 1911–12 | Huddersfield | Wigan |
| 1912–13 | Huddersfield | Wigan |
| 1913–14 | Salford | Huddersfield |
| 1914–15 | Huddersfield | Leeds |
| 1919–20 | Hull | Huddersfield |
| 1920–21 | Hull | Hull K.R. |
| 1921–22 | Wigan | Oldham |
| 1922–23 | Hull K.R. | Huddersfield |
| 1923–24 | Batley | Wigan |
| 1924–25 | Hull K.R. | Swinton |
| 1925–26 | Wigan | Warrington |
| 1926–27 | Swinton | St Helens Recs. |
| 1927–28 | Swinton | Featherstone R. |

*The Story of Rugby League*

| YEAR | WINNERS | RUNNERS-UP |
|------|---------|------------|
| 1928–29 | Huddersfield | Leeds |
| 1929–30 | Huddersfield | Leeds |
| 1930–31 | Swinton | Leeds |
| 1931–32 | St Helens | Huddersfield |
| 1932–33 | Salford | Swinton |
| 1933–34 | Wigan | Salford |
| 1934–35 | Swinton | Warrington |
| 1935–36 | Hull | Widnes |
| 1936–37 | Salford | Warrington |
| 1937–38 | Hunslet | Leeds |
| 1938–39 | Salford | Castleford |
| 1945–46 | Wigan | Huddersfield |
| 1946–47 | Wigan | Dewsbury |
| 1947–48 | Warrington | Bradford N. |
| 1948–49 | Huddersfield | Warrington |
| 1949–50 | Wigan | Huddersfield |
| 1950–51 | Workington T. | Warrington |
| 1951–52 | Wigan | Bradford N |
| 1952–53 | St Helens | Halifax |
| 1953–54 | Warrington | Halifax |
| 1954–55 | Warrington | Oldham |
| 1955–56 | Hull | Halifax |
| 1956–57 | Oldham | Hull |
| 1957–58 | Hull | Workington T. |
| 1958–59 | St Helens | Hunslet |
| 1959–60 | Wigan | Wakefield T. |
| 1960–61 | Leeds | Warrington |
| 1961–62 | Huddersfield | Wakefield T. |
| *1962–63 | Swinton | St Helens |
| *1963–64 | Swinton | Wigan |
| 1964–65 | Halifax | St Helens |
| 1965–66 | St Helens | Halifax |
| 1966–67 | Wakefield T. | Hull K.R. |
| 1968–69 | Leeds | Castleford |
| 1969–70 | St Helens | Leeds |

*Division One

| YEAR | WINNERS | RUNNERS-UP |
|------|---------|------------|
| 1970–71 | St Helens | Wigan |
| 1971–72 | Leeds | St Helens |
| 1972–73 | Dewsbury | Leeds |
| 1973–74 | Warrington | St Helens |
| 1974–75 | St Helens | Wigan |
| 1975–76 | Salford | Featherstone R. |
| 1976–77 | Featherstone R. | St Helens |
| 1977–78 | Widnes | Bradford N. |
| 1978–79 | Hull K.R. | Warrington |
| 1979–80 | Bradford N. | Widnes |
| 1980–81 | Bradford N. | Warrington |
| 1981–82 | Leigh | Hull |
| 1982–83 | Hull | Hull K.R. |
| 1983–84 | Hull K.R. | Hull |

## Challenge Cup Finals (1897–1984)

| YEAR | WINNERS | RUNNERS-UP | VENUE |
|------|---------|------------|-------|
| 1897 | Batley | St Helens | Leeds |
| 1898 | Batley | Bradford | Leeds |
| 1899 | Oldham | Hunslet | Fallowfield |
| 1900 | Swinton | Salford | Fallowfield |
| 1901 | Batley | Warrington | Leeds |
| 1902 | Broughton R. | Salford | Rochdale |
| 1903 | Halifax | Salford | Leeds |
| 1904 | Halifax | Warrington | Salford |
| 1905 | Warrington | Hull K.R. | Leeds |
| 1906 | Bradford | Salford | Leeds |
| 1907 | Warrington | Oldham | Broughton |
| 1908 | Hunslet | Hull | Huddersfield |
| 1909 | Wakefield T | Hull | Leeds |
| 1910 | Leeds | Hull | Huddersfield |
| Replay: | Leeds | Hull | Huddersfield |
| 1911 | Broughton R. | Wigan | Salford |
| 1912 | Dewsbury | Oldham | Leeds |
| 1913 | Huddersfield | Warrington | Leeds |
| 1914 | Hull | Wakefield T. | Halifax |

| Year | Winners | Runners-up | Venue |
|------|---------|-----------|-------|
| 1915 | Huddersfield | St Helens | Oldham |
| 1916–19 | No competition | | |
| 1920 | Huddersfield | Wigan | Leeds |
| 1921 | Leigh | Halifax | Broughton |
| 1922 | Rochdale H. | Hull | Leeds |
| 1923 | Leeds | Hull | Wakefield |
| 1924 | Wigan | Oldham | Rochdale |
| 1925 | Oldham | Hull K.R. | Leeds |
| 1926 | Swinton | Oldham | Rochdale |
| 1927 | Oldham | Swinton | Wigan |
| 1928 | Swinton | Warrington | Wigan |
| 1929 | Wigan | Dewsbury | Wembley |
| 1930 | Widnes | St Helens | Wembley |
| 1931 | Halifax | York | Wembley |
| 1932 | Leeds | Swinton | Wigan |
| 1933 | Huddersfield | Warrington | Wembley |
| 1934 | Hunslet | Widnes | Wembley |
| 1935 | Castleford | Huddersfield | Wembley |
| 1936 | Leeds | Warrington | Wembley |
| 1937 | Widnes | Keighley | Wembley |
| 1938 | Salford | Barrow | Wembley |
| 1939 | Halifax | Salford | Wembley |
| 1940 | No competition | | |
| 1941 | Leeds | Halifax | Odsal |
| 1942 | Leeds | Halifax | Odsal |
| 1943 | Dewsbury | Leeds | Dewsbury and Leeds (two-leg) |
| 1944 | Bradford N. | Wigan | Bradford and Wigan (two-leg) |
| 1945 | Huddersfield | Bradford N. | Huddersfield and Odsal (two-leg) |
| 1946 | Wakefield T. | Wigan | Wembley |
| 1947 | Bradford N. | Leeds | Wembley |
| 1948 | Wigan | Bradford N. | Wembley |
| 1949 | Bradford N. | Halifax | Wembley |
| 1950 | Warrington | Widnes | Wembley |
| 1951 | Wigan | Barrow | Wembley |

| YEAR | WINNERS | RUNNERS-UP | VENUE |
|------|---------|------------|-------|
| 1952 | Workington T. | Featherstone R. | Wembley |
| 1953 | Huddersfield | St Helens | Wembley |
| 1954 | Warrington | Halifax | Wembley |
| Replay: | Warrington | Halifax | Odsal |
| 1955 | Barrow | Workington T. | Wembley |
| 1956 | St Helens | Halifax | Wembley |
| 1957 | Leeds | Barrow | Wembley |
| 1958 | Wigan | Workington T. | Wembley |
| 1959 | Wigan | Hull | Wembley |
| 1960 | Wakefield T. | Hull | Wembley |
| 1961 | St Helens | Wigan | Wembley |
| 1962 | Wakefield T. | Huddersfield | Wembley |
| 1963 | Wakefield T. | Wigan | Wembley |
| 1964 | Widnes | Hull K. R. | Wembley |
| 1965 | Wigan | Hunslet | Wembley |
| 1966 | St Helens | Wigan | Wembley |
| 1967 | Featherstone R. | Barrow | Wembley |
| 1968 | Leeds | Wakefield T. | Wembley |
| 1969 | Castleford | Salford | Wembley |
| 1970 | Castleford | Wigan | Wembley |
| 1971 | Leigh | Leeds | Wembley |
| 1972 | St Helens | Leeds | Wembley |
| 1973 | Featherstone R. | Bradford N. | Wembley |
| 1974 | Warrington | Featherstone R. | Wembley |
| 1975 | Widnes | Warrington | Wembley |
| 1976 | St Helens | Widnes | Wembley |
| 1977 | Leeds | Widnes | Wembley |
| 1978 | Leeds | St Helens | Wembley |
| 1979 | Widnes | Wakefield T. | Wembley |
| 1980 | Hull K.R. | Hull | Wembley |
| 1981 | Widnes | Hull K.R. | Wembley |
| 1982 | Hull | Widnes | Wembley, replay at Elland Road, Leeds |
| 1983 | Featherstone R. | Hull | Wembley |
| 1984 | Widnes | Wigan | Wembley |

## Premiership Trophy

| YEAR | WINNERS | RUNNERS-UP | VENUE |
|------|---------|------------|-------|
| 1975 | Leeds | St Helens | Wigan |
| 1976 | St Helens | Salford | Swinton |
| 1977 | St Helens | Warrington | Swinton |
| 1978 | Bradford N. | Widnes | Swinton |
| 1979 | Leeds | Bradford N. | Huddersfield |
| 1980 | Widnes | Bradford N. | Swinton |
| 1981 | Hull K.R. | Hull | Leeds |
| 1982 | Widnes | Hull | Leeds |
| 1983 | Widnes | Hull | Leeds |
| 1984 | Hull K.R. | Castleford | Leeds |

# Index